D0207500

MENTORING students & young people

MENTORING students & young people

A HANDBOOK OF EFFECTIVE PRACTICE

ANDREW MILLER

**KOGAN
PAGE**

First published in 2002

Kogan Page Limited
120 Pentonville Road
London N1 9JN
UK

Stylus Publishing Inc.
22883 Quicksilver Drive
Sterling, VA 20166–2012
USA

British Library Cataloguing in Publication Data

A CIP record for this book is available from the British Library.

ISBN 0 7494 3543 7

Typeset by Jean Cussons Typesetting, Diss, Norfolk
Printed and bound in Great Britain by Clays Ltd, St Ives plc

January 16, 2004

Contents

List of case studies	*viii*
List of figures	*ix*
List of tables	*x*
List of abbreviations	*xi*
Ages and stages of education in the US, Canada, UK and Australia	*xii*
Preface	*xiv*

PART I   UNDERSTANDING MENTORING

1 The context of mentoring   **3**
Introduction 3; Origin of modern mentoring programmes 3;
The United States 5; Canada 8; Case study 8; Israel 9;
Australia 10; Mainland Europe 11; Development of
mentoring in the UK 12; Case study 18; Conclusions 20

2 The concept of mentoring   **23**
Introduction 23; History of the concept 24; Natural
mentoring 25; Definitions of planned mentoring 26;
Mentoring and helping behaviours 31; Aims and objectives
33; Aims for mentors 38; Classification of mentoring
programmes 39; Issues 43; Mentoring and learning 46

PART II   THE FORMS OF MENTORING

3 Business mentoring   **53**
Introduction 53; The extent of business mentoring in the
United Kingdom 53; Aims and objectives 54; One-company
versus multi-company schemes 54; Role of the company
coordinator 56; Business aims and benefits 56; Case studies
59; Research and evaluation evidence 64; Issues 67; Setting
up a business mentoring scheme 70; Future trends 72

4 Community mentoring: intergenerational programmes   **73**
Introduction 73; Aims and objectives 74; Case studies 75;
Research and evaluation evidence 79; Issues 82; Setting up
intergenerational mentoring programmes 83; Future trends
85

5 Minority ethnic mentoring   **86**
Introduction 86; Aims and objectives 87; Case studies 88;
Research and evaluation evidence 95; Issues 97; Setting up a
minority ethnic mentoring programme 100; Future trends
102

6 Mentoring for students 'at risk' of exclusion   **103**
Introduction 103; At-risk students 104; Exclusion from
school 104; Mentoring for young offenders 105; Aims and
objectives 106; Case studies 107; Research and evaluation
evidence 113; Issues 115; Setting up at-risk mentoring
schemes 117; Future trends 119

7 Peer mentoring   **120**
Introduction 120; Types of peer mentoring 121; Aims and
objectives 122; Benefits 123; Case studies 124; Research and
evaluation evidence 127; Issues 129; Setting up a peer
mentoring scheme 130; Future trends 132

8 Telementoring   **133**
Introduction 133; Aims and objectives 136; Telementoring
versus traditional mentoring 136; Case studies 138; Research
and evaluation evidence 141; Issues 142; Setting up a
telementoring programme 144; Future trends 146

9 Higher education student mentoring in schools   **148**
Introduction 148; US college-school mentoring 149;
GEAR UP 150; UK university and college volunteering 150;
Aims and objectives 151; Key skills 151; Case studies 152;
Research and evaluation evidence 157; Issues 159; Setting up
a higher education schools mentoring programme 162;
Future trends 163

PART III   GUIDE TO EFFECTIVE MENTORING

**10 Planning and managing mentoring programmes
for young people**   **167**
Introduction 167; A model mentoring programme 168; Pre-
planning 169; First steps 169; Objectives and forms of

mentoring 173; Mentoring documentation 173; Information
for mentors 175; Roles and responsibilities 176; Resourcing
179; Whole-school approaches 181; Case study 182;
Leadership and management of staff 184; Planning and
managing a mentoring programme for young people 185;
Future trends 187

11 **Focus on mentors**   188
Introduction 188; Mentor aims 188; Mentor characteristics
189; Mentors and emotional intelligence 191; Recruitment
194; Mentor Point 199; Selection 200; Training 201; Codes of
practice 205; Support and supervision 207; Accreditation
208; Case studies 209; Summary of good practice points 210;
Future trends 212

12 **Mentoring processes**   213
Introduction 213; Mentee selection 213; Mentee preparation
214; Matching 216; Gender issues 217; Meeting parameters
218; The mentoring relationship 220; Other activities 221;
Stages of the mentoring relationship 222; Learning mentors
in action 225; Experiential learning 226; Contracting 228; The
role of parents 229; Relationship problems 231; Endings 232;
Summary of good practice points 234; Future trends 235

13 **Evaluation and quality**   237
Introduction 237; The language of programme measurement
237; Measuring performance in the voluntary sector 238;
'Grey' evaluation 239; Evaluation and related concepts 240;
Case study 246; Developing an evaluation strategy 247; A
model for external evaluation 248; Empowerment
evaluation 250; Programme versus systems evaluation 251;
Quality standards 252; Quality assurance 255; Summary of
good practice points 258; Future trends 259

PART IV   CONCLUSION

14 **The future of mentoring for students and young people**   263
Case study 263; Benefits 265; Towards a mentoring culture
267

Glossary of mentoring terms   270
Web guide   275
References   278
Index   293

List of case studies

1.1 Big Brothers and Sisters of Canada 8
1.2 Learning mentors in England 18
3.1 Roots & Wings at Deptford Green School (UK) 59
3.2 Deloitte & Touche (UK) 62
3.3 Merrill Lynch ScholarshipBuilder® Program (USA) 63
4.1 Generations in Action in Salford (UK) 75
4.2 School Volunteer Program in Western Australia 77
4.3 The Across Ages programme in Philadelphia (USA) 78
5.1 ASELU Black mentoring programme (UK) 88
5.2 Southwark Black Mentor Scheme (UK) 90
5.3 North London Mentor Trust (UK) 93
6.1 Chance primary programme (UK) 107
6.2 Dalston Youth Project (UK) 109
6.3 Juvenile Mentoring Program (USA) 111
7.1 The peer-buddy programme at McGavrock High School, Tennessee (USA) 124
7.2 Coca-Cola Valued Youth Program (UK/USA) 124
7.3 Peer mentoring at South Wigston High School (UK) 125
8.1 The Hewlett-Packard E-Mail Mentoring Project (USA) 138
8.2 The Electronic Emissary Project (USA) 139
8.3 City of Leeds School (UK) 140
9.1 The National Mentoring Pilot Project at South Bank University (UK) 152
9.2 Mentoring at Middlesex University (UK) 154
9.3 Local GEAR UP Programs (USA) 155
10.1 Pershore High School: towards a whole school approach (UK) 182
11.1 Mentoring Draft Occupational Standards (UK) 209
11.2 Diploma in Mentoring at Leeds Metropolitan University (UK) 210
13.1 Experimental Evaluation Design – Big Brothers/Big Sisters of America 246
14.1 Telemachus High School 2015 263

List of figures

10.1 Model mentoring programme 170
11.1 A model of emotional intelligence 193
12.1 Examples of risk and protective factors in the JUMP
programme 215
12.2 The experiential learning cycle (adapted from Kolb) 227
13.1 The countenance model of evaluation 249
13.2 The Business Excellence Model applied to school mentoring 257

List of tables

0.1 Education system in case study countries: schools, ages, grades and years — xiii

6.1 Risk domains of JUMP youth — 112

10.1 The main objectives associated with the different forms of mentoring — 174

10.2 Typology of mentoring development in a school — 182

11.1 Ten attributes of 'good' mentors — 190

11.2 Roles of mentors — 192

11.3 Mentor training topics and processes — 203

12.1 The mentoring learning cycle: key questions — 229

12.2 Common relationship problems and programme responses — 233

13.1 Examples of key performance indicators for student mentoring — 241

13.2 Empowerment evaluation: self-evaluation — 250

List of abbreviations

BEM	Business Excellence Model
BITC	Business in the Community
CPIL	Campus Partners in Learning
CSV	Community Service Volunteers
DfEE	Department for Education and Employment (UK to 2001)
DFES	Department for Education and Skills (UK from 2001)
DYP	Dalston Youth Project
EAL	English as an additional language
EAZ	Education Action Zone
EBP	Education Business Partnership
EI	Emotional intelligence
GEAR UP	Gaining Early Awareness & Readiness for Undergraduate Programs
HP	Hewlett-Packard
GCSE	General Certificate of Secondary Education (UK exam at 16)
IT	Information technology
ICT	Information and communications technology
JUMP	Juvenile Mentoring Program
KPI	Key performance indicator
MAP	Mentoring Action Project
NMN	National Mentoring Network
NMPP	National Mentoring Pilot Project
OFSTED	Office for Standards in Education
SDQ	Strengths and Difficulties Questionnaire
SME	Subject matter expert (Electronic Emissary term)
VYP	Coca-Cola Valued Youth Program
YELLIS	Year Eleven Information System
Y5, Y6	Year 5, Year 6 (UK school year groups)

Ages and stages of education in the US, Canada, UK and Australia

Table 0.1 *Education system in case study countries: schools, ages, grades and years*

Age	11–12	12–13	13–14	14–15	15–16	16–17	17–18
US	Grade 6	Junior high school Grade 7	Junior high school Grade 8	Senior high school Grade 9	Senior high school Grade 10	Senior high school Grade 11	Senior high school Grade 11
Canada	Middle Grade 6	Middle Grade 7	Middle Grade 8	Senior 1 Grade 9	Senior 2 Grade 10	Senior 3 Grade 11	Senior 4 Grade 12
UK	Secondary school Year 7 Key stage 3	Secondary school Year 8 Key stage 3	Secondary school Year 9 Key stage 3	Secondary school Year 10 Key stage 4	Secondary school Year 11 Key stage 4	Secondary school or college Year 12	Secondary school or college Year 13
Australia	Year 6	Junior high school Year 7	Junior high school Year 8	Junior high school Year 9	Junior high school Year 10	Senior high school Year 11	Senior high school Year 12

Preface

This book represents a culmination of five years' involvement with mentoring beginning in 1997 at the University of Warwick. A qualitative research study into the impact of business mentoring on students' achievement involved interviewing many 15-year-old students and their mentors. This experience, in several schools around the country, confirmed the anecdotal evidence that is often presented at mentoring conferences and events. I was convinced of the power of mentoring to help young people to learn and develop. Since that time I have worked closely with the UK's National Mentoring Network and the Department for Education and Skills (DfES) in the development of student mentoring.

My experience of the mentoring field is that there is a lot of good practice and 'how to' guidance available, especially in the United States and on the World Wide Web. There is also much that can be learned from examining practice in parallel mentoring fields, for example, within the corporate setting, youth justice and education. At the level of individual schools, mentoring practice has developed incrementally, with new programmes being grafted on to the curriculum. The most innovative schools may have peer, business and community, teacher and minority ethnic programmes. A key argument advanced in this book is that these programmes need to be coordinated and managed (see Part IV). Schools, colleges and communities would benefit from the development of a mentoring culture, where individuals, as they pass through their education, training and work careers, experience both being mentored and acting as mentors to others. I believe that this will prove to be an effective way of developing learners, learning organizations and more cohesive communities.

AUDIENCE

The book has been written as a guide to current practice in a rapidly developing field. It aims to bridge the gap that is often found between research and practice by appealing to both constituencies. It can be read in the conventional way from start to finish or used in different ways. However, Part I should be the starting point for all readers as it sets the conceptual framework used in later chapters. Readers interested in particular forms of mentoring may want to start with individual chapters in Part II. People wanting an overview of mentoring programmes may want to begin with Chapters 10 to 12. Researchers and policy makers concerned with the effectiveness of programmes may want to read the sections on 'research and evaluation evidence' in Chapters 3 to 9. Readers wanting concrete examples of what is involved in mentoring programmes may want to start by reading some of the case studies.

The book also aims to appeal to a wide readership in different regions, in particular the English-speaking countries where student mentoring has 'taken off'. Case studies are largely drawn from the United States and the United Kingdom, although there are also Canadian and Australian examples. In order to help the reader, a table illustrates the relationship between schools, ages, years and grades in case study countries (see page xiii). References are drawn from across the English-speaking world. The book is aimed at everyone involved in operating mentoring schemes for young people who wishes to compare and contrast their own schemes with others. It is addressed to mentoring practitioners with experience and to people who are considering setting up their own mentoring programme. These may be teachers and lecturers, or staff in voluntary sector or community organizations. However, the book goes beyond the 'how to' manual in attempting to identify the findings of research and evaluation into effective mentoring programmes. It should, therefore, also be of interest to policy makers and researchers in higher education.

STRUCTURE

The book is organized into four parts. Part I examines the idea of mentoring and its links to the curriculum, and the social and political context within which mentoring for young people has emerged. In Chapter 1, on the context of mentoring, the development of mentoring in the United States, Canada, the United Kingdom, Australia and Israel is described. This chapter also includes a case study of the evolution of government policy on student mentoring in the United Kingdom. Chapter 2 explores the concept of mentoring from its origins to its rapid evolution in the past 20 years.

Part II comprises seven chapters on the forms of mentoring for young people. Each chapter has a similar structure, beginning with a definition and a discussion of the particular form or type of mentoring programme. Three extended case studies follow to inform the reader how programmes work and are managed. These have been selected as examples of interesting practice and, where possible, international examples have been used. The next section summarizes research and evaluation evidence on this form of mentoring and, where available, includes evaluation findings on the case study programmes. There is a discussion of the main issues arising from the form of mentoring, and a 'how to' guide. The good practice 'bullet points' on setting up and running a programme are drawn from the literature, discussions with practitioners and from mentoring Web sites across the world. Each chapter concludes with some 'crystal ball gazing' about the future of the form of mentoring.

Chapter 3 explores programmes that bring business people into schools. Business mentoring in schools has been at the forefront of the growth of mentoring in the United Kingdom and United States. Chapter 4 on community mentoring focuses on the involvement of senior citizens as mentors for students. Minority ethnic programmes (Chapter 5) have proved popular in the United States and United Kingdom as a means of providing role models to help raise the achievement of minority youths in schools. Chapter 6 examines mentoring schemes aimed at students who are 'at risk' of exclusion, although it does not go into detail on programmes within a youth-justice context. The peer mentoring programmes described in Chapter 7 have long been popular in the United States and Canada and they are about to expand within the United Kingdom, encouraged by government policies on citizenship, literacy and raising standards. Telementoring or e-mentoring (Chapter 8) is well established in the United States, and other countries are beginning to pilot programmes as schools and students go online. Chapter 9 tackles the final form involving higher education students mentoring school students.

Part III provides a guide to establishing mentoring programmes, drawing on the lessons of the case study projects and published good practice guidelines from the United States, Canada, United Kingdom and Australia. Chapter 10 deals with the organizational and management issues involved in establishing a mentoring programme. Chapter 11 focuses on all aspects of mentors including recruitment, selection and training. The next chapter, on the processes of student mentoring, includes matching, the stages of the mentoring and ending mentoring relationships. Monitoring, evaluation and the quality assurance of mentoring programmes are covered in Chapter 13.

Part IV offers a vision of a school of the future with a strong mentoring ethos and culture.

ACKNOWLEDGEMENTS

I am very grateful to Professor Ian Jamieson and Professor Tony (AG) Watts, who have acted as mentors in my writing career and spurred me into writing this book. A special thanks to Carol Ainslie and colleagues at Focus Central London and the London Central Learning and Skills Council for their support over the past two years. I am particularly grateful to my partner, Julia Fiehn, for her tolerance, ideas and critical input. I would like to thank my son, Charlie, for help with the diagrams. I have also appreciated the support and encouragement of Jonathan Simpson at Kogan Page.

I am particularly indebted to all those mentoring programme managers who gave their time and commitment: Eddie Bayardelle of Merrill Lynch; Kylie Brown and Nicholas Foster of Hammersmith and Fulham Mentoring Project; Clive Corbett of Pershore High School; Gaynor Day of Roots & Wings Lewisham; Diana Edgecombe of Greenwich EBP; Alan Evans of the National Mentoring Pilot Project; Laura Foley of Mentoring Works Oregon; Professor Tim Newburn of Goldsmith's University; Dr Balwant Singh of Chance UK; Brian Gay; Gillian Granville of the Beth Johnson Foundation; Judy Harris of the University of Texas; Paul Hill of the Dalston Youth Project; Ray Hope and Peter Collins of Salford Business Education Partnership; Amanda Howells of Crime Concern; Keith Hughill; Des Malone of Deptford Green School; Howard Jeffrey of North London Mentor Trust; Professor John Annette and Jane Iremonger of Middlesex University; Pam Maras of Greenwich University; Helen O'Donnell of Central London Mentor Point; Heather Sinclair of CM; Victoria Olisa of Southwark Black Mentor Scheme; Angela Slaven of the Divert Trust; Gary Toward of South Wigston High School; Sue Tuttlebury of South Bank University; Nikki Marsh, Maxine Walker and Kate Amis of the University of Westminster; Ruth Walker of Help the Aged Millennium Volunteers; and Sophie Wellings of RPS Rainer.

A special thanks to colleagues in the National Mentoring Network, in particular Marie Jones, Marie Costigan and Michelle Turner, and members of the UK Mentoring Strategy Group. Alison Lockwood and Leila Seals of the DfES have been helpful over the years in supporting my interest in mentoring. I am grateful to Judith MacCallum and Susan Beltman whose work was important in providing insights into mentoring in Australia. Thanks to former colleagues at the Centre for Education and Industry at the University of Warwick. Finally, I would like to thank all those people who take the time to publicize their mentoring programmes on the World Wide Web and have made the research for this book so much easier and more enjoyable.

Part I

Understanding mentoring

1

The context of mentoring

INTRODUCTION

We begin at the turn of the twentieth century in North America with an account of the modern origins of mentoring programmes. This leads into a description of the development of student mentoring internationally. Mentoring programmes have developed widely across the English-speaking world and the chapter provides a brief overview of mentoring in the United States, England, Australia and Canada. However, there are notable examples of student mentoring in Israel and in Europe. The next section examines the development of government policy towards mentoring for young people, using the experience of England in the past ten years as an example. It includes an account of the role of the National Mentoring Network and an extended case study on the role of learning mentors. The chapter ends with some broad conclusions on the role of government and the international spread of mentoring programmes for young people.

ORIGIN OF MODERN MENTORING PROGRAMMES

The most illuminating account of the modern development of the mentoring movement in America can be found in Marc Freedman's book, *The Kindness of Strangers* (Freedman, 1992). The so-called 'third wave' of mentoring developed rapidly in the 1980s and early 1990s as the administrations, first of Ronald Reagan, and then of George Bush, turned to voluntarism, rather than federal action, as a vehicle to address deep-seated social problems. 'The current wave of mentoring is a particular form of voluntarism, one focusing on the poor, primarily involving middle-class volunteers and promoting personal relationships as an instrument for helping the disadvantaged' (Freedman, 1992: 2).

This was, however, the latest manifestation of a recurring phenomenon in American society. During the economic depression of the later 19th century a social reform movement began. It was based upon a network of charitable societies with paid male agents supporting female 'friendly visitors'. Friendly visitors were middle-class evangelists who aimed to serve as role models for the children of the poor, and to dispense sympathy and wise advice. Philip (2000) comments on the irony of middle-class women, whose own children were being cared for by servants, attempting to rescue children of the poor from following their parents' example. The intrinsic difficulty of the task, the overwhelming nature of the economic hardship and poverty, and a shortage of volunteers led to the demise of the Friendly Visitor movement and their eventual replacement with social workers (Lubove, 1965).

Big Brothers/Big Sisters

The first mentoring programme, Big Brothers/Big Sisters emerged at the beginning of the 20th century in New York (Beiswinger, 1985). Ernest K Coulter served in the first Children's Court in New York, where he felt that the lack of concern shown for the children in sending them to the harsh reformatory school contributed significantly to high rates of recidivism. In an address to civic leaders, middle-class businessmen and professionals, he discussed the plight of one young offender.

> There is only one possible way to save that youngster, and that is to have some earnest, true man volunteer to be his big brother, to look after him, help him do right, make the little chap feel that there is at least one human being in this great city who takes a personal interest in him; who cares whether he lives or dies.
>
> (Freedman,1992: 8)

Coulter ended his speech with a call for volunteers to join his personal crusade. That night the first 39 big brothers were recruited. The Big Brothers movement caught on and in April 1916 a rally at the Casino Theatre in New York attracted an audience of 2,000 people, both black and white, and from all denominations. As with the earlier Friendly Visiting movement, Big Brothers/Big Sisters was driven by the desire to prevent social breakdown through socializing, guiding and building personal relationships. In 1921 the Big Brother/Big Sister Federation was founded, and established the first ground rules for one-to-one relationships. The movement evolved into Big Brothers/Big Sisters of America, probably the largest mentoring programme in the world today (see Chapter 13 for evaluation findings).

THE UNITED STATES

The current mentoring movement within education in the United States was sparked by an upsurge of interest in an 'instrumental' concept of mentoring within the corporate world (Freedman, 1992: 14–16). During the 1970s, what Freedman calls the 'second wave' of mentoring was viewed as an effective way to boost the achievement of women in corporations, in order to help them to break through the 'glass ceiling'. This movement spawned its own industry of 'how to' manuals, seminars and corporate schemes. Eventually the goals of corporate mentoring programmes were widened to include employees from minorities.

Big Brothers/Big Sisters of America was the original mentoring programme for young people. Other programmes grew up to address some of the perceived limitations of Big Brothers/Big Sisters, which:

- targeted the under-10s for the start of the programme;
- focused on one-parent families;
- had a lengthy recruitment and training process for mentors.

The third wave of mentoring spread rapidly across the United States in the late 1980s as a tool to help disadvantaged and at-risk children and young people. The 1983 report, *A Nation At Risk*, produced by the National Commission on Excellence in Education, recommended collaboration between schools, corporations and universities to provide mentors for youth (Guetzlow, 1997). Mentoring increasingly gained high profile and influential backers, including many leading politicians. Milestones of the third wave included:

- 1989: President Bush endorsed mentoring in a television commercial.
- 1989: New York's First Lady, Mathilda Cuomo, declared 1989 'The Year of the Mentor'.
- 1990: several large corporations and national organizations, such as the United Way of America and the National Education Association, announced their support for mentoring.
- 1990: the First National Mentoring Conference was held with Elizabeth Dole, Secretary of Labor, giving the keynote address and federal endorsement.
- 1994: The Office of Juvenile Justice launched the Juvenile Mentoring Program (see Case Study 6.3)
- 1997: at the Presidents' Summit for America's Future it was announced that every child in America should have access to 'an ongoing relationship with a caring adult mentor, tutor, or coach' (Lauland, 1998).
- 1998: Gaining Early Awareness and Readiness for Undergraduate

Programs received large-scale federal funding to encourage children from low-income homes to go to college (see Chapter 9).

● 2001: President George W Bush backed a big expansion of Big Brothers/Big Sisters working with four leading service organizations.

The Presidents' Summit of 1997 was important as it made having a mentor a cornerstone of the nation's approach to tackling young people's problems through active citizenship and volunteering. In 1996, it was estimated that between 5 and 15 million of the nation's youth would benefit from a caring adult mentor (Lauland, 1998). The Presidents' Summit established the America's Promise organization chaired by General Colin Powell, which stimulated Communities of Promise across America to meet the five promises set out in the Presidents' vision. The fact that it included both Republican and Democratic Presidents heralded continuing bipartisan support for mentoring. This translated into many pledges, such as that of the Governor of California that there would be a further 250,000 mentoring relationships across the state during the next few years.

Mass mentoring

Freedman divides US mentoring programmes into large national programmes, small-scale local programmes and corporate programmes (see Case Study 3.3). In addition to organizations running mentoring programmes, there are also mentoring support organizations at national, state and local level. By 1992, the youth mentoring field was described as being in a 'start-up phase', 'highly decentralised and extraordinarily diverse' (Freedman, 1992: 27).

Big Brothers/Big Sisters of America has grown dramatically in the past few years. In 1992, there were 483 local affiliates in 49 states involving 60,000 young people with 'Bigs' and a further 40,000 on the waiting list. It is a good example of what has been referred to as 'mass mentoring' (Withers and Batten, 1995). The 1997 Presidents' Summit led to a pledge to boost the number of mentees to 200,000 by the year 2000. A similar mass-mentoring programme is Campus Compact, which has a goal of a million college and high school students to act as mentors for at-risk children in grades 4 to 9. President George W Bush showed his support for mentoring, which began when he was Governor of Texas (see pp 206–07), by announcing a partnership between Big Brothers/Big Sisters and four leading service organizations: the Kiwanis, Lions, Optimist and Rotary International (Philadelphia, 2 July 2001). The aim was to recruit a million mentors over five years to support the estimated 14 million at-risk young people across the United States.

Another example of mass mentoring supported by the Federal Government came during the Clinton-Gore administrations. Gaining

Early Awareness and Readiness for Undergraduate Programs (GEAR-UP) was expanded to help 750,000 low-income, middle-school children complete their schooling and prepare for college (see Case Study 9.3). Federal GEAR-UP funding aimed to bolster mentoring efforts among states and to provide new grants to partnerships involving middle schools, higher education institutions, private companies and community organizations. The 2001 budget sought to expand services to 1.4 million students, a 63 per cent increase on the previous year. The programmes were distinctive in being:

- based on solid educational research;
- extremely well funded;
- a catalyst for establishing extensive local and state-wide partnerships;
- responsible for a wide range of activities to raise achievement in schools, with mentoring as a key component.

Factors behind growth

Freedman attributes the popularity of mentoring in America to three main factors (1992). The first was the focus in the media on the increasing isolation of young people from caring adult attention, which was deemed responsible for the lack of opportunity, exclusion (see Chapter 6) and poor quality of life for young people, and potentially serious problems of crime and disorder for society. The second factor was the trend towards volunteering and charitable giving among a section of the socially concerned middle class, particularly those 'baby boomers' whose formative years had been around the 1960s. It may also be true that many people reacted to the widening gulf between rich and poor during the 1980s. A third factor was the need identified by psychologists for middle-aged adults to want to transfer their knowledge and culture to the young through direct contact (Goleman, 1990). Mentoring has emerged as an excellent vehicle for 'matching spirit with need' (Freedman, 1992: 33).

According to Freedman the popularity of mentoring also rests in several properties. Mentoring is:

- *Simple*: complex social issues can be tackled by focusing on the needs of an individual.
- *Direct*: mentoring enables an adult to give direct help to a young person in order to make a difference to their lives.
- *Cheap*: mentoring is a low-cost alternative to expensive government programmes and to the work of public institutions.
- *Sympathetic*: to be called a mentor is a kind of honour that links to a noble tradition.
- *Legitimate*: it is recognized as a proper role for unconnected adults to play in the lives of young people.

- *Flexible*: in that it can be used for a range of purposes and appeals to all shades of political opinion.

Mentoring has managed to avoid the controversy that has sometimes embroiled the volunteering movement. However, there was a risk in the early 1990s of its effectiveness being over-hyped. According to Freedman (1992), the evidence of overall impact was 'modest' amid the anecdotal claims of success which have characterized the movement. Indeed, he warned the mentoring movement of the dangers that fervour without a supporting infrastructure could lead to more harm than good being done for young people.

CANADA

An upsurge of interest in mentoring in Canada also occurred during the 1990s, according to the Peer Resources Network (Carr, 2001). The Peer Resources Network is a Web-based organization that provides information on mentoring and tutoring, and has the most extensive mentoring database in North America. The database lists 7,500 peer and mentor programmes around the world, with around 5,200 programmes and individuals in Canada, most of them managed by educational or not-for-profit organizations. Carr argues that, from the data available, Canada is a world leader in the per capita percentage of people involved in tutoring and mentoring. Case Study 1.1, Big Brothers and Sisters of Canada, illustrates the spread of mentoring programmes and models internationally. The case study also shows the diversity of mentoring practice and programmes in a mature mentoring organization and culture.

Case Study 1.1 Big Brothers and Sisters of Canada

Big Brothers and Sisters of Canada is the Canadian version of Big Brothers/Big Sisters of America. The Burlington, Ontario, office manages the mainstream mentoring programmes for children and youth. However, it also acts as a catalyst for local agencies to develop innovative programmes. Mentorship activities include:

- *Mobilising Community Partners*: where a student spends three to four hours once a week at the workplace of his or her mentor.
- *Terra Buddy Program*: where young women with children or who are pregnant are paired with an adult volunteer who provides friendship and support.
- *Roots and Wings*: where 'at-risk' families are matched with adult mentors who provide guidance, support, and friendship to the whole family.

- *Life Choices*: where girls learn about life choices during weekly group meetings with adult volunteers.
- *Right for Me*: where boys facing difficulties during adolescence meet in groups with adult volunteers.
- *In-school Mentoring*: where an adult mentor works with four student mentors, who in turn are matched one-on-one with younger students.

A recent Peer Resources telephone survey of the 2,000 corporations listed as the most productive by the *Canadian Business Magazine* investigated their involvement in mentoring. A third had structured mentoring programmes. One in ten reported that their employees worked as volunteer mentors, typically working with local young people.

A Canadian example of a mass-mentoring programme is the influential Stay-in-School Initiative that was launched in 1992 to tackle the problem of the rising drop-out rate from high schools across the country. The Initiative included various elements:

- a training-the-trainers in mentoring and peer-assistance campaign;
- consultancy for community and school-based mentoring and tutoring programmes;
- dissemination of services to support mentoring and peer assistance across Canada.

From the initial training of 30 National Mentor Leaders in Victoria in 1992 until the end of the Initiative in 1995, more than 65,000 mentors were recruited and 130,000 students were matched with mentors (3 per cent of the youth population aged 14–25). The national school drop-out rate has shown a steady decline since the introduction of the Initiative. A glance at the Peer Resources Web site shows that all forms of mentoring for students and young people continue to thrive in Canada.

ISRAEL

Israel provides a very different experience from the diversity of programmes to be found in North America. One of the main issues in the Israeli education system is achieving equality of opportunity and reducing gaps in achievement from such a diverse population. Since 1975, the *Perach* project has involved university students working as tutors and mentors with school students. *Perach* means 'flower' in Hebrew, but it is an acronym for a 'tutoring project'. The *Perach* project was a compromise outcome of a strike by 150,000 university students protesting at the high costs of tuition (Carmeli, 1999). The idea was to award students scholarships to cover around half their tuition costs in return for them spending a few hours each week helping and motivating disadvantaged Jewish and Arab children.

The number of university students involved in the project has steadily risen and in 2001 it stood at over 25,000 student-mentors (20 per cent of all higher education students) working with over 50,000 children in 800 schools. Typically around twice as many students apply to join *Perach* as there are places available (Carmeli, 1999). The head office of *Perach* is the Weizmann Institute of Science and there are eight regional offices located in the universities, with around 500 staff to supervise the students. The student mentors work closely with the children's families, schools and social services to develop their self-esteem and academic potential. Students typically meet their mentees on a one-to-one basis twice a week for two-hour sessions during the school year. Meetings take place outside school, generally in the child's home, but they are also held at the child's school or at local *Perach* enrichment centres. Mentors are not primarily concerned with academic learning as enrichment; motivation to learn and serving as a role model are given greater priority. *Perach* has traditionally focused on children in elementary and junior high schools, and there has been a trend for the average age of participants to fall (Fresko and Kowalsky, 1998).

Perach has been much evaluated over the years (see, for example, Fresko and Carmeli, 1990). More recently Eisenberg has evaluated the programme, using a control group of non-mentored children to compare with the mentored group (Topping and Hill, 1995). The results showed little impact on standardized tests of academic achievement, but significant gains in attitudes towards school, self-reported participation in school, and leisure time allocated to reading. The studies also reported a lower drop-out rate among the mentored group.

Policy borrowing

Other countries have turned to the *Perach* model as a way of off-setting rising tuition fees following government policies to widen participation in higher education. Probably the most notable example of this policy borrowing is the National Mentoring Pilot Project in England (see Case Study 9.1). However, there are also examples of individual universities using the model in Sweden. For example, students at Malmö University are paired with children in local schools where they meet outside school hours to raise self-esteem and to serve as a role model. In return they are paid 6,000 kronor for their work between October and May.

AUSTRALIA

A 1999 study of mentoring in Australia found a wide range of both small and large-scale programmes (MacCallum and Beltman, 1999). However, these have tended to grow from the bottom-up rather than as a result of a national government policy drive. In another contrast with the US and UK experience, there has tended to be less private sector involvement with education. Consequently, it has been less common for corporations to give employees paid time to act as volunteer mentors in schools. By 2000, sufficient progress had been made for a national mentoring network to be founded, the National Mentoring Association of Australia. However, mentoring organizations in Australia were still looking to the United States for information, experience and resources (Tobin, 2000). An early task of the Australian network was to produce national quality standards to serve as a good practice 'benchmark' to everyone setting up mentoring programmes across the country.

MAINLAND EUROPE

A literature review on mentoring in mainland Europe in the corporate and voluntary sectors found that during the 1990s there were numerous examples of corporate schemes aimed at career development for women (Walton, 2001). There were relatively few examples of mentoring programmes aimed at raising standards in education or to combat social exclusion among young people. However, an interesting feature of the review was an hypothesis that used the concepts of 'uncertainty avoidance' and 'power distance' in an attempt to explain cultural differences in the response to mentoring (Hofstede, 1991).

Uncertainty avoidance and power distance

According to this theory, societies and organizations with a strong tendency towards 'uncertainty avoidance' would perceive the unpredictability associated with mentoring as threatening. In contrast, those tending towards patterns of 'weak uncertainty avoidance' might more easily see the challenge and relish the risks involved in one-to-one mentoring. Similarly, in cultures with 'large power distance', people accept inequalities in the distribution of power in organizations. Teachers, managers and 'successful' individuals would thus be perceived as being at a considerable 'power distance' from school students. The essentially egalitarian notion of mentors 'getting alongside' their mentees would be difficult for mentors and mentees to accept in such an environment.

Walton hypothesizes that the countries in Western Europe that have 'small power distance' and 'weak uncertainty avoidance' are those that have embraced mentoring. These countries include: Sweden; the UK; the

Republic of Ireland; Norway; and the Netherlands. Countries falling into the 'high power distance' and 'strong uncertainty avoidance' categories would include the Southern European countries, such as France, Italy and Spain.

Parrainage

In order to exemplify this theory, Borredon offers the example of a mentoring scheme, which was introduced into a French *Grande École* (Borredon, 1995). The first problem was that the students rejected the term 'mentoring' preferring the term *parrainage* (godparenting). Mentees were called *filleuls* (godchildren). Administrative and academic staff were recruited as *parrains* or 'godparents' for 25 students. Interestingly, all the students allocated administrative *parrains* only attended one meeting. Mentoring was seen as too personal and outside the training of lecturers, who feared that they might lose their credibility if they were unable to advise and solve problems for the students. The mentoring scheme was rejected as a failure by the school.

Clearly, more research needs to be done to test out these hypotheses, and to investigate the extent and spread of mentoring for young people in European education systems.

DEVELOPMENT OF MENTORING IN THE UK

The most common form of mentoring in schools until recently was the mentoring of newly qualified teachers by more experienced staff (see, for example, Fletcher, 2000; McIntyre and Hagger, 1996; Wilkin, 1992). The term 'primary mentoring' was also applied to describe the mentoring of teachers by teachers during training in primary schools (see, for example, Yeomans and Sampson, 1994). This form of mentoring in schools is outside the scope of this book, which focuses exclusively on the mentoring of students and young people.

Business mentoring in schools

The origins of the current wave of mentoring in UK schools began in the early 1990s with the spread of business mentoring programmes (see Chapter 3). The first major quantitative study of school-based mentoring schemes for students in the UK was undertaken in 1997 (Golden and Sims, 1997). The focus was on so-called 'industrial mentoring' of students, which provided the context for the development of mentoring in schools. The study found a total of 16,834 student mentees and 4,527 mentors, from at least 518 schools and 1,978 companies in the 72 schemes that responded to the survey. By the 1998–99 academic year, a survey of 7,000 secondary schools found that of 3,000 respondents, 2,043 secondary schools had mentoring schemes, with 1,257 using business, community or peer mentors, and a further 786 using teacher mentors (DfEE, 1999a). Around 700 schools had business mentoring schemes, and the same number used mentors recruited through education business partnerships. The study also showed that a large number of schools were planning to establish mentoring schemes in the coming year. In 1997, the enthusiasm for mentoring shown by the incoming New Labour government led to a proliferation of national programmes and initiatives.

National Mentoring Network

The National Mentoring Network (NMN) was set up in 1994 following a suggestion made at the annual National Mentoring Conference, now in its tenth year (Costigan, 2000). The aims of the NMN were to:

- promote the development of mentoring;
- offer advice and support to those wishing to set up or develop mentoring programmes;
- provide a forum for the exchange of information and good practice.

The NMN has grown steadily from 350 members in 1998, to 700 in 2000 and over 1,000 by 2001.

An early Network survey indicated that there were 178 mentoring programmes operating throughout the UK during the 1993–94 year (Anderson, 1994). In its early years, the Network membership comprised people concerned with education business partnerships and with mentoring by business people in secondary schools. This reflected the fact that responsibility for mentoring in government rested with the same division of the Department for Education and Employment (DfEE) that was responsible for links between schools and businesses.

By 1997, the DfEE agreed to fund a full-time Network Co-ordinator. This gave added impetus to the drive to expand membership, commission new publications (for example, Miller, 1998) and influence government policy towards mentoring. A further spur to Network growth was provided by DfEE funding of a Mentoring Bursary Scheme, which was administered by the NMN. The aims of the Mentoring Bursary Scheme were to:

- stimulate mentoring activity where none exists already;
- develop quality frameworks within which progammes can operate;
- harness existing evidence in a systematic way to help raise the profile of mentoring and spread its use in schools.

Mentoring Bursary Scheme

In 1998–99, 20 projects received funding to develop innovative approaches to student mentoring (Golden and Sims, 1999). The scheme was expanded in 1999–2000 to cover 40 projects, including funding earmarked for inner-city areas and for minority-ethnic programmes at a total cost of £450,000. The Bursary Scheme was re-focused on the social-inclusion objectives favoured in government policy 'around gender, ethnicity, promoting equality of opportunity, combating disadvantage and disability' (Rt Honourable Paul Boateng, Minister of State for the Home Office). By 2000, education-focused projects accounted for about half of Network membership, with the remainder comprising youth and community organizations, careers services and charitable trusts.

In 1998, the UK Mentoring Strategy Group was formed in order to:

- draw together the public, private, government and voluntary sectors;
- provide a national voice for mentoring;
- influence the development of government policy (NMN, 1999).

The NMN provides the secretariat for this cross-sectoral group, which has representatives from various government departments and different mentoring schemes. The network has increasingly been used as a vehicle for implementing aspects of government policy towards mentoring in the UK.

Government policy towards mentoring

During the years of the last Conservative administration the policy towards mentoring in schools was supportive. The focus was on business mentors developing employability skills among young people and motivating borderline students to achieve the five GCSE A*–C benchmark (Miller, 1998). The incoming New Labour government was prepared for a major expansion of mentoring programmes as a contribution to several policy areas. Increasingly, ministers used the annual National Mentoring Conference as an occasion to make policy announcements about government-sponsored mentoring initiatives.

Policy developments in 1998

At the 1998 Conference Estelle Morris, Minister for School Standards, outlined how mentoring was underpinning several policies on education, training and employment, including:

- The New Deal 'Gateway' for unemployed 18–24 year olds offered them 'independent, volunteer mentors'.

- Modern apprentices were to be given opportunities for mentors, especially to encourage progression into higher education.
- The 'New Start' strategy for re-engaging 'disaffected' 14–17 year olds had mentoring as a key element.
- The *Excellence in Schools* White Paper included plans for government collaboration with the charity Age Concern, to provide older mentors for young people (DfEE, 1997).
- *Excellence in Schools* also acknowledged the contribution of business, voluntary and public organizations in providing mentors to help raise standards and motivation in schools (Morris, 1998).

The Minister also announced the start of the Mentoring Bursary Scheme (see above).

Policy developments in 1999

One area in which mentoring could make an obvious contribution was in the drive to encourage more volunteering. Volunteering was seen as part of the process of rebuilding healthy communities, and mentoring was viewed as an appropriate activity for volunteers. At the 1999 National Mentoring Conference, Paul Boateng, Minister of State at the Home Office, described the role of the newly established Active Community Unit in promoting mentoring. The Active Community Unit would:

- examine the scope for sharing resources and good practice;
- identify and explore generic mentoring issues, such as recruitment, training and development;
- develop the role of mentoring in combating social exclusion and tackling some of society's more intractable problems, such as youth crime, drugs and homelessness.

He also explained the important role of mentoring in the youth justice reforms based around the Crime and Disorder Act. The role of the Youth Justice Board was to identify and spread good practice in mentoring, using some of the £30 million funding given over the following three years. He highlighted two good practice examples that are featured in this book: the Dalston Youth Project (see Case Study 6.2) and the Chance project, working with difficult primary pupils (see Case Study 6.1).

'Mentoring will prove a useful tool in supporting the range of community sentences that will now be available to the courts' (Boateng, 2000). Paul Boateng had a particular interest in the subject that stemmed from his own origins. His personal philosophy of mentoring was based on an old Ashanti saying: 'If you go into the forest be sure you take an elder with you. They are sure to have travelled the path before you.' 'A mentor is someone who represents another way, some stability in a troubled world' (Boateng, 2000).

Policy developments in 2000

An inter-departmental study of mentoring programmes supported by government during 1999–2000 produced some interesting findings (Home Office, 2000b). Four parts of government were mainly involved in sponsoring mentoring programmes: the Home Office, the Department of Health, DfEE (Department for Education and Employment) and the Social Exclusion Unit. The study found that:

- A third of schools used mentoring and there were around 750,000 volunteers supported through DfEE programmes (primarily in schools).
- There were an estimated 2,000 organizations providing mentoring.
- Nineteen different client groups were identified as the subject of mentoring programmes, including: people with mental health problems; pre-release prisoners; clients of the New Deal for those aged 18–24 who were moving into work; and young people wanting to set up a business.

The great diversity of mentoring situations, with the resulting plethora of projects and range of government departments involved, was given as an important reason why there had been only limited studies of the impact and effectiveness of mentoring. The report concluded that it was essential to safeguard vulnerable young people and to ensure the quality of mentoring programmes through an improved infrastructure.

Learning mentors

The key feature of the Minister for School Standards' speech at the 2000 National Mentoring Conference was to explain the central role of mentoring within the Excellence in Cities and Connexions Service policy initiatives (Morris, 2000). Under the first phase of the Excellence in Cities programme, 800 learning mentors were appointed in six conurbations 'to help pupils to overcome barriers to learning, sometimes within the school, and sometimes outside of it' (see Case Study 1.2 below). The Minister sought to distinguish between the role of learning mentors and volunteer mentors (see Case Study 1.2). Learning mentors would be:

- paid employees of the school, not volunteers;
- only located in inner-city schools;
- working one-to-one, as one part of their job;
- responsible for ensuring the flow of information about pupils at the point of transfer from primary to secondary school;

- coordinating external, volunteer mentors;
- selecting students for volunteer mentoring;
- signposting students to wider support services outside the school, including study support, counselling or social services.

In the programme's second year, 'excellence clusters' were introduced in new areas across the country. In each Excellence in Cities area, a 'link learning mentor' was appointed to facilitate networking and support among learning mentors. By the end of the 2000–01 school year an estimated 1,500 learning mentors in secondary schools and 900 in primary schools were in post (Hansard, 2001). This was set to rise to over 3,000 learning mentors by 2004, at an average cost of £33,000. Schools outside targeted areas were also encouraged to appoint learning mentors to help reduce truancy and exclusion.

The Minister highlighted various policy initiatives aimed at increasing the supply of volunteers, and hence of volunteer mentors. These included:

- *Timebank*: a Web-based programme to encourage people to volunteer their time.
- *The Experience Corps*: which aimed to increase the number of volunteers aged 50 and over.
- *Millennium Volunteers*: the Prime Minister's 'flagship programme' to engage thosse aged 16–24 in voluntary activity.

Policy developments in 2001–2004

At the same conference, the Minister also launched the Mentor Point Initiative with the establishment of three pilot points in Excellence in Cities areas to support volunteer mentors working with young people in schools (see Chapter 11). She also announced that DfEE would work with the NMN to produce a set of generic quality standards to apply across all mentoring programmes (see Chapter 13). In January 2001 the Chancellor of the Exchequer, Gordon Brown, announced £5.3 million additional money to support mentoring during 2001–04. The Active Community Unit of the Home Office was allocated funding to set up three more 'mentor points' targeting one or more of three groups:

- young people outside the school context;
- mentoring for, and by, people over 50 years of age;
- mentoring serving a rural community.

Funding was also made available to the NMN to support the creation of a 'mentoring infrastructure' to aid mentoring projects to meet minimum national quality standards (NMN, June 2001). This included the development of resources to support projects nationally, training and professional development workshops, and the creation of a register of approved providers of mentoring programmes. The Active Community Unit was given funding to establish The Mentoring Fund with priority being given to bids in the following areas:

- non-school-based mentoring working with children;
- transition mentoring, eg school leaver to employment;
- peer mentoring, eg adult-to-adult;
- intergenerational mentoring;
- mentoring by those aged over 50.

The launch of this mentoring initiative involved four Ministers and it even captured the attention of the leading UK tabloid, the *Sun*, which featured it in an editorial.

> Gordon Brown's bid to bring mentoring to Britain should be applauded. Not all children have the loving support of parents. Many do not. The idea of mentoring is for successful adults to spend time encouraging children – raising their sights and lifting their ambitions. It has worked across America; it can work here. It is interesting that Brown is involving himself in social and education issues. We like this move towards 'joined up government'. Mentoring in Britain has our full support. We will do all we can to help.
>
> (*Sun*, 16 November 2000: 8)

In 2001, the Standards and Effectiveness Unit at the DfEE supported the expansion of the National Mentoring Pilot Project linking 21 Education Action Zones to 16 higher education institutions. The project has supported young people in deprived neighbourhoods and raised aspirations towards higher education (Barber, 2001). By spring 2001, there were 800 mentors working with around 2,500 students.

Case Study 1.2 Learning mentors in England

This case study describes the learning mentors programme in England as a special form of mentoring in schools (DfEE, 1999b). Although learning mentors were employed by and answerable to head teachers in schools, there were four key objectives that all schemes should aim to meet:

- All students in the designated areas would have access to a learning mentor to help them overcome barriers to learning.
- Help would be targeted at those most in need.
- Standards would be raised, truancy and exclusions reduced in the target areas.
- The service provided would complement that of teachers and other support agencies.

Role of the learning mentor

The role of learning mentor involved:

- diagnostic assessment of students' strengths, weaknesses and learning support needs using a variety of methods, including one-to-one interviews, behavioural assessment tools, parental feedback, observation and school reports;
- producing an action plan for the support of students identified as needing extra support;
- working to support students through a range of methods, such as one-to-one mentoring, support with tasks, in-class support, mediation, home visits, group work, peer mentoring, work with external mentors and youth projects;
- monitoring and evaluating students' progress and developing an 'exit strategy'.

Learning mentors played an important role in the transfer of pupil information from primary to secondary school, within school and between schools and external agencies. They were also involved in the assessment of all pupils entering or returning to school. They worked closely with Special Educational Needs Coordinators and staff responsible for 'gifted and talented' students. Learning mentors provided a contact point for student access to external mentors and out-of-school study support. The government also viewed learning mentors as an important element of its anti-bullying strategy (DfEE, 2000a).

According to government, learning mentors can come from a range of backgrounds including teaching, social work, youth work, education welfare, human resource departments in the private sector or counselling (DfEE, 1999b). Guidance stressed that young people should view learning mentors as focusing on their needs as individuals, and 'not simply as additional members of school staff'.

Training

In addition to local training schemes, a national five-day training programme was developed. The programme covered a wide range of subjects and introduced theoretical frameworks to guide learning mentors' decision making:

- The stages of work: before and at referral; initial contact; action planning; and exit strategy.
- Managing behaviour in order to raise achievement: applying theoretical frameworks for understanding behaviour; selecting appropriate tools to develop learning skills; and appreciating the issues of personal safety and anger management.
- Developing strategies and skills in effective monitoring and evaluation, including an examination of 'hard' and 'soft' indicators of progress.
- Raising achievement through group work.

Mentoring and learning mentors

Clearly, the role of learning mentors goes way beyond the role of volunteer mentors as described elsewhere in this book. Some of the key differences between learning mentors and more conventional, volunteer mentors are that they:

- are paid employees of the school;
- are not always engaged in voluntary mentoring, since students are targeted;
- are given longer and more thorough training that includes both theory and practice;
- play a key role in accessing, developing and communicating information on students;
- take an interventionist and advocacy role in meeting with teachers;
- can offer qualified careers guidance and counselling methods (depending on their background and training);
- focus on raising achievement through group work.

It is probably true to say that mentoring is one aspect of the complex role of the learning mentor. Learning mentors in England approach the role of the holistic, professional mentor described in the next chapter. However, it can also be argued that learning mentors are an example of pseudo-mentoring, because, like teachers they are members of school staff, and so their work is neither independent, nor voluntary.

CONCLUSIONS

Policy borrowing

In this chapter we have explored the international dimension of student mentoring. Undoubtedly, the development of the World Wide Web has facilitated the spread of mentoring by providing countless examples of programmes and good practice information. The major mentoring Web sites are based on North American mentoring programmes. It is, therefore, inevitable that the United States has had a major influence on student mentoring in other countries. The problem of youth disaffection and school drop-out has been recognized for much longer in the United States, and student mentoring has developed as one response to this crisis. Other countries facing similar problems with their young people have also looked to the US for solutions. The *Perach* programme in Israel has also been influential in the development of paid mentoring by higher education students in schools. This programme has been borrowed and modified by the government in England and by universities in Sweden. However, when borrowing policies and practices from other countries it is important to consider the political, educational and social contexts that allow particular programmes to thrive.

Patterns of evolution

The countries we have focused on have had different starting points for their student mentoring. In the UK, the current range of mentoring programmes evolved from the business mentoring schemes, which developed in the early 1990s. These were part of what has been termed the schools-industry movement, which saw the development of local education-business partnerships to broker links between schools and business (Jamieson, 1985). The main focus of these early programmes was on developing employability skills, as well as increasing motivation and achievement. In Israel the emphasis was on bridging the gap in achievement between children from different Jewish and Arab communities. In the United States, Canada and Australia the major impetus was to reduce the school drop-out rate and combat the social exclusion this caused. Since 1997 the UK has followed these other countries in focusing on mentoring as a vehicle for promoting social inclusion.

In the United States, Canada and the UK we have seen a similar pattern of evolution in student mentoring programmes. The first phase saw pioneering, primarily local, programmes targeting particular groups of students. In the second phase, there was a proliferation of local and some national pilot programmes using different 'forms' of mentoring. Finally, we have seen the emergence of 'mass mentoring' programmes, often supported by government funding and policies to spread practice across the whole country.

Politics of mentoring

It is also interesting to note how mentoring has been a strategy that has appealed to politicians at different ends of the spectrum. The Presidents' Summit in the United States signalled this bipartisan approach. However, as the mentoring field has become more differentiated, so politicians are able to put a different 'spin' on what mentoring aims to achieve. Thus for President Clinton support for the GEAR UP mentoring programme (see Case Study 9.3) was a means to promote social and educational mobility for middle-school children from poor families. President George W Bush, on the other hand, seems to view mentoring by certain types of volunteers (including ex-military personnel) as a way of instilling family values and developing 'character' education. Another Bush policy was to support faith-based organizations in providing mentors for the 1.5 million children of incarcerated parents.

Thus we see the emergence of a colour-coded mentoring curriculum (Law, 1983), where mentoring can serve goals of various hues. Those with a red or pinkish (left-wing) hue tend to:

● promote equal opportunities for females and minority students;

- raise the education aspirations of students from poor families;
- increase the proportion of students from poor families graduating and going into higher education.

Those with a blue (right-wing) perspective aim more to:

- redress faulty socialization within dysfunctional families;
- instil values in young offenders;
- promote character education, faith and family values.

Mentoring has also been attacked from the left as a form of social control, as predominantly white, middle-class mentors pass on their values to working-class students (Gulam and Zulfiquar, 1998). According to this view, mentoring practitioners have been naïve in colluding with the dominant ideologies and contradictions of an unequal and divided society. Far from empowering young people, mentoring can reinforce the status quo. The New Labour government in the UK has typically managed to embrace both ends of the spectrum in its support for mentoring in school, community, employment and youth-justice contexts.

The role of government

In the early 1990s, Marc Freedman highlighted the dangers of 'fervour without infrastructure', which might undermine the emerging mentoring movement (Freedman, 1992). It would seem that in both the United States and the United Kingdom the warning was heeded as governments played an increasingly important role in developing the infrastructure to underpin mentoring. Government funding has obviously enabled mass mentoring programmes to be introduced. Well-funded and managed schemes have been able to act as beacons of good practice, which have helped other programmes avoid pitfalls.

Support for national networks and networking events has also helped to disseminate good practice. The publication of, and government support for, national quality standards and quality assurance programmes has aided the development of minimum standards. Government action has promoted the supply of volunteers, coupled with support for mentoring organizations that can train and place mentors. Education departments have also identified areas of school improvement where mentoring can contribute to the twin goals of raising standards and countering social exclusion. In other words, governments have helped stimulate the demand for mentoring and the supply of mentors to satisfy the demand. In these ways, the ongoing fervour has been supported by the emerging infrastructure.

2

The concept of mentoring

INTRODUCTION

Mentoring is an idea and a practice that has evolved over time in different cultures and contexts. This book is concerned with 'planned' or 'structured' mentoring, as contrasted to 'natural mentoring'. Natural mentoring occurs incidentally in a variety of life settings through friendship, teaching, coaching and counselling. 'Planned' mentoring involves structured programmes with clear objectives, where mentors and mentees are matched using formal processes. It is unsurprising, therefore, that today there is considerable confusion over its meaning.

The purpose of this chapter is to explore the concept of mentoring, drawing on some of the extensive theoretical and operational literature. It begins with an account of the origins of the term in Greek mythology, and of recent work on natural mentoring relationships. After an initial review of the literature on the concept of mentoring, there is a discussion of the aims of mentoring programmes for mentees and mentors. The possible links between mentoring and the curriculum of educational institutions are identified. Distinctions are then drawn between mentoring and other types of 'helping relationship' such as counselling and coaching. There follows an account of various ways of classifying mentoring programmes. The chapter concludes with a discussion of some key conceptual issues, such as competing mentoring philosophies, paid and voluntary mentoring, and one-to-one compared to small-group mentoring. Finally, the concept of mentoring used in the rest of the book is described, and the links between mentoring and current debates in learning theory are discussed.

HISTORY OF THE CONCEPT

It is customary for trainers, mentoring programme managers and authors to refer to the origins of the term 'mentor' in Greek mythology. In Homer's *Odyssey*, Odysseus prepares to fight in the Trojan War and entrusts his friend, Mentor, with the care of his son, Telemachus. Mentor was responsible, as a wise and trusted adviser, for guiding all aspects of the boy's development. Later Athena, Goddess of both war and wisdom, assumed the form of Mentor to offer prudent counsel. The example of Athena's (Mentor's) advice below was given to boost his confidence, as the young Telemachus was about to meet Nestor on Pylos.

> *Telemachus: Mentor, how am I to go up to the great man? How shall I greet him? Remember that I have had no practice in making speeches; and a young man may well hesitate to cross-examine someone so much his senior. Athena: Telemachus, where your native wit fails, heaven will inspire you. It is not for nothing that the gods have watched your progress ever since your birth.*

However, Mentor was only one of several forms, both animal and human, that Athena assumed to advise both Telemachus and Odysseus (Roberts, 1999). Indeed Mentor himself seems to have been particularly ineffective in handling the suitors that harassed Telemachus's mother, Penelope, and in generally protecting his friend's household. In the myth it was not he but Athena – in the guise of Mentor – who was the wise and trusted adviser. Roberts argues convincingly that the modern interpretation of the role of Mentor is based on *Les Aventures de Telemaque*, published in 1699 and arguably the most popular book in the 18th century. Fenelon engaged his hero, Telemaque, in a series of adventures designed to illustrate the wise and ideal monarch in contrast to the absolutist Louis XIV. In these stories, unlike in the original *Odyssey*, Mentor did play the wise adviser role, and the book's popularity explains the introduction of the term 'mentor' into the English language after 1750 (Roberts, 1999).

This classical model of mentoring is also an embodiment of sexism (Philip, 2000). Penelope, as a single parent, is deemed incapable of bringing up her son to follow in the footsteps of his heroic father. The nurse, Euricleia, is also mentioned in the myth, but her advice is treated dismissively. Although it was Athena who provided Telemachus with guidance, Mentor takes all the plaudits. This negative attitude towards women, who are deemed incapable of imparting manly behaviour, is continued in the influential modern work by Levinson *et al*, *The Seasons of a Man's Life* (1978).

NATURAL MENTORING

Although this book is concerned with planned mentoring programmes established by adults to benefit students, it is important to be aware of the range of natural mentoring relationships available to young people. A Scottish study by Philip and Hendry (2000) investigated natural mentoring relationships using a broad sample of young people and adults. Five types of natural mentoring relationship were identified:

- Classic mentoring was a one-to-one relationship where a more experienced adult would provide support, advice and challenge to a younger person. This might occur within the context of a shared interest or hobby, where the adult would act as a role model and treat the younger person as 'special'. Historically the classic model was that of the expert and the apprentice in craft enterprises; a more recent model is that of the mentor and protégé in corporate settings.
- Individual-team mentoring was where a group of young people would look to an individual or small number of individuals for support, advice and challenge. This was often found in the context of youth work in groups such as the guides and scouts. The young people tended to respect mentors who had relevant experience and who understood their expectations.
- Friend-to-friend mentoring was most common among young women who were 'best friends', and provided a 'safety net' for those who were mistrustful of adults. They were able to share sensitive information and discuss options prior to action.
- Peer-group mentoring occurred among groups of friends, often in the context of exploring an issue, such as drug misuse within a specific context.
- Long-term relationship mentoring with 'risk-taking' adults was similar to classic mentoring, but in a situation where the mentee has a history of rebellion and challenging authority (pp 216–17).

Philip (2000) concludes that natural mentoring can take place within a wide range of relationships and that it takes on greater importance at times of crisis or as the relationships develop. Characteristics of natural mentoring were the mutual benefits, and the equality of power between mentors and mentees. The mentoring relationships represented a safe and confidential setting in which issues could be explored. Trust was a key theme raised by young people interviewed.

African-American patterns

Rhodes and colleagues in the United States have examined the role of natural mentoring networks among African-American families (Rhodes,

Ebert and Fischer, 1992; Rhodes, Gingiss and Smith, 1994). Young mothers often had older natural mentors who acted as a bulwark against depression and who would support them through difficulties. This was traced back to the tradition of 'other mothers' within African-American families. These were women who were close to the family, but sufficiently independent to become confidants of younger women. Philip (2000) concludes that it is important to examine mentoring in the context of differing cultural and social patterns.

DEFINITIONS OF PLANNED MENTORING

In the UK there are demands for a tighter definition of mentoring. This stems from the increasing amounts of public, private and voluntary-sector resources that are being channelled into supporting mentoring programmes. When funding groups put money into a mentoring programme, they clearly like to know what the core processes are and what the outcomes are likely to be. The fact that programmes with 'mentoring' in their title tend to attract funding has led programme designers to 'stretch' the term to include a wide range of helping and learning processes. Such trends have encouraged the Home Office to include its own definition of mentoring in bidding literature.

> A one-to-one, non-judgemental relationship in which an individual mentor voluntarily gives time to support and encourage another. This relationship is typically developed at a time of transition in the mentee's life, and lasts for a significant and sustained period of time.
>
> (Carrad, 2002)

The development of mentoring networking organizations has also promoted very broad definitions. It is in the interests of membership organizations to define mentoring in a way that will include as wide a range of practitioners as possible. This 'big tent' approach is also visible in the numerous mentoring Web sites developed in the United States, Canada and the UK, which also aim to attract as wide an audience as possible. However, the very flexibility of the concept of mentoring may also have become a barrier to stakeholders accepting it as a definable and credible process (Langridge, 1998).

Contract mentoring

It can be argued that attempts to define mentoring are futile because mentoring relationships or mentorships are constructed by each mentor and mentee (Monaghan, 1992). The concept of 'contract' mentoring emphasizes the importance of the agreement struck at the initial meeting between mentor and mentee as to the nature and objectives of the relationship. Mentors are involved in negotiating the form of their duties and are, therefore, involved in defining what mentoring is and what mentors do. The term 'mentorship' is used to describe the relationship between the mentor and the mentee or student. Mentoring can then be judged in relation to these negotiated objectives and processes, which will be different in each relationship. Although it is often the case that mentorships are constructed, this is generally in the context of an overall framework of objectives and ground rules set by the programme organizers.

'Popular consensus' approach

One approach to defining mentoring is to accept the broad range of practitioners' descriptions. This is based on the idea that everyone knows what mentoring is, but they are all working with their own definitions (Lunt *et al*, 1992). This 'popular consensus' approach to defining mentoring accepts what is offered by descriptions of mentorship at an operational level. For example, Peer Resources, a Canadian Web-based network providing useful resources on mentoring, gives a typical popular consensus definition (see Web guide).

Formal mentorship is held to have the following characteristics:

- It is a deliberate, conscious, voluntary relationship.
- The relationship may or may not have a specific time limit.
- It is sanctioned or supported by the organization.
- It occurs between an experienced, employed or retired person and one or more other persons.
- There is generally no direct, hierarchical or supervisory chain of command.
- The outcomes are expected to benefit all parties for personal growth, career development, lifestyle enhancement, spiritual fulfilment, goal achievement, and other mutually designated areas.
- It has a benefit to the community in which it takes place.
- It takes place through one-to-one relationships or small groups, and by electronic or telecommunication means.
- It typically focuses on interpersonal support, guidance, mutual exchange, sharing of wisdom, coaching and role modelling.

Such definitions, however, tend to exclude some forms of mentoring, such as 'involuntary' mentoring in a youth-justice context or 'paid' mentoring in a small business support context. They also fail to distinguish between mentoring and other forms of helping such as coaching, tutoring and counselling.

The 'continuum' approach

A second approach to defining mentoring is to view it as a continuum of helping behaviours from which the mentor can choose. Different behaviours may be appropriate at different stages in the relationship. Gay (2000) argues that mentoring is about helping people in transition. This involves the passage from being 'unconsciously incompetent' to being 'consciously incompetent' and then through being 'consciously competent' to a final condition of being 'unconsciously competent'. The role of the mentor in this process is to challenge and to 'tug the sleeve' of the mentee. According to Gay there is a continuum of helping behaviours during the mentoring relationship from 'exploring' to 'directing':

- *Exploring*: informal and mutual exploration of issues.
- *Revealing*: making known.
- *Guiding*: leading the way.
- *Advising*: considering in company.
- *Teaching*: enabling.
- *Training*: coaching.
- *Directing*: showing the way.

The continuum has at one end the 'exploring' behaviour, which involves the mentor in supporting the mentee, promoting his or her independence and encouraging risk taking. These behaviours provide encouragement for lifelong learning, and involve mutual personal growth and a learning partnership. At the 'directing' end of the mentoring spectrum, the mentor is confirming, creating greater dependence and encouraging safe options. According to Gay, as the mentoring relationship moves down the list, the behaviour of mentor and mentee is increasingly constrained by external protocols.

'Key characteristics' approach

A third approach to defining mentoring combines the search for key characteristics with the continuum of mentor behaviours. Thus, Anderson and Shannon (1995) review the historical origins of mentoring and conclude that mentoring exhibits five key features. Mentoring:

- is intentional;
- is a nurturing process to help people grow towards their full potential;
- is an insightful process involving the acquisition of wisdom by the mentee;
- is supportive and protective;
- involves role modelling as a key feature.

Their definition of mentoring involves five elements:

- the process of nurturing;
- the mentor as role model;
- the five functions of teaching, sponsoring, encouraging, counselling and befriending;
- a focus on personal and/or professional development;
- an ongoing, caring relationship.

The mentor actions associated with the five functions – which all flow out of the history of the concept – are as follows:

- *Teaching* involves modelling, informing, confirming, disconfirming, prescribing and questioning behaviours.
- *Sponsoring* means protecting, supporting, and promoting or advocating (advocacy) behaviours.
- *Encouraging* includes affirming, inspiring and challenging behaviours.
- *Counselling* involves listening, probing, clarifying, advising and problem-solving behaviours.
- *Befriending* includes accepting and relating behaviours.

Phenomenological definition

Following an exhaustive literature review on the concept of mentoring using a phenomenological approach, Roberts advances this definition of mentoring:

> A formalized process whereby a more knowledgeable and experienced person actuates a supportive role of overseeing and encouraging reflection and learning within a less experienced and knowledgeable person, so as to facilitate that person's career and personal development.
>
> (Roberts, 2000: 162)

He argues that there appears to be a consensus that mentoring has a number of essential attributes. Mentoring involves a:

- process;
- supportive relationship;
- helping process;
- teaching-learning process;
- reflective process;
- career–development process;
- formalized process;
- role constructed by or for a mentor.

Mentoring also has a number of contingent attributes:

- coaching;
- sponsoring;
- role modeling;
- assessing;
- being an informal process.

Roberts argues that people will inevitably perceive and experience mentoring in different ways and the debate over the meaning of mentoring is therefore bound to continue.

Power or experience

Clutterbuck (1998) contrasts two distinct schools of thought about mentoring in the context of corporate programmes. In the United States concept of mentoring, older and more powerful mentors support their protégés in developing their careers, with relatively little emphasis on learning. In the European concept the mentor relies on greater experience, rather than power, to help the mentee, and the focus is on learning and development. According to Clutterbuck developmental mentors have a complex role, because they need to be reasonably competent in all four of the other roles: coach, counsellor, guardian and networker/facilitator. Effective mentors know when to move from one role into another. Again mentoring is used as an overarching concept that links together the range of other forms of helping behaviour.

'Holistic' mentoring

The term 'holistic' can be used to describe the mentor who deploys a wide range of interpersonal skills to help another person reach towards academic, work-related learning and personal goals. A 'holistic' mentor uses a full range of helping skills: befriending, counselling, coaching and tutoring. It is likely that holistic mentors will be very experienced, well-trained individuals who are able to operate at a high level of skill and who may be paid professionals. It may be that the new role of learning mentor in the UK will involve holistic mentoring (see Chapter 1). They will be people who understand the often complex linkages between:

- a student's knowledge, skills and attitudes;
- academic performance and personal life;
- motivation, classroom performance and achievement;
- career aspirations, self-esteem and self-confidence.

The idea of holistic mentoring draws a clear distinction between mentoring and other forms of helping relationship. However, it is also true that most mentoring programmes do not aspire to holistic mentoring, but have much more modest goals. It is important, therefore, to examine the aims and objectives of mentoring programmes and to see how they fit into the curriculum of educational institutions.

MENTORING AND HELPING BEHAVIOURS

As stated before, part of the confusion over the definition of mentoring arises from the fact that mentors employ 'helping' behaviours, which themselves are often the subject of separate intervention programmes aimed at young people. These behaviours include befriending, counselling, coaching and tutoring.

Befriending

Befriending is a form of helping relationship generally undertaken by volunteers, who agree to provide emotional and social support for someone else. Befriending schemes offer help to people with a wide range of needs, which can range across the lonely, the suicidal and those facing life-threatening illnesses. The befriending relationship involves 'getting alongside' and supporting the person to be helped. It can also involve regular meetings and social outings. While mentoring may include befriending, it does not have to, and generally involves less extensive emotional support than in the cases just mentioned. Mentors are also unlikely to offer the kind of practical support by 'doing things' for their mentee that a befriender might undertake.

Befriending is sometimes conflated with 'buddying'. 'Buddy schemes' often help new members settle in to an organization by providing a supportive and encouraging network (Conway, 1997). They therefore provide an integrative function. Buddying is often used in schools when an older student aids a student who is new to the school to settle in. Such schemes tend to be less concerned with emotional support and are much shorter term than befriending programmes. They are more likely to be seen as part of the induction of students aiding the transition to new schools by 'showing them the ropes'. However, they can be much more extensive in their goals and have been applied to the integration of students with special needs into mainstream schools (see Case Study 7.1).

Counselling

Langridge (1998) refers to the 'Janus-faced nature of mentoring', which uses both counselling and coaching behaviours, but is different from either of these forms of helping relationship. Counselling is often regarded as the preserve of the trained counsellor using a range of skills and styles to help the client move forward. It clearly involves a set of skills that well-trained, experienced mentors need to deploy if they are to be effective. In particular these include active listening, identifying problems and encouraging the mentee to 'own' their solutions. However, mentors are more likely than counsellors to have contact with their mentees outside formal sessions, and generally have to engage in self-disclosure to help win the trust of their mentee, whereas counsellors tend to avoid self-disclosure. The latter are also likely to use particular diagnostic and therapeutic techniques, which will not be available to mentors who lack specialist training.

Coaching

Conway distinguishes between coaching and mentoring in organizations. 'Coaching is more directive and focused on the job. It is a process often carried out by line managers. Mentoring is a non-directive relationship and more broadly focused. The mentor takes a longer perspective for the individual and the organization' (1997: 54). In his view, coaching is directly related to performance issues. He also uses the concept of 'technical mentors', who sometimes offer assistance in addition to skills coaching undertaken by the line manager. Parsloe and Wray (2000) have explored the distinctions between coaching and mentoring in a corporate context. In educational institutions the term 'coaching' is more often applied to teaching skills within a sporting context. Some mentoring programmes involve sporting role models coaching mentees to develop their skills, but also to help their personal development.

Tutoring

Tutoring can be distinguished from mentoring, although the mentor will often employ tutoring skills as part of the mentoring process (see also Chapter 7). According to Goodlad (1995) the key differences are that tutoring focuses on subject learning, usually takes place in the classroom, involves groups of tutees and generally lasts a few weeks. Mentoring, in contrast, concentrates on 'life skills', often occurs outside the classroom, is one-to-one and lasts for several months or years. Clearly, where mentoring focuses on subject learning, is relatively short term and involves a group, then this sharp distinction becomes blurred.

AIMS AND OBJECTIVES

A review of the literature and an examination of programme objectives in many different mentoring programmes indicate that there are three main aims of student mentoring. First, the 'developmental' aim focuses on the personal and social development of the student, and may involve changing attitudes. This developmental purpose is sometimes referred to as the 'psychosocial function' of mentoring, and is contrasted with so-called 'career' or 'instrumental' mentoring (Galbraith and Cohen, 1995). The psychosocial function results from the interplay between the interpersonal dialogue of mentor and mentee, and the inner dialogue within the mentee. It represents the value of the relationship to the self of the mentee. The instrumental function is the external value of the relationship, that is, when mentees benefit from their mentors' knowledge, contacts, support and guidance. The second, 'work-related learning', aim refers to goals concerning the career choice of the students, their knowledge of the world of work and their employability skills. Third, the 'subject' aim of mentoring concerns students' achievements in their courses, and includes basic skills support and work on study skills.

The three broad aims of student mentoring can include a wide range of content:

- *Developmental* mentoring may involve social skills, attitudinal change, social inclusion, anti-drug strategies, self-esteem, self-confidence, feelings about self and others, spiritual development, motivation, attitudes and values and so-called 'soft' skills.
- *Work-related* mentoring can include employability and work-related skills, key skills, enterprise, career progression and management, and future goals and aspirations.
- *Subject* mentoring may relate knowledge acquisition, subject-specific skills and study skills.

Each of the three broad aims of student mentoring has a number of more specific objectives. These are introduced in Box 2.1.

Box 2.1 Possible aims of student mentoring schemes

Developmental aims

1. *Self-esteem objective*: to raise students' self-esteem and positive feelings of self-worth.
2. *Personal and social skills objective*: to develop interpersonal and 'life' skills.
3. *Motivational objective*: to develop students' motivation to learn and achieve in school.

---

4. *Maturational objective*: to aid transition from one phase of development to another.
5. *Attitudinal change objective*: to change negative or anti-social attitudes into positive, pro-social attitudes.
6. *Behavioural change objective*: to alter negative, anti-social behaviours or those infringing institutional norms.

Work-related aims

7. *Aspirational objective*: to raise students' sights and broaden horizons in terms of career or learning goals.
8. *Employability objective*: to develop knowledge, skills and personal qualities that are valued by employers.

Subject aims

9. *Vocational objective*: to develop students' knowledge and skills, and raise achievement in one or more vocational subjects.
10. *Academic objective*: to develop students' knowledge and skills, and raise achievement in one or more academic subjects.
11. *Learning-skills objective*: to develop students' study and 'learning to learn' skills.

Developmental aims and objectives

The developmental aim has the broadest range of objectives, as it includes various forms of personal and social development, as well as various types of mentoring for at-risk students. Developmental mentoring may have one, some or all of the objectives discussed below. However, programmes aimed at socially excluded or at-risk young people are more likely to include *behavioural-* and *attitudinal-change* objectives.

Improved self-esteem is often noted as a main outcome of student mentoring programmes (Golden and Sims, 1999). A widely accepted definition of healthy self-esteem is that of Branden (1994), who defines it as 'the disposition to experience oneself as competent to cope with life's challenges and being worthy of happiness'. Self-esteem is often confused with the idea of self-concept. Self-concept can be seen as a conscious perception of how one sees oneself, whereas self-esteem is the evaluation of how one feels about one's self-concepts. Thus some people may perceive themselves as being bad at team games, but because this is unimportant to them it does not necessarily affect their self-esteem.

Student mentoring often aims to make students feel better about themselves, particularly when they have a pre-existing low self-esteem that may be holding them back academically or result in challenging behaviours that put them at risk of school exclusion. Enhanced self-esteem may be a by-product of being made to feel 'special', rather than 'labelled' as a problem, during selection and matching. Self-esteem is also likely to be raised by mentor behaviours that are non-judgemental, encouraging, positive and sustained over a period of time. The befriending function of mentoring can play an important role in raising self-esteem: the message is 'this person wants to be and is my friend'. Minority-ethnic programmes that pair mentees with successful role models also often aim to raise students' self-esteem.

The *personal and social skills* objective includes such aspects as building the self-confidence of the mentees, which is often quoted as a positive outcome of mentoring programmes (Golden and Sims, 1999). The self-confidence gained from mentoring may partly be a product of having sustained one-to-one discussions with an adult over a long period of time. Early discussion of situations that are to be encountered and agreeing coping strategies can build confidence. Similarly mentors often encourage students to try personal challenges that allow the mentees to succeed and to feel more confident as a result. Mentors can also assist with developing interpersonal skills, for example, how to behave when greeting and meeting new people. In some forms of mentoring the mentor has an explicit role to develop the life skills of the student.

The *motivational* objective is critical in providing the link between developmental and subject-oriented mentoring. Mentors can use their questioning skills to discover why students are underperforming in certain subjects. They can encourage students to set aside personal dislikes of particular teachers and to work harder in a subject because it is important for them in their future career. Mentors can also help students to overcome the demotivating impact of negative peer pressure. Grades are only likely to improve if students are making more effort in class and at home, and the mentor has a role in providing added extrinsic motivation, as well as encouraging students to want to perform better for themselves.

Mentoring has often been seen as critically important at times of transition in a young person's life (Levinson *et al*, 1978; Gay, 1997). The *maturational* objective of mentoring recognizes the role of mentors in helping the transition process. Mentors are generally people who have greater experience and can share their insights with their mentees. Mentoring as a process involves reflection and forward thinking, which are two facets of a more mature approach to life. The regular engagement with an older, more experienced person is likely to aid the maturation process. The fact that most mentoring relationships bring mutual benefits and are non-hierarchical also promotes maturation. Mentoring programmes are often timed to coincide with times of transition, for example, from primary to secondary school, from middle to high school, from school to college or university.

The *attitudinal-change* objective is more controversial, as it involves being judgemental about certain attitudes held by the student, which may either be acting as a barrier to their development or be leading to other problems. These can include fundamental values, or rather the absence of them. For example, some young people in trouble with the youth-justice system may believe that there is nothing wrong with stealing or violence. The role of the mentor in these circumstances is often to challenge these anti-social belief systems and to introduce alternative sets of values that are acceptable to society. In addition to the helping skills listed is the skill of advocating or advocacy, where the mentor may have to speak on behalf of their mentee, sometimes in a court setting. On a less extreme level students may have negative attitudes to school and learning that the mentor tries to break down.

The *behavioural-change* objective seeks to change negative behaviours that are damaging the student's progress through their education. In school settings these might involve truancy and disruption in class. Mentors will need good counselling skills to help students explore the reasons for and the consequences of their behaviour. Positive behavioural change is more likely to follow from a change in attitude, although the two things do not always necessarily go together in this way. For example, the first step to changing attitudes towards a subject or teacher may be to change negative behaviour in class.

Work-related objectives

The work-related aim incorporates both career and employability objectives. The *aspirational* objective can involve pairing mentees to mentors from the industry to which mentees aspire. This is sometimes an objective of minority-ethnic mentoring programmes where successful role models are sought to help raise the aspirations of students. Other programmes are designed to support (generally female) students making non-traditional course and career options. Typically, this would involve women choosing science, technology, engineering or mathematics courses. Again, mentor role models are recruited who can work with students during their course and give them tips on possible career paths. Mentors will not usually be experts in careers guidance and their role is to broaden horizons, not to make judgements about the suitability or otherwise of particular careers. The role should involve helping the students to analyse their career preferences and explore possible further education and work routes that they may not be aware of or have fully considered.

The *employability* objective involves the mentor assisting the mentee to develop the kinds of work-related knowledge, skills and attitudes that are required by employers when recruiting young people (Miller, 2000c). This objective is most closely associated with business mentoring, which can involve meetings at the mentors' workplace and work experience or internship. Students on extended work-experience placements lasting a year or longer may have workplace mentors, who are most likely to use coaching skills to help their mentee develop their work skills. College students can also use mentoring as a way of demonstrating employability skills and personal qualities such as reliability, punctuality, persistence and the capacity to motivate others.

'Subject' objectives

The subject aim is concerned with developing students' achievement in their academic or vocational subjects. In programmes that have an *academic* objective, the mentor may be a 'subject matter expert' (see Chapter 8) who has detailed knowledge of the area of the student's assignment and can offer responses to questions, advice, insights and challenging questions. In mentoring linked with a vocational objective, the mentors are likely to be experienced in using *vocational* skills in work contexts and will be able to relate coursework to the world of work. Teacher mentors, who are as it were 'experts in learning', are probably best placed to offer students advice in 'learning to learn' or study skills where there is a *learning-skills* objective. However, some people would argue that mentoring by teachers is more appropriately described as academic tutoring and is a form of pseudo-mentoring. Mentoring programmes with a subject aim are most likely to need mentors who have the skills associated with teaching and tutoring.

Multi-focused programmes

A key difference between mentoring programmes is whether they have a:

- holistic approach to the mentor role, with multiple aims and objectives;
- more limited approach to the mentor role and dual aims;
- highly focused approach to the mentor role and a single aim.

Clearly holistic, multi-focused programmes will tend to demand much more of their mentors, and training programmes will need to be longer. Mentoring for at-risk young people tends to fit this description. Holistic mentoring programmes aim to promote the personal development of the mentee, but at the same time to encourage work-related skills, broader career choices and achievement across a range of subjects.

Mentoring programmes with a dual focus can have:

- developmental and work-related aims;
- developmental and subject aims; or
- subject and work-related aims.

Although programmes may profess a single focus in practice, there may be a dual- or multi-focus to interactions between mentors and mentees. It can be argued that all mentoring programmes must include one or more developmental objectives, because without this dimension other objectives are unlikely to be achieved.

The confusion over the distinction between mentoring and the other helping behaviours most often arises in those programmes that have a single focus. Thus mentoring schemes that are only developmental tend to overlap with befriending and counselling. Programmes focusing on developing work-related skills or career management skills often are very similar to coaching programmes. Mentoring programmes that target achievement in subjects overlap with teaching or tutoring. It is where there are multiple aims and a holistic approach that the distinctive, integrative role of mentoring can be clearly seen.

AIMS FOR MENTORS

One the distinctions between mentoring and other helping behaviours, such as coaching, counselling or teaching, is that learning is an important goal for the mentor. That is not to say that learning should not also be an important goal for people engaged in those other activities. The nature of outcomes for mentors will vary with the form of mentoring and especially with the type of mentor.

Emotional intelligence

There are a number of potential beneficial outcomes for mentors in the development of their own emotional intelligence. Models of emotional intelligence were first developed in the 1990s (Salovey and Mayer, 1990; Mayer and Salovey, 1997; see Chapter 11). Mentoring provides the opportunity to practise, improve and demonstrate various emotional-intelligence skills and capabilities, such as:

- intrapersonal capabilities, such as emotional self-awareness, assertiveness and self-reliance;
- interpersonal skills, such as empathy for the feelings of others, ability to establish a mutually beneficial personal relationship and taking social responsibility;

- mood and optimism – the abilities to maintain hope in adverse situations and to generate happiness in oneself and others.

Although emotional intelligence is most likely to be a concept understood in a business context and therefore appreciated by mentors from business, these outcomes are likely to be of benefit to a much wider range of mentors.

Business benefits

A second set of positive outcomes for mentors comes from the use of counselling, coaching, teaching, tutoring and mentoring skills. It is a well-established fact that having to teach knowledge or skills to another person is an excellent way of reinforcing and broadening one's own knowledge. These benefits seem particularly appropriate for peer mentoring and for business mentors in situations where mentoring and coaching are regarded as important competencies in the workplace (see Chapter 3). Corporate mentoring schemes are increasingly being introduced into public and private sector organizations as a major vehicle for staff induction and development. The opportunity to develop mentoring skills in a relatively risk-free environment is, therefore, an important benefit for mentors and the organizations from which they come.

There are also outcomes that pertain to particular forms of mentoring. In particular a major aim of intergenerational programmes (see Chapter 4) is to include older citizens within schools, which are a key feature of the local community. Older people can feel isolated from the community, and from younger people in particular, and intergenerational mentoring involves building their network of relationships with their mentees, with other mentors and with the school. Social inclusion is also an aim of some peer-mentoring programmes, for example the Coca-Cola Valued Youth Programme, which targets at-risk youth to be mentors to primary-aged pupils (see Chapter 7).

CLASSIFICATION OF MENTORING PROGRAMMES

This book is about student mentoring, but a range of descriptors is applied to mentoring programmes. 'Business mentoring' describes the scheme by the work origin of the mentors; 'socially excluded mentoring' programmes are defined by their goal in relation to the mentees; and 'telementoring' is concerned with the means of communication between mentors and mentees. (The glossary contains a full listing of mentoring phrases used throughout the book.)

Mentoring programmes have been classified in four main ways, according to:

- the aims and objectives of the programmes;
- the main characteristics of the mentee target group;
- the main characteristics of the mentors;
- the main characteristics of the programme.

Classification by aim

The first approach describes mentoring schemes according to their principal aims. Thus, there are *developmental* mentoring programmes, *work-related* mentoring programmes and *subject-focused* mentoring programmes. This approach is perhaps not particularly illuminating, because as we have observed all mentoring programmes have some developmental purpose as a defining characteristic, and many schemes have multiple aims and objectives.

Classification by mentee characteristics

A second, more common approach is to classify mentoring programmes according to the selection criteria applied to mentees.

- *At-risk, socially excluded,* or *social-inclusion* mentoring programmes (see Chapter 6): mentees range from pupils at risk of under achievement in mainstream schools to young people who are outside the school system and at risk of drifting into crime or drug and alcohol abuse. School mentoring programmes are also targeted at students who are 'at risk' of being permanently excluded from school because of their behaviour. Another at-risk group often targeted for mentoring initiatives is young people leaving care, where mentors can help in the transition to independent living.
- *Minority ethnic* mentoring programmes (see Chapter 5): these are targeted at young people from one or more minority ethnic groups. Some programmes cater for refugee students, who often face additional language barriers and who can have emotional problems stemming from recent traumatic experiences.
- *Gifted-and-talented* mentoring programmes (see Chapter 9): these cater for students who have special abilities, but who may come from disadvantaged backgrounds. Mentoring can be focused on sports or general educational achievement, and mentors are frequently role models who can help with raising aspirations and career routes in addition to developing skills in a particular area.
- *Enterprise* and *work-experience* mentoring programmes: these can include small business mentors working with young people setting

up their own businesses, and business people working as Young Enterprise advisers with a Young Enterprise team. Students on work experience of varying lengths can also have designated workplace mentors who support them during their placements.

- *Subject* mentoring programmes: these are established within a course to enable the group or individual students to have a mentor who can assist them with their subject learning.

Classification by mentor characteristics

A third approach is to classify mentoring programmes according to the characteristics of the mentors:

- *Community mentoring* programmes (see Chapter 4): the mentors are drawn from the school's local community. The programme would include intergenerational or third-age mentoring by older mentors, aiming to bring 'inclusion' benefits for the mentors, as well as mentee gains. Minority ethnic programmes typically recruit local mentors from the minority ethnic communities that are represented in the student body.
- *Business mentoring* programmes (see Chapter 3): these include one-company schemes where a company is twinned with a particular school and provides all the mentors for a particular year group's scheme. However, more common are multi-company schemes where mentors are drawn from a range of small to large enterprises in both the private and public sectors. Business mentoring programmes are often focused on teachers, with the aim of developing management skills. Consequently, they tend to target head teachers and other senior managers in schools and pair them with senior managers in businesses.
- *Business-and-community* mentoring programmes: these schemes draw mentors from both business and the community.
- *Student mentoring* programmes (see Chapter 9): these may be in further or higher education. Mentoring relationships in higher education vary quite widely and include tutors acting as mentors to students, experienced students mentoring less experienced students and university students mentoring school students. A key distinction is between paid and volunteer student mentors working with school students. Further education college mentoring programmes, as in higher education, can include peer mentoring within the college and external mentoring of students from local schools.
- *Peer mentoring* programmes (see Chapter 7): these can be further categorized by the relative ages of the mentor and the mentee. Thus there are same-age (same year group) and near-age (one or three years' difference) and far-age (four years' difference or more) programmes.

- *Teacher mentoring* programmes: these include teacher-teacher mentoring, which is the most well-researched form of mentoring in schools, and teacher-student mentoring. Some people would argue that teachers cannot mentor students in the same way as mentors from the community, on the grounds that they are in a power relationship because of their role *in loco parentis*. A similar argument applies to learning mentors or personal advisers in schools: because they are employed by the school and have an authority role in relation to students, this precludes acting as a mentor (see Chapter 1).

External and internal mentoring

This mode of classification can be further subdivided into external and internal mentoring programmes. In external programmes the mentors are drawn from outside the educational institution. These schemes have the merit of the mentors having no personal history of their mentee, so that it is easier to start the mentoring sessions with a 'blank piece of paper' and no preconceptions. Internal mentors – whether teachers, paraprofessionals based in the school or other students – are more likely to know or know of their mentees, and previous history, institutional knowledge and unstated assumptions are more likely to influence the relationship.

Classification by programme characteristics

Another approach to the classification of mentoring programmes is to examine the features of each programme. For example, a recent study in the United States by Big Brothers, Big Sisters classified programmes used the following criteria:

- One-to-one or group programmes: the former have one mentor to one mentee, the latter one mentor to two or more mentees. One-to-one mentoring can also be face-to-face or non-face-to-face, as in the case of telementoring or e-mentoring. A further distinction is between small-group mentoring, where the maximum is around four or five mentees per mentor, and large-group mentoring where the unit is often a class of students (as in some telementoring programmes, see Chapter 8).
- Site-based or community-based programmes: site-based mentoring meetings are held at the educational institution or building of the organizing body, whereas community-based mentoring meetings can be held at the mentor's workplace or a neutral public venue, such as a café.
- The duration and intensiveness of programmes also vary. Long-term intensive programmes last a year or more with weekly meetings, short-term intensive programmes in contrast last less than a year (often around three months). In non-intensive programmes meetings are held less frequently than once a week.

- The degree of structure of the mentoring programmes depends on the organizing agency. High, medium and low structuring can be found depending on the extent of mentor screening procedures, the length of training, the regularity and extent of monitoring of mentor-mentee pairs, and presence of mentor support group meetings.

ISSUES

Philosophies of mentoring

There are three potentially conflicting philosophies of mentoring, and these influence the training and subsequent behaviour of mentors, and the preparation of mentees. The mentoring philosophy of the programme organizers may be student-led, school/college/programme-led or mentor-led. In student-led mentoring programmes, the mentor is briefed to be responsive to the expressed needs of the student, so that the content of mentoring meetings is largely determined by the mentee.

In school/college/programme-led mentoring programmes, the scheme managers aim to provide a structure for mentor meetings, often based around target setting to reflect the objectives of the scheme. There may be mentee diaries and recording sheets for mentors, so that a record of discussions, agreements and progress against targets can be monitored to ensure that pairs are 'on task'. Lists of suitable discussion topics might be provided.

In mentor-led mentoring programmes, the school is happy to leave mentors to be the main determinants of what is transacted during mentoring meetings. This is probably the least common or advised approach, and most often arises from a perceived lack of direction from the school and a lack of understanding on the part of the student of the purpose of the mentoring. In the context of telementoring, however, subject-matter experts will often take the lead in e-mail interactions with students (see Case Study 8.1).

In a study of seven school schemes across England, the most dominant philosophy was student-led, where mentors were briefed to be reactive in response to their students' needs (Miller, 1998). However, some schools were considering a more school-led approach, where the agenda would involve mentors being proactive in monitoring students' performance to meet coursework and other targets. There were some examples of a mentor-led approach, which resulted from mentors being encouraged to use particular knowledge and skills that they brought to the sessions. For example, one mentor was using group-mentoring sessions for a series of teambuilding exercises.

Where scheme organizers believe that the essence of mentoring is the constructed relationship between mentor and mentee, there is a tendency to advocate the student-led approach as the only legitimate mentoring philosophy. Such practitioners often talk about the indefinable 'chemistry' that makes certain mentorships especially effective. It is clearly important that mentees are able to articulate their needs and concerns to their mentors. However, it is also important in educational settings that this occurs within an overall structure of defined goals and processes. In other words, there is scope for an amalgam of both student-led and programme-led approaches within most mentoring programmes.

Paid versus volunteer mentors

There is a view that an essential prerequisite for a helping relationship to be described as mentoring is that both mentor and mentee are volunteers (Costigan, 2000). However, there have been paid external mentors within corporate mentoring for some time and this has spread to mentoring for students and young people. It may be that the perceptions of the young person about their mentor will be different, if they know that they are being paid for their time as opposed to giving their free time voluntarily.

Paid mentors in education

Paid mentors can be found working with young people of school age in three contexts: higher education student mentoring (Chapter 9), learning mentors (Chapter 1) and mentors assigned by the criminal justice system (Chapter 6). Payment has been a central part of the *Perach* mentoring and tutoring system in Israel since its foundation 25 years ago (Chapter 1). In the National Mentoring Pilot Project, university students are paid £5 an hour to mentor students at risk of underachievement in Education Action Zone secondary schools (see Case Study 9.1). This has prompted debate within the universities about the merits and drawbacks of 'paid' compared with 'volunteer' mentoring, including the impact of paid mentoring on other forms of volunteering. Learning mentors in the Excellence in Cities programme are full-time employees of the school, part of whose job is to mentor selected students (see Case Study 1.2). Paid mentors are also employed in some projects working with young people who have been prescribed a mentor under court orders.

Business mentors

It is also the case that business mentors, particularly those who participate in company-coordinated partnerships with particular schools, are also in a sense paid for mentoring. Large companies often allow employees so many hours per month to work on worthwhile programmes, as part of the corporate social responsibility policy (see Case Study 3.1). The company may also have objectives that they want to achieve for their employee mentors in terms of self-development and in meeting corporate objectives. Many company staff also give their own time to mentoring. It seems improbable that there are any discernible differences between the kinds of mentoring styles or strategies used by volunteer, free-time mentors as opposed to in-company-time mentors. For these reasons it seems inappropriate to reserve the term mentoring exclusively for volunteers.

One-to-one versus group mentoring

The main mentoring models used in schools are one-to-one, small groups and a combination of the two approaches. Schools offering group rather than one-to-one mentoring may have limited mentor resources or they may wish to include more students (Gibb, 1994). A UK study found that although 60 per cent of schemes used one-to-one mentoring, these programmes only involved 49 per cent of mentors and 13 per cent of students (Golden and Sims, 1997). Small-group mentoring was the predominant model in 10 per cent of schemes and a combination of one-to-one and group mentoring was used in the remaining 30 per cent of schemes. These figures were broadly similar to those of an earlier study carried out by the National Mentoring Network, which identified 95 schemes of which 59 per cent used one-to-one, 19 per cent involved small-groups and 22 per cent had a combined model of mentoring (Collins, 1994).

The processes and outcomes of group mentoring are likely to be different from one-to-one programmes. Some commentators would dispute the use of the term mentoring to describe such small-group models (Gay, 1994). One of the case-study schools in the business and community mentoring programmes investigated by Miller (1998) used small-group mentoring, and this provided an opportunity to investigate its strengths and weaknesses in practice. However, in some of the groups, mentors focused on teambuilding and study skills, two purposes for which group mentoring seemed well suited. In this school, 15 mentors had originally been involved in mentoring 36 students. Group sizes ranged from two to four. Twelve students were asked their views on group mentoring and they identified two advantages and two disadvantages to the approach.

Pros and cons of small-group mentoring

The advantages were that it was less frightening or embarrassing to meet a mentor with other students, and that students learned to work as a group and listen to each other. A few students also mentioned that it was a way of making new friends among students they might not otherwise know. The disadvantages were lack of time allocated by the mentor to each student, and the difficulty of discussing personal issues with the mentor. A further disadvantage, not mentioned by the students but apparent from the research, was the difficulty of making appointments when a number of mentees were involved. If one could not make the appointment, there was a tendency to cancel the meeting. In a small study of group mentoring for women running small businesses, the problems of confidentiality and difficulties in raising personal issues in a group setting were evident (Mitchell, 1999). A further difficulty of group mentoring was the tendency for certain individuals to dominate and the need for the mentor to have good facilitation skills to prevent this from happening.

The main problem in small-group mentoring is that the individuals are unlikely to be able to establish the same degree of trust in their mentor as in a one-to-one situation. There is also the issue of the lack of privacy and confidentiality, making it difficult for personal issues to be aired and addressed. When small-group mentoring examples are examined, it is often the case that the behaviours and relationships are more akin to groupwork, workshops, group counselling, tutoring or teaching than to mentoring.

MENTORING AND LEARNING

Mentoring defined

The concept of mentoring has proved difficult to define, but the popularity of the term is undeniable, with new forms arising all the time. Any attempt to be precise will inevitably face the accusation of an arbitrary drawing of the line between mentoring and other forms of support for students. Nevertheless, it is important to have some clarity in the use of the term for stakeholders, educational institutions, students and their mentors. Objectives are more likely to be achieved when there is a clear relationship between intended outcomes and planned processes.

We have defined an ideal-typical mentoring programme as 'holistic' where there is an intention to develop the whole student – personally, vocationally and academically – and the mentor skillfully uses a range of helping behaviours in this task. However, it is clear that very few schemes approach this model. We suggest that the minimum criteria for a mentoring programme are as follows:

- A prime goal of mentoring relationships is the personal development of the mentee. The mentorships seek to shape, change and examine attitudes and values. In other words the focus is not exclusively or largely upon developing the knowledge and skills of the mentee.

- The mentorships involve a one-to-one relationship between mentor and mentee based on trust and an attempt to establish a non-hierarchical, equal relationship. This would preclude small-group work and situations where there was an obvious power relationship that is invoked, as is often the case with teachers acting as mentors to students.
- The programme involves mentors who are more experienced than the mentee, who use a range of interpersonal skills or helping behaviours, and who are also seeking to learn from the experience. This would preclude situations where one skill, such as coaching or tutoring, is used or where the mentor was an expert with no personal learning agenda.

There is a range of activities that might be described as pseudo-mentoring; that is, they are called mentoring by those involved, but they fall outside the scope of our definition. I have not included a chapter on teacher mentoring, which generally is an extension of tutoring and tends to focus on academic tutoring. The case of learning mentors in the UK is an interesting one and the debate will continue as to whether as employees of the school they can be anything other than pseudo-mentors. National evaluation of their work is awaited and in the meantime the principles and current evidence of practice is included, because of the approximation of their work to holistic mentoring. There is coverage of telementoring, which is often not developmental or one-to-one, because of the widespread interest in this form of communication among the mentoring community. As Roberts (2000) has observed, the definition of mentoring is probably best left as fluid and provisional, as new forms continue to emerge.

Learning theory and mentoring

The way in which we have defined mentoring precludes the conventional transmission model of learning involving knowledge being poured into the learners by the teacher. It is in the social constructivist theory of Vygotsky that advocates of mentoring find most support for the role of mentoring in promoting young people's learning. He stressed the importance of culture and social context in learning or cognitive development (1994). A key concept is the 'zone of proximal development', which suggests that young people with the support of more experienced peers or adults understand ideas that they would not be able to grasp alone. Some of the key principles derived from Vygotsky's thinking will be familiar to advocates of school-community or school-business links. These include the ideas that:

- Learning is a social and collaborative activity.

- School learning should be developed in meaningful contexts and should be closely linked to learning developed in the 'real' world beyond the school gates.
- Out-of-school experiences should be related to the young person's school experience.

Building on the foundation provided by Vygotsky, the proponents of situated learning argue that to be useful knowledge must be situated in a relevant or authentic context. Knowledge is to a great extent a product of the situation, culture, activity or context in which it is used. The idea of cognitive apprenticeship is used in situated learning theory to describe the role of coach or mentor in providing cognitive 'scaffolding' (Brown, Collins and Duguid, 1989). This 'scaffolding' helps learners to make sense of the topic by relating it to personal experiences and to the context in which it will be applied. The support provided by the mentor can gradually be reduced as mentees begin to construct their own knowledge and understanding. 'Mentors provide authentic, experiential learning opportunities as well as an intense interpersonal relationship through which social learning takes place' (Kerka, 1998; see Chapter 12 for a discussion of experiential learning). The proponents of situated learning also advocate collaborative problem solving as a strategy.

Situated learning

Situated learning can be seen as a framework for the design of learning environments (Evans and Hoffmann, 2000). Planned mentoring programmes exhibit many of the features of constructed, situated learning environments:

- Mentees are encouraged to experiment and experience between mentoring meetings.
- Mentors and mentees discuss work-related contexts for learning and development and mentors pass on the lessons of their own experience.
- Mentees meet adults from a wide range of occupations and varying cultures and thus they gain insights into different perspectives on problems.
- Knowledge is created through the collaborative construction of knowledge between mentor and mentee.
- Mentoring provides 'scaffolding' that can aid mentees' learning.
- In mentoring meetings mentees are often encouraged to engage in systematic reflection of their experiences and discussion about what has been learnt that can be applied in new situations.
- Mentors ask questions to encourage mentees to make tacit competencies explicit.

It is impossible to discuss mentoring and situated learning without highlighting the work of Jean Lave and Etienne Wenger (1991). Historically a form of mentoring was evident in the master-apprentice model of the medieval guild system. Lave and Wenger studied learning in five traditional and non-traditional apprenticeships in Mexico, Liberia and the United States. Their study showed how, in work settings, learning occurred within 'communities of practice'. Apprentices moved from 'legitimate peripheral participation' in the workplace as newcomers to a central role over time as they learnt, recreated and finally replaced the craftspeople from whom they had learnt. Much of the learning that occurs is tacit rather than intentional as apprentices become expert through observation and noting what is valued in their community of practice. Novice learners gradually move from the periphery to the centre of their community's activities. Some forms of student mentoring do allow young people to become involved in communities of practice at a business, at the local university or college, and in local community organizations. In this way they can be engaged in forms of learning which are 'more personally and socially meaningful and [allow] students to foresee their participation in activities that matter beyond school' (Greeno, 1997: 11).

Part II

The forms of mentoring

3

Business mentoring

INTRODUCTION

The term business mentoring describes people from business acting as mentors to students and young people. It is, however, an ambiguous term as it is also commonly used to refer to mentoring where the subject matter is small-business start-up and development, and where the mentor is a small-business adviser or experienced business person. In this chapter we examine the use of business mentors in mentoring programmes for students.

We begin with an account of the growth of business mentoring in the United Kingdom and the advantages of single-company compared to multi-company schemes. The aims and objectives for students and the benefits to business are then discussed, together with the role of the company mentoring coordinator. Three case studies provide contrasting examples of business mentoring programmes: Deloitte & Touche in the United Kingdom; Merrill Lynch's ScholarshipBuilder® Program in the United States; and Deptford Green School's Roots & Wings scheme with Warburg Dillon Read, Citibank and IPC Magazines. This is followed by a summary of research and evaluation evidence, and issues arising from the case studies. The chapter concludes with a good practice guide to setting up and running a business mentoring programme, and a discussion of possible future trends.

THE EXTENT OF BUSINESS MENTORING IN THE UNITED KINGDOM

A 1995 UK study of employers' views of education-business link activities found that 13.5 per cent of a sample of 1,389 employers engaged with education were involved in mentoring programmes (Hillage, Hyndley and Pike, 1995). Larger businesses were more likely to be involved in mentoring than smaller companies, but the differences were far less marked than for other forms of link such as careers events, schools visits or teacher placements. A 1997 study of 'industrial mentoring' found that from an initial base of four programmes in 1991 and ten in 1992, there was a marked expansion with 19 schemes starting each year between 1993 and 1995 (Golden and Sims, 1997). The survey of 72 business mentoring schemes in England, Scotland and Wales found that there were 1,978 companies and 4,527 mentors involved with 518 schools and 16,834 mentees. Of these programmes, 60 per cent were one-to-one mentoring, 10 per cent were group mentoring and the remaining 30 per cent were a combination of both approaches. A survey of 7,000 secondary schools during the 1998-99 academic year found that of 3,000 respondents, 2,043 secondary schools had mentoring schemes, with about 700 schools involved in business mentoring schemes (DfEE, 1999a).

AIMS AND OBJECTIVES

Business mentoring is used for all three aims of student mentoring. The most common objectives within the developmental aim are:

- *the self-esteem objective*: students tend to be more positive about themselves when someone from business is prepared to put time and energy into their development;
- *the personal and social skills objective*: most business managers have experienced interpersonal skills training and will use these skills in one-to-one discussions with their mentees;
- *the motivational objective*: students will often respond to calls for increased effort at school from people perceived to be in the 'real world' rather than their parents or teachers.

Within the subject aim, business mentors are most likely to contribute towards the vocational objective by supporting students taking particular vocational courses. However, the most obvious goal for business mentoring is the employability objective within the work-related aim. Business mentors also often help students with their basic skills of literacy, numeracy and information technology.

ONE-COMPANY VERSUS MULTI-COMPANY SCHEMES

Business mentoring schemes tend to fall into two main categories. In the first category are schemes where all the mentors working with a particular school are drawn from one company. These are most often the result of large companies developing their existing school links programme or working with a national brokerage agency such as Business in the Community (BITC). The best-known UK example of a one-company approach is BITC's Roots & Wings Programme, which is described more fully in the case study below.

The second, more common, approach is where mentors are drawn from a range of different businesses. This is the typical approach of many of the UK's education business partnerships (EBPs), which are local brokerage agents that help schools and businesses to work together for mutual benefit. Mentors are generally recruited from across a range of small-to-large business partners, public sector and voluntary organizations. Recruitment, selection and training of mentors tend to be undertaken centrally by the EBP.

One-company schemes have a number of potential advantages over multi-company programmes.

- There is usually a formal agreement between the company and the school, which means that there is likely to be high-level support within both organizations for the programme. Therefore, the programme is likely to be more adequately resourced and sustainable.
- It is easier for mentors to see how volunteering can benefit them in their corporate career when the company has seen the benefits and included the review of learning outcomes in the appraisal process.
- There is often an in-company coordinator whose role is recognized by the company. This greatly facilitates communication between the school and the company. The company coordinator can also use the Intranet to aid recruitment, training, support and monitoring.
- It is much easier for mentors to meet each other to share common issues. This also brings further benefits to the company through the promotion of cross-company networking. It is also easier to bring mentors together for joint events with the mentees.
- The school is more likely to benefit from a widening of links with the company. Such benefits may include: the offer of work experience placements for mentees; company involvement in related curriculum projects; donations of surplus office furniture; and exchanges of personnel and expertise.

However, although one-company schemes have distinct advantages, the majority of schools are unlikely to have a large business on the doorstep, which is keen to make a strong link with just one school. Thus multi-company and mixed business and community schemes are much more common than single-company schemes in the UK.

ROLE OF THE COMPANY COORDINATOR

In mentoring partnerships between a large or medium-sized company and a school or college, it is important to appoint a coordinator from within the business. This often provides an excellent development opportunity for a junior member of staff, as it entails meeting with a cross-section of people from the business who volunteer to become mentors. It is estimated that the role can take about 20 per cent of someone's time, or around 40 to 50 days per annum. Coordinators also need some administrative support, as will become clear when reading through the main tasks associated with the role, which are shown in Box 3.1.

Box 3.1 Key tasks of the company mentoring coordinator

- planning the programme with the external and school coordinators;
- preparing briefing materials for line managers and publicity about the scheme;
- discussing their involvement with interested would-be mentors;
- administering the mentoring programme budget;
- making the in-company arrangements for mentor training;
- giving talks at mentor training sessions about the company perspective;
- helping match mentors to mentees;
- liaising with the school on arrangements for initial mentoring meetings at the school and the company;
- attending and possibly servicing steering group meetings and review meetings with the school and external coordinator;
- advising mentors on problems that arise;
- helping to plan social events and mentor support sessions;
- publicizing the programme both inside and outside the business;
- gathering data on the programme for monitoring and evaluation;
- arranging an end-of-year celebratory event and certificates for mentees and mentors;
- writing up testimonies from mentors, and a case study of the programme as a whole, for the purposes of dissemination and reporting.

(adapted from BITC, 1997b)

BUSINESS AIMS AND BENEFITS

There are five main aims for businesses that become involved with education (Miller *et al*, 1995):

- raising educational standards, both among potential recruits and more widely;
- developing existing staff;
- fulfilling social and community responsibilities;
- improving young people's knowledge and understanding of industry and commerce, and influencing attitudes to them;
- enhancing the reputation of the company and its products.

One reason for the extraordinary increase in the popularity of business mentoring as a strategy for corporate involvement with education is the versatility of mentoring in addressing all five of these aims.

The main educational rationale for mentoring has been its contribution to the so-called 'raising standards agenda'. The funding of the majority of UK business mentoring schemes has been through EBPs, and developing young people's employability has been a key objective. Employed role models serve as examples to young people of what can be achieved through gaining qualifications, having ambition and working hard. Mentoring programmes are often part of the company's strategy for demonstrating corporate social responsibility. Company volunteers are generally linked to schools that are near to the company's offices. Head teachers, who are often respected local figures, tend to speak warmly of companies that are supporting students in this direct way. Mentors often bring other benefits with them, such as access to surplus equipment, donations and access to other types of work-related activity. Mentoring schemes generally have celebratory events and success stories that make good copy for local newspapers. The company's reputation for doing good works in the local community can be enhanced in this way. For companies, therefore, mentoring offers a low-cost way of achieving a number of goals.

Staff development

There is an even greater benefit to companies from involvement in mentoring programmes, and that is the staff development opportunities. Benefits to business are most likely to accrue when there is a planned programme of community investment linked to staff development (Miller *et al*, 1998). Encouraging staff to become mentors with local students can generate positive feelings towards the company that is prepared to put something into the community and to help often disadvantaged young people. Mentoring in schools is a cost-effective way of developing a range of competencies that are increasingly important in today's workplace. The benefits of mentoring tend to be greatest where the company is seeking to develop the mentoring skills of its staff, and mentoring of school students provides an opportunity to practise those skills in a different context (Miller *et al*, 1998). 'If you can successfully manage a group of secondary school students, then you can cope with almost anything you might encounter in the workplace' (Deloitte & Touche employee quoted by Stone, 2000). These competencies include interpersonal skills in general, and mentoring and coaching skills in particular. The ability to practise and refine these skills in a non-commercial setting may be important to the individual's career development plan in the business.

Research on benefits to business

In a survey of 59 business mentors working in seven school programmes from across England, it was found that only one in five mentors identified specific learning goals for themselves at the start of the mentoring programme (Miller *et al*, 1998). The majority were unclear about what the benefits of mentoring might be for them at the outset. Mentors were asked to rate the benefits to them personally and to their organizations. The most highly rated personal benefits for mentors in rank order were:

- feeling good about doing something worthwhile for young people;
- understanding the needs and problems of young people today;
- gaining insights into how young people think;
- improving interpersonal skills.

A recent survey of six business mentoring schemes by the Runnymede Trust found that seven out of ten business mentors felt more confident about talking to young people and valued the opportunity to learn about different cultures and religions (Appiah, 2001: 7).

The most highly rated benefits to the mentors' organizations were:

- contributing to the local community;
- developing the mentoring skills of staff;
- gaining good PR;
- developing the interpersonal skills of staff (Miller *et al*, 1998).

Some mentors who were interviewed described very positive personal benefits:

> I've got a phenomenal amount out of meeting my student. Until I met him I was an operational person.... Since I met him I am viewed as someone with management potential. I now act as a mentor for people in my team. My boss has seen the benefits of my mentoring and has been impressed by the changes that have taken place in me.

This outcome was achieved in a climate where the mentor's organization, an international bank, was fully supporting the mentoring scheme.

Mentors were more likely to perceive personal benefits related to their work when their company endorsed and supported staff involvement in mentoring. Other companies also view mentoring as a development opportunity for staff. For example, Marks & Spencer, the leading UK retailer, selected mentors on the basis of their potential for taking on increased responsibility (BITC, 1998). Staff in a London store demonstrated increased confidence, motivation and assertiveness as a result of acting as mentors to 16-year-olds in a local school. This enabled managers to spot those with potential and to give them additional responsibilities.

It is particularly important to identify benefits to the organization when recruiting mentors and/or persuading companies to commit resources to a mentoring scheme. A former mentoring coordinator involved with the Roots & Wings Programme identified eight key benefits to the bank (see Box 3.2).

Box 3.2 Benefits of student mentoring to a bank

- As an investment bank we can be seen to be just concerned about money; mentoring is good in terms of general PR and our community programme has a youth emphasis.
- Our company seeks to recruit high-calibre graduates; they want to join an employer who has this kind of approach, and it may sway them.
- Mentors are drawn from all parts of the organization and it provides an opportunity for networking with people from different parts of the business.
- Individuals can learn skills in a non-threatening environment. The 'soft skills' involved in mentoring are more important as the organization flattens. It helps develop in-company mentoring skills.
- It generally helps with morale as we feel we are doing something worthwhile. Mentors want to feel that they are putting something back, and it spills over into their work.
- It gives insight into schools and children; the mentors may be parents themselves.
- It provides contact with other cultural values. It may challenge prejudices and assumptions and it may make personnel more open to different styles and people from different ethnic groups.
- It is an inexpensive form of training.

(adapted from Miller, 1998)

Case Study 3.1 Roots & Wings at Deptford Green School (UK)

The Roots & Wings Mentoring Programme began as an initiative of BITC in 1992. The distinctive feature of the programme is that a member company of

BITC is twinned with a school and mentoring meetings at the company are an important dimension. The success of the programme is dependent on a trained external programme facilitator and an in-company facilitator. These are full- or part-time personnel, paid for through a variety of local funding sources.

Organizational issues

Deptford Green School is an 11–18 comprehensive school of 1,066 pupils in the London Borough of Lewisham. The starting point for the scheme was a situation of 'challenging home environments, sometimes difficult racial/social balancing acts and a lack of employed adult role models' (Alexander and Day, 1995). About half of the students were from minority ethnic groups. Although examination results at 16 had been improving, progression to further and higher education was still low. An analysis of statistics on student destinations suggested that they tended to choose careers from a relatively narrow range of locally available occupations.

Since 1994, there had been a part-time programme facilitator who developed the mentoring scheme, so that by 1999 there were 60 mentees paired with mentors from three City of London companies: Warburg Dillon Read, IPC Magazines and Citibank. The strategy of working with a limited number of companies placed constraints on the supply of mentors, and rapid change in the City of London meant occasional 'downsizing' with a resulting sudden loss of mentors. However, there were several spin-off benefits for the school from involvement with large corporations, including work experience (internships) for mentees, donations of surplus furniture and funding.

The facilitator also supported Roots & Wings mentoring in two other local secondary schools, supported by a part-time project worker. She was line-managed by the deputy head teacher, which ensured that the programme was closely linked to the school's overall strategy for raising achievement. There was a management group, which included company representatives and governors, for the general oversight of the programme. Overall the scheme averaged 100 mentor pairs per year, involving students in each year group from ages 14 to 18.

The main aims of the business mentoring programme were to:

- raise the aspirations of young people towards higher academic achievement;
- help develop confidence, self-esteem and social skills;
- provide access to world-of-work experiences and skills for employability.

Mentor recruitment and training

Once a partner company had signed up to the programme, the company's mentoring coordinator took a lead in recruiting staff to act as mentors. For example, the coordinator at Citibank used 'everybody' e-mails, staff bulletins, notices on bulletin boards and word of mouth to recruit mentors. The company had 40 mentors, and several others awaiting matches. The programme facilitator, working with the company coordinator, managed mentor induction. A mentor-induction pack included: ideas for mentoring activities; case histories of personal experiences; lists of existing company mentors; the annual programme of events; and press cuttings.

Mentee selection

Students were introduced to the mentoring programme at a year assembly, and there were always many more volunteering to take part than there were mentors available. The ones selected were representative of the ethnic composition of the school and were those who were thought to be likely to benefit from the programme. Non-attenders and the 'bottom 10 per cent' of students, in terms of behavioural problems, were excluded from the scheme. Once students were selected, following discussions between the facilitator and pastoral staff, a mentee-induction pack was distributed, parental permission was sought and an induction programme was organized. Training in the use of the telephone was given to those students who needed it. Guidelines were set at the outset for the duration and frequency of meetings. The Roots & Wings guidelines indicated that pairs should meet at least every two weeks for about an hour. After an initial period, however, it was left up to the pairs to decide how often they met. Pairs in their third or fourth year, for example, often met every month, but communicated in between via the telephone or e-mail.

Mentors occasionally visited the school, but students mainly travelled to meet them at their place of work after school every two to three weeks. A representative of a rail transport company briefed the students on travelling safely in London. Mentees were also encouraged to contact their mentors by telephone, fax or e-mail (using the facilitator's office as a base) in order to encourage greater independence and self-confidence. A number of social events were held throughout the school year for mentors and mentees and a social dimension was also encouraged, so that pairs might undertake visits to theatres, cinema, museums and restaurants. This strong befriending or social strand to the programme meant that there was no clear endpoint to the mentoring; if pairs wanted to carry on then they were able to.

Feedback to mentors on the progress of the students was provided informally by the mentoring coordinator, and twice a year at review meetings where the completed 'teacher forms', which give their perceptions on the impact of mentoring, were made available to mentors.

Parental involvement

There were attempts to encourage mentor-parent contacts; for example, one mentee had taken the mentor home for a social visit, and this proved very successful. A parents' group was kept informed about the scheme. The facilitator attended parents' evenings and regularly contacted families about the programme. Parents were also invited to mentoring social events. One said that it made her daughter 'wake up to the big world' and the need for good qualifications to be able to get jobs in the 'big league'. Another said that her son's confidence and independence had increased and this had had a knock-on effect on schoolwork, so that a recent report showed a marked improvement in all subjects.

Evaluation

Subject teachers were asked to give an impressionistic assessment of the impact of mentoring on various aspects of progress, including attendance, punctuality, motivation and enthusiasm, attitude, confidence, maturity and social skills. They were asked to indicate whether there had been a large or small improvement or no difference. They were also invited to offer advice to mentors on how they could help their mentees. There was an annual evaluation report based on questionnaires distributed to students, mentors, tutors and parents/guardians with a good response rate. The programme won a number of awards and was a pilot for the Excellence in Mentoring Quality Award (Miller, 2000a).

Case Study 3.2 Deloitte & Touche (UK)

Deloitte & Touche, a global professional services company, provided a good example of a business that had embraced student mentoring (Stone, 2000). A range of mentors played an important role in the development of staff, from 'buddies' who offered regular support to new joiners, to development advisers who support senior managers. The role of mentor in the business was to give honest and constructive advice about a range of learning issues, including the individual's development plan. The firm's core competencies that could be developed through student mentoring had been identified as:

- leadership and management skills;
- service and relationship skills;

The mentoring of students was generally one-to-one and continued for 18 months in the lead up to GCSE examinations at age 16. The objectives were to develop the confidence and motivation of students so as to ensure success in their examinations, and in transition to further education and the world of work. According to the Director of Community Investment, the real learning came from winning the confidence of the students and developing their active participation.

Staff mentors were allowed to spend half a day a month of the firm's time on their mentoring activities. This formal recognition added to the status of student mentoring as a legitimate vehicle for personal and career development. Volunteer mentors identified individual objectives linked to the firm's core competencies with their appraiser before they commenced the mentoring. Illustrative examples were shown to the volunteers to help them shape their own objectives. The achievement of objectives and the mentoring experience itself were discussed with their line managers in their annual appraisals.

Case Study 3.3 Merrill Lynch ScholarshipBuilder® Program (USA)

Merrill Lynch is a good example of a company with a philanthropic ethos eager to make social investment over the long term. In 1988, the Merrill Lynch Foundation, in partnership with the National Urban League and ten schools across ten big US cities, established ScholarshipBuilder®. The programme randomly selected 249 first-grade students with 'limited resources but unlimited potential' and aimed to support their educational progression from grade school to college. ScholarshipBuilder® is a 12-year, multi-million dollar initiative funded by the company, with additional funding of $1.2 million from Merrill Lynch employees. The programme aims to instil the value of higher education in students and their families, and to inspire similar business and community efforts.

Mentoring was central to the programme and many employees had had the same mentees for 12 years. This must give the programme some of the longest-running mentorships in the world. By 2000, 97 per cent of students were still in the programme and 90 per cent were expected to graduate from high school. Each student who graduates will receive a grant of up to $16,000 ($4,000 each year) to cover the costs of tuition, housing, books and transport. Students not attending college will receive a lump sum payment of $2,000 upon entering the military or becoming fully employed. In addition to this funding, ScholarshipBuilder® offers tutoring, parental involvement, cultural enrichment, work experience, community service and life skills development. Merrill Lynch volunteers give their time to provide intensive help in middle and high schools through SAT preparation, college counselling, academic summer camps, conflict-resolution workshops and college tours. This on-going academic and developmental support has enabled students to stay in school and to overcome challenges they faced. The National Urban League supports the parents of students through information and training on post-secondary education process, career counselling, skills training and help with job placements.

The company has received many plaudits and awards for ScholarshipBuilder® because it is a long-term commitment, a scholarship scheme to fund disadvantaged youth, a community partnership, a way of involving employees as volunteers and a model of corporate social responsibility. In 1999, senior executives and high school graduates were invited to the White House for a special briefing session and to receive the President's Service Award. This followed a Presidential Award for Private Sector Initiatives in 1989.

RESEARCH AND EVALUATION EVIDENCE

Roots & Wings internal evaluation

The Roots & Wings Programme featured in the case study has been evaluated both internally and externally. The most recent evaluation was of the 1998-99 programme, which involved three schools and four companies. Questionnaires were used as the main method of evaluation and there were 280 returns with a 50 per cent response rate from students, 52 per cent from parents, 63 per cent from mentors and 92 per cent from teachers. The impact of mentoring upon mentees was measured through teacher assessment on a range of outcomes. According to the teachers, the outcomes showing greatest impact were self-confidence (57 per cent showing improvements), motivation and enthusiasm (50 per cent) and social skills (44 per cent). The outcomes where mentoring appeared to have less impact were the behavioural areas of attendance (20 per cent) and punctuality (25 per cent), and academic progress (32 per cent showing gains).

The internal evaluation compared the examination grades and the post-school destinations of 35 mentored students with the control group of all other non-mentored students. In their predicted grades, in their 'mock' examination results and in their actual GCSE examination, the mentored group performed slightly better than the non-mentored group. However, this also suggests that the mentored group would be expected to perform better without having a mentor. Mentored and non-mentored students were also compared by student ability bands, which range from band 1 (higher ability) to band 4 (lower). This analysis suggested that the lower the ability the greater the impact of mentoring, as the differences between the mentored and the non-mentored group increased in the lower bands. There were also significant differences between the post-16 destinations of the mentored and non-mentored groups, with 71 per cent of mentees opting for further education compared with 45 per cent of the non-mentored group. The relatively small numbers involved in this sample mean that these conclusions should be interpreted with caution.

Business mentoring national evaluation

A study sponsored by the DfEE compared the impact of business mentoring on mentees compared to a control group in seven schools across England (Miller *et al*, 1998). Mentees tended to have a more instrumental view of the purposes of mentoring than mentors. Two-thirds of students saw the main purpose of mentoring as improving their GCSE coursework and exam results. About half the students saw a main purpose as increasing their self-confidence and improving their personal and social skills. Almost two-thirds of mentors saw the main purpose as increasing students' self-confidence, and the second most important purpose was raising motivation. Mentors regarded curriculum-related purposes, such as helping with GCSE subjects (28 per cent) and support with study skills (17 per cent), as less important. In some schemes, the differing perceptions of mentors and students as to the purposes of mentoring caused difficulties, which might have been avoided with clearer briefing.

In the majority of case-study schools, business mentoring was regarded as one part of a general strategy for raising attainment. Most of the schools had schemes where teachers mentored a small group of Year 11 students. The relationship between staff mentoring and business mentoring schemes was not always thought through. For example, some students might have both business and staff mentors, but the latter were not always aware of the role of their business counterparts. In general, school coordinators regarded the impact of business mentoring on attainment as indirect. According to this view higher self-esteem and improved motivation would tend to lead to improved GCSE performance. Although mentor training tended to emphasize general support and encouragement for students, both mentors and students were able to give examples of help provided in a range of GCSE subjects.

Mentors reported helping students with their GCSE assessed coursework and homework in a range of subjects, particularly English (27 per cent), mathematics (22 per cent), technology (12 per cent), business studies (10 per cent) and science (9 per cent). Students reported that mentoring had helped them to improve their work in English (38 per cent), mathematics (28 per cent), science (18 per cent), geography (14 per cent) and business studies (12 per cent). However, many of the mentors preferred to give general encouragement rather than specific help. In some schools, mentoring meetings focused on helping students to structure their revision for mock GCSE examinations. Students particularly valued this support with study skills, which is one area where group mentoring may provide a cost-effective approach.

Impact of business mentoring

In order to judge the impact of mentoring on GCSE performance, 183 students (90 mentored and 93 control group) from the study schools took the Year Eleven Information System (YELLIS) test. YELLIS involves a vocabulary test, a mathematics test and a questionnaire to identify students' 'cultural capital' (which includes social background). Their GCSE results were matched against the YELLIS predictions using the standard scoring system (ranging from A* = 8 points to G = 1 point). The resulting number indicates whether, across the subjects, a student had under-achieved (-) or over-achieved (+) against the YELLIS prediction. However, any conclusions must be interpreted with caution given the relatively small size of the sample.

Overall there were significant differences between boys and girls, and between mentored and control-group students. Girls tended to out-perform boys in all the schools. The 46 mentored girls scored an average 2.26 GCSE points above YELLIS, compared with 1.87 GCSE points for the 43 control-group girls. The difference between these scores gives a measure of the value added by mentoring of 0.39 of a grade across all subjects. The 44 mentored boys had an average score of –1.72 GCSE points below YELLIS, compared with –2.13 for the 49 control-group boys (mentoring value added = 0.41). On average the impact of mentoring seems to be an improvement in GCSE performance of almost half a grade. However, these broad results mask wide differences between schools. Students in three case-study schools performed well against YELLIS predictions. In the four other schools, however, students tended to under-achieve against the YELLIS predictions.

Impact on motivation

There were a number of other positive impacts. The majority of students (70 per cent) said that mentoring had affected their wish to do well at school. Three-quarters of these students stated that mentoring had a lot of impact on their motivation; of these, 42 per cent said it had affected most (ie 5–9) of their GCSE subjects; another 18 per cent reported it had affected some (ie 3–4) subjects; and 14 per cent said this applied to one or two GCSE subjects. Many of the students who said that there was no impact on their motivation regarded themselves as well motivated already. This was a reflection of the school's selection criteria when students were chosen for reasons other than low or falling motivation. Most mentored students said that the evidence of their improved motivation was shown by: spending more time on coursework (66 per cent); spending more time on homework (55 per cent); paying more attention in class (55 per cent); and being more interested and enthusiastic in class (51 per cent). Other significant improvements were handing work in on time more often (38 per cent) and working more thoroughly (35 per cent).

Most students (84 per cent) had discussed career choices with the mentor. Over a third of students (38 per cent) said that their mentor had influenced their choice of career, but this was generally to help confirm the choice already made. In one school the mentors sought to encourage students to aim higher in their career aspirations. In a small number of cases mentors helped students to identify possible careers where they had none before, and there were a few examples of students changing their career choice as a result of the mentoring.

Business benefits at Deloitte & Touche

A company survey of the perceptions of 60 mentors working with school students in 1999 yielded very positive results (Stone, 2000). When asked how mentoring had helped develop their competencies:

- 91 per cent acted as a role model.
- 89 per cent managed relationships.
- 87 per cent developed their communication skills.
- 85 per cent practised counselling and coaching skills.
- 67 per cent demonstrated leadership and management skills.

ScholarshipBuilder®

The programme was evaluated by the Yale Child Study Center during its twelfth year (Ben-Avie, Steinfeld and Vergnetti, 2000). The methodology used was interviews with 167 participants across ten cities and statistical analysis of data provided by the project. The evaluation aimed to document the ScholarshipBuilder® process, analyse its impact and identify the lessons learnt.

The evaluation report observed that the expected high graduation rate of 93 per cent over a three-year period contrasts starkly with the typical inner-city rate of 50–70 per cent. Despite high student mobility, the programme was still in touch with 96 per cent of students. A key factor in the programme's success was the sustained intervention over many years, which enabled students to be able to build on prior success. Interviews with students and their families consistently demonstrated the impact of the scholarship and support services on raising aspirations. Easy access to effective adult support enabled students to tackle personal, social and academic challenges over the life of the programme. In particular the links to Merrill Lynch and the National Urban League opened doors to sources of personal and social power. Internships with close supervision and mentoring in Merrill Lynch developed strong employability skills.

The support of Merrill Lynch mentors encouraged a strong connection to the education process among the students. Mentors also acted as befrienders by supporting students through 'traumatic life events'. The mentors were important in 'pushing' the students towards successful academic careers and success in life. The 'pull' of the scholarship raised the students' aspirations and, most importantly, those of their parents. The programme was also impressive in binding the mentees together as a 'cohesive, long-lived group'. It also engaged siblings and parents in a holistic approach, which proved vital in securing positive support for the programme.

ISSUES

Business mentoring schemes have proved a popular approach to developing links between education and business. Business mentors can provide effective mentoring relationships that can motivate young people and develop their employability skills and personal qualities. One-company programmes in particular can bring a wider range of benefits to schools and to the businesses, in addition to the individual benefits to mentors and mentees. However, there a number of issues that should be considered when setting up business mentoring schemes.

Supply of business mentors

There is usually a shortage of business mentors, which is why many schemes that began as 'business mentoring' ended as 'business-and-community mentoring'. Community mentors tend to be used to 'top-up' the supply when it falls short. However, the cultural background of business mentors is often relatively homogeneous when compared with the heterogeneity of most inner-city schools. The introduction of community mentors can thus be viewed as a way of increasing the diversity of the mentor population (Appiah, 2001: 3).

The excess demand for business mentors can result in inadequate vetting of potential mentors to ensure that they are likely to make good mentors. In the past, business mentors have tended to be accepted uncritically by EBPs, because they are in short supply and because of a desire to please the company in building wider partnerships. It is desirable to apply some selection criteria to business mentors, but to be in a position to offer a range of other volunteering opportunities to business people who wish to work with schools. As schools and businesses go online it is likely that telementoring may become the main means of communication between business mentors and their student mentees.

Selection of students

The selection of students who are most likely to benefit from a business mentor can also prove problematic. Business mentors are more likely to have an impact on motivated underachieving students than in turning round disaffected students. Students will sometimes seek mentors who work in sectors where they have a career interest, and this can act as a powerful additional motivator. However, career interest is not often used as a key matching criterion by scheme coordinators. Some schools with a relatively poor reputation may be tempted to select their 'best students' as mentees to enhance their school's reputation, rather than choose those students who might gain most benefit. While understandable, this route can lead to lack of clarity on the part of students and mentors about the purpose of the programme.

Developing employability

Business mentoring schemes often cite 'developing employability' as a key goal, but how this is to be achieved and what precisely is meant by 'employability' is rarely spelt out. Employability goals are more likely to be met when there is a 'mentoring plus' programme, which includes: employability workshops, work experience and residential or other developmental approaches. An interesting case study from Australia involving an inner-city high school in New South Wales and a bank is a good example of this 'mentoring plus' approach (MacCallum and Beltman, 1999). There were three phases to the mentoring programme:

- The initial meeting at the school.
- The teambuilding phase, which began with a canoeing expedition over a weekend and was followed by weekly meetings alternating between the school and the bank as a venue. The programme included opportunities for one-to-one meetings and teambuilding exercises for the whole group.
- The project phase when mentor and student chose a project to work on together, such as a remote-control boat, a photographic history of the area. This culminated in the presentation evening followed by a formal dinner.

Mentoring can also provide opportunities for situated learning, especially when accompanied by work experience as part of a school-to-work transition process (see Chapter 12). Business mentors who meet students at their workplace can be seen as inducting them into the community of practice (Lave and Wenger, 1991). They are able to reflect with their mentees on how knowledge is used and developed in work situations. Business mentors can help students to articulate the key skills that they have developed and to see how they are valued in the workplace. In this way business mentoring can be seen as an induction into the culture of work.

Problems of sustainability

There is an inherent contradiction within business mentoring programmes that makes sustainability problematic. In some schemes mentors are encouraged to develop their own learning goals, which fit with the company's set of staff competencies. This is especially true where the company has targeted young managers for staff development reasons. However, once these objectives have been achieved or demonstrated through the mentoring scheme, the incentive to continue as a mentor can disappear. Fortunately the majority of mentors do not seem to join schemes for purely instrumental, job-related motives. Single-business mentoring programmes are also more subject to the vicissitudes of the economic cycle, and downturns can result in large-scale culls of mentors.

Unreliability and turnover

Finally, business mentors are frequently working in pressurized environments, which may result in meetings being postponed at short notice. Schools have also observed the high turnover, particularly among young professionals. This puts additional responsibilities on the school coordinator to facilitate and monitor the arrangement and completion of meetings in business mentoring schemes. Again the development of a telementoring dimension to the scheme can help address some of these communication problems.

SETTING UP A BUSINESS MENTORING SCHEME

There are clearly differences between brokerage agencies setting up a local scheme covering a number of schools and a school establishing its own business mentoring scheme. Generally it will be more difficult for individual schools to devote sufficient resources of staff time to set up and run an effective scheme. Local agencies are able to take advantage of economies of scale in mentor recruitment and training, and division of labour in appointing specialist, mentoring coordinators. There are also clear advantages in managing one-company schemes as described above. The good practice points set out below are drawn from both one- and multi-company schemes.

Planning

- Explain to the school or college partners the distinctive culture and values of the company and make sure that the company understands the goals and priorities of the school or college.
- Encourage the company to designate a coordinator with a clearly defined set of functions.
- Write a guidance document for would-be mentors and their line managers, making it clear what the role entails, what can be done in company time and what demands there are on free time.
- Explain what the costs are likely to be and the need for a budget, where there is no other source of funding for the scheme (costs might include: police vetting, training, in-house literature, travel, refreshments, outings, subsidies for students from low-income families to attend events).

- Write down ways in which involvement in the mentoring programme would help the company achieve wider goals.
- Draw up a log so that mentors can record the time they have spent on the mentoring programme. This should include: travel time, mentoring time, other activity time (such as social events and meetings of mentors), company time and their own time.
- Assist the company in developing 'SMART' objectives: specific, measurable, achievable, realistic and timebound.
- Encourage a wider partnership between the school and the company.
- Consider whether meetings will be held after the end of the working day or during the working day (if company policy allows this) and how line managers' approval will be gained.
- Target members of staff who live near to the school or college to minimize travel times for mentees and mentors and the knock-on effect on work loads, and to maximize meeting times.
- Consider buying pagers for the programme coordinator so company staff can contact them. Telephone cards issued to students or access to the coordinator's phone in the school can also help communications.
- Involve an experienced mentor pair when training business mentors, especially people who can talk articulately about their experiences and a business mentor who can spell out business benefits.
- Ensure that the first meeting is at the school so that the mentor can understand better the context in which the student is operating.
- Secure the support of line managers for the programme and try to engage them in evaluating the impact of the programme on mentors.

Implementing

- At the first meeting invite the head teacher and a senior company champion to launch the programme.
- Ensure that there is a system in place for students to pick up their messages and to record when they are meeting their mentors, to facilitate monitoring.
- Consider organizing a programme of team events, educational and social outings to help break down barriers, to make participants feel part of a larger programme and as a means of recruiting new mentors.
- Encourage mentoring pairs to present the outcomes of their relationship in the form of case studies for the purposes of evaluation, dissemination and mentor recruitment.
- Encourage the company to produce and present certificates, incorporating the company logo, to their students on completion of the programme, which they can include in the record of achievement.
- Involve the head teacher and a senior company representative in presenting certificates at an end-of-scheme celebratory event.

- Think about the opportunities for other links that build on the mentoring programme, for example, work-experience placements.
- Invite one of the business mentors to keep a scrapbook of cuttings from newsletters and the local press about the scheme.

FUTURE TRENDS

The development of vocational pathways in schools, and of specialist or magnet schools, will increase demand for business mentors in education. Business mentoring will be seen, alongside work experience, as the most important contribution business can make to young people's development. Businesses will support mentoring for young people as part of corporate support for employee volunteering. This will be seen as an important way of increasing the loyalty of staff and the attractiveness of the company. Company support for mentoring programmes will come to be viewed as a way of encouraging greater work–life balance. Some large companies will support long-term, flagship mentoring programmes as a vehicle for corporate community investment. Telementoring will be seen as an attractive alternative to face-to-face mentoring. Programmes such as the Hewlett-Packard E-Mail Mentoring Project will be replicated in the UK and other countries.

4

Community mentoring: intergenerational programmes

INTRODUCTION

Community mentoring programmes involve members of the local community providing mentors for a school. Community mentors are local residents, but they can be further segmented by age. Senior citizens are sometimes targeted for social intervention, as they too can be excluded from society. Intergenerational mentoring programmes generally involve men and women over the age of 50 in acting as mentors to students in their local primary or secondary school.

In this chapter we begin by discussing the mutual benefits to be gained by old and young from intergenerational mentoring. Case studies from England and Australia illustrate practice in intergenerational mentoring. The Across Ages project in Philadelphia shows that elder mentors from an African-American background can make effective mentors for at-risk students. The findings of research and evaluation evidence are followed by a discussion of issues arising from intergenerational mentoring programmes. Good practice points on planning and implementing mentoring programmes that use older mentors are listed. Finally, some future trends in intergenerational mentoring programmes are highlighted.

Intergenerational programmes

Intergenerational mentoring is one activity within the much broader area of intergenerational programmes. Such programmes are designed to bring together different generations for mutual benefit. Intergenerational programmes are based upon non-familial relationships between the generations. Most intergenerational programmes are concerned with the two groups at the opposite ends of the age spectrum: the young and the old. In most cases this means under-18s and the over-50s. There is a 'skipped' generation; that is, the two generations involved are non-adjacent.

There is a view that there are three generations: 'those that believe in Father Christmas, those that don't believe in Father Christmas and those that are Father Christmas' (*Countdown*, Channel 4 Television, October 2000). However, a more sophisticated categorization would include:

- children, aged 0–12;
- young adolescents, aged 12–18;
- adolescents, aged 18–24;
- young adults, aged 24–30;
- adults aged 30–45;
- mature adults, aged 45–60;
- the young old, aged 60–75;
- the old, aged 75 plus.

According to this model, intergenerational mentoring programmes tend to involve mature adults and the young old working with children and young adolescents.

AIMS AND OBJECTIVES

Intergenerational mentoring programmes, unlike most other forms of mentoring, aim to bring mutual benefits to mentors and mentees. For young people the aims of intergenerational mentoring tend to be developmental, with a focus on the self-esteem, motivational and personal and social skills objectives. However, a major goal of intergenerational mentoring is also often to improve basic literacy and numeracy skills in young people. In the United Kingdom many older people serve as reading volunteers in primary schools and the mentoring is an incidental add-on to the main function of improving reading skills. The academic objective is also, therefore, highly important in intergenerational mentoring programmes.

For the older mentors a prime objective of mentoring in schools is that of social inclusion. Older people are frequently isolated in their communities and distanced from younger people, whom they may find threatening. Intergenerational mentoring helps to break down stereotypes, and to build cross-generational bridges with mentees and friendships with other mentors. Mentoring can help senior citizens to feel a valued part of the community again.

Mutual benefits

A rationale for intergenerational programmes is that young and older people share certain problems, but seldom have the opportunity to meet naturally. This is one by-product of an age-segregated society. Intergenerational programmes 'provide spaces and opportunities for young and old to meet where stereotypes, myths and misconceptions can be broken down' (Mercken, 1999: 9). Common issues shared by young and old include the following:

- They do not form part of the workforce and are, therefore, more dependent on the middle generations for economic support.
- They lack clear social roles.
- They may feel more isolated than other generations.

However, young and old also have considerable differences in their experience and views of life. Each has assets that can benefit the other. So intergenerational programmes are above all powerful vehicles for the social inclusion of both young and older people.

Case Study 4.1 Generations in Action in Salford (UK)

Generations In Action is an intergenerational programme that enables mentors aged 50 and over to work in primary and secondary schools (Hope and Davies, 2000; Salford BEP, 2000). The programme began in 1996 in Salford, Manchester, and by 2001 there were around 60 mentors working in 30 schools. The mentors either worked in primary schools on paired reading or in secondary schools on reading support and/or one-to-one mentoring of 14–16-year-old students. The older mentors were recruited separately from other mentors, but the training and programmes they joined involved business and other community mentors. In this sense the intergenerational programme was integrated with other mentoring programmes. The paired-reading programme involved the older mentors being attached to a particular class and pupil, and visiting the school at least once a week over a year to hear their pupil read. Once the relationship was formed over a period of time, the coordinator noted that a developmental dimension of mentoring often resulted.

Objectives

In the primary schools the main objective of the programme was to improve reading scores and literacy, and in the secondary schools it was to meet the wide range of objectives of mentoring schemes from employability to personal development to subject support. According to the scheme coordinator, the objectives for the mentors in participating were to:

- use their experience and expertise;
- combat ageism;
- bring the generations together;
- feel valued and included;
- promote activity and a healthier lifestyle: 'I get aches and pains but because I know I am going into school I put those aches and pains to the back. If you're not going into school you may concentrate more on the aches and pains' (senior mentor).

Recruitment

Salford Business Education Partnership (Salford BEP), which runs the programme, appointed a project coordinator who took an important role in recruiting mentors. This involved researching the 'community map', which illustrated those locations and times when different groups of retired and older people met. These included church groups, bowling clubs, community centres and 'keep-fit' classes. The coordinator then arranged to speak to the groups and to bring along marketing literature about the programme. One of the messages he tried to put across was that it is important to 'move your mind, as well as your body' and that the Generations programme encouraged greater mental flexibility. The coordinator conceded that people who are inflexible in their thinking and nostalgic for a bygone golden era may not make suitable mentors, and indeed tend not to put themselves forward to be mentors.

Another good means of recruitment was existing mentors, who were asked to bring along a friend to mentor support meetings. Local voluntary groups referred people to Salford BEP if they expressed an interest in working with schools. It proved difficult to recruit men to the programme and 80 per cent of mentors were female. Most of the mentors had a long employment history, but were now retired and yet wished to remain active in their communities. Some mentors had recently been bereaved and had been referred to the programme by relatives who were keen for them to re-engage with the wider world. Some mentors have been attached to the same school for five years, and this continuity has been important (in contrast to other business and community mentors).

Support mechanisms

It was important for the coordinator to accompany the mentors on their initial visit to the school to meet the teacher. This was part of the process of encouraging the school to value the contribution of the older mentors. In addition to termly networking meetings, which enabled them to feel part of a wider team, there was an annual celebratory event at which the Director of Education formally thanked them for their contribution. There was also a regular newsletter to publicize successes and to make the older mentors feel included. Although mentors sometimes dropped out of the programme, because their own elderly parents had become demanding and needed more care, the coordinator did not perceive any particular problems with older mentors. Indeed they tended to be more reliable than business mentors, who often had to prioritize other work activities. Travel expenses were offered to older mentors and they generally wanted to be within easy reach of the school.

Case Study 4.2 School Volunteer Program in Western Australia

The School Volunteer Program (SVP) was set up in Western Australia in 1994 and by 1999 it involved over 1,000 community mentors aged 50 and above, working with more than 2,000 primary and secondary-age students. The aims of this intergenerational mentoring scheme are to:

- encourage children to achieve their full potential by developing improved life skills, thus enhancing their quality of life;
- support and guide children who have difficulty coping with formal education;
- help children to improve their literacy skills;
- promote the value of seniors in the community.

Interestingly the SVP has received a prestigious crime prevention award for three years running, because of its perceived role in reducing the threat of violence by young people.

Most students are targeted because of low self-esteem, poor communication skills, low reading scores and/or poor achievement in mathematics. The students vary from year 7 in primary schools to years 8-12 in secondary schools.

Recruitment

The SVP organization coordinates the scheme in local areas, promotes intergenerational mentoring, recruits, trains and supports mentors and schools. School coordinators manage groups of local volunteers. Promotion occurs through word of mouth, local media, the churches, signs in shopping centres and doctors' surgeries, and talks to community groups. Nine out of ten mentors have had previous volunteering experience, and four in ten read about the scheme in the local press. Volunteers contact the local SVP coordinator who sends them the pack of information about the programme and application forms. References are taken up on all volunteers as part of the screening process, and those accepted are sent a name badge and are invited to a half-day workshop at the school they have requested. Volunteers' names are sent to the school and it is the responsibility of the school coordinator to contact them and interview them.

Mentor training workshops

The workshop is run by SVP and includes the school coordinator. Key elements of the programme are introduced and mentors receive a comprehensive manual. Ongoing support includes one-day training workshops on subjects such as anger management, working with aboriginal children and how to use newspapers. Mentors generally meet their mentees once a week for one hour and have some choice in the work they select from a bank of materials provided by the school coordinator. Students see their mentors during lesson time. In the primary schools mentors tend to come at the same time each week, and this allows for informal contact between mentors and the parent coordinators who attend at the same time.

Case Study 4.3 The Across Ages Program In Philadelphia (USA)

The Across Ages Program was developed by the Center for Intergenerational Learning at Temple University in Philadelphia (Taylor and Dryfoos, 2001). The programme was evaluated during the period from 1991 to 1998 and so a lot of data is available on its impact. It was designed to address a number of risk and protective factors affecting young teenagers in the city's most deprived neighbourhoods that are characterized by poverty, a high incidence of substance abuse and drug-related crime, and general dereliction. Many of the students were at least one year behind at school, and they often lived with other relatives as their parents were unable to care for them.

The mentors

The mentors ranged in age from 60 to 85 years and were mainly African-American, reflecting the ethnicity of the students. A typical mentor was formerly a skilled or semi-skilled worker, widowed or divorced and a grandparent. Two-thirds were female and many had not found retirement as fulfilling as they had hoped. Mentors were all carefully screened, trained and supervised by project staff. Prior to matching, mentors and students worked on classroom-based activities so that they could get to know each other and so that natural pairings might arise. Once matched the pairs would typically spend four or five hours each week together on a range of activities:

- attending sporting and cultural events;
- joining in weekend activities organized by the project;
- attending school plays, assemblies and school trips;
- helping with work in class and with homework.

Some mentors helped their students get to school on time, and others acted as a bridge between the school and the parents.

Mentoring plus

There were three other elements, which supported the mentoring programme. First, resiliency was built as students undertook work to benefit other people in a 'direct and personal' way. The mentors generally accompanied the students on visits to frail elders in nursing homes. Prior to these visits project staff briefed students on the problems of advancing age and failing health. Second, the students' teachers were trained by project staff to run weekly social competence, or life skills, lessons to enable students to resist negative peer pressure and unhealthy behaviour. Third, Across Ages provided opportunities for family learning, with parents and students learning together. Workshops were held on understanding adolescent sexuality, and setting goals and limits. Activities included African dance, storytelling and student talent shows.

RESEARCH AND EVALUATION EVIDENCE

UK evaluation

The Beth Johnson Foundation carried out research into three intergenerational mentoring programmes in Salford, North Staffordshire and London (Granville, 2000). Interviews were held with 45 people aged over 50 involved in a variety of programmes in primary and secondary schools. Females were three times as likely as males to volunteer as mentors. The main benefits of school-based intergenerational mentoring for mentors were:

- It enhanced their engagement with life and quality of life. 'It gets me out in the morning, provides structure to the day and you feel you're doing a good job.'
- They enjoyed working with children and the equality of a relationship which brings mutual benefits. 'It does give me a thrill to see the children develop.'
- They felt better about themselves, enjoying health benefits and general well-being. 'The work keeps me young and healthy. I'm often faced with difficult questions which I enjoy.'
- The work promoted interaction with other people and increased their circle of friends.
- It led to greater confidence.

The particular benefits of using older volunteers for young people were:

- the non-judgemental attitude born out of experience which contradicted a prevailing stereotype of older people;

- the capacity to see broader priorities or 'the bigger picture' beyond an immediate problem or circumstance;
- the initiative they are able to show because of their greater reservoir of life experiences that can be drawn upon.

Young people said that mentors teach, help, befriend and like them. The mentees did not have age-related stereotypes; they described their mentors as 'special, intelligent, wise, funny, kind and significant in their lives'. In the secondary-school setting, mentoring resulted in a positive change in the attitudes of the young people towards older people in general.

High-school teachers noted that older mentors brought a maturity and respect to the classroom environment. Granville observes that older mentors bring greater diversity to the school and that this brings a humanizing effect. She notes a special empathy between two segregated generations that comes from mutual understanding of the way both groups tend to be marginalized in society.

The main benefits for the local community through including older people in mentoring programmes were, first, that they acted as 'champions' for young people and teachers and, second, that they became more visible in the community; thus counteracting the stereotype of older people.

Australian evaluation

MacCallum and Beltman (1999) undertook a qualitative evaluation of the SVP scheme as part of the International Year of Older Persons Mentoring Research Project. The evaluation involved interviews with mentors, mentees and school coordinators in primary and secondary schools. School coordinators were very positive about SVP based on their behavioural observations:

> Students enjoy going to the programme, those not in the programme ask for a mentor, students give Christmas presents to their mentors, and invite them to see them play sport, go to concerts etc., teachers ask for mentors for students, and mentors send postcards from overseas holidays.
> (MacCallum and Beltman, 1999: 46)

Although teachers thought that there were academic benefits, the personal development outcomes were viewed as the greatest benefit of the mentoring scheme.

Six out of ten mentors believed that the students they mentored gained in self-esteem, improved their basic skills, were less likely to show violence and frustration, and were more tolerant towards others. The research showed that most mentors went to great lengths to meet the individual needs of their mentee and in some cases the mentorship had lasted a number of years. For example, one mentor decided to take a maths class when his mentee had asked for maths support. Generally mentors were unsure of the outcomes of the mentoring, and this was partly attributed to a lack of feedback from the school. Six in ten mentors thought that their skills and interests were not matched to the needs of students. This tended to happen when the training led them to believe that they would be dealing primarily with literacy issues, only to be faced with social and emotional difficulties. Students tended to be more certain about the positive outcomes than mentors.

US evaluation

An early study by Freedman (1988) examined the relationships between 'elder' mentors and at-risk young people in a range of contexts: youth offending, dropping out of school and teenage pregnancy. Interviews with 47 pairs showed significant bonds bringing benefits to both parties in 37 cases. Freedman placed the relationships into two categories, primary and secondary. Primary relationships were characterized by attachments 'approximating kinship, great intimacy and a willingness on the part of elders to take on the youth's full range of problems and emotions'. In contrast, secondary relationships exhibited greater 'emotional distance' and the emphasis was on positive reinforcement by elders acting as 'friendly neighbours'.

Mentees reported improvements in the quality of their daily lives and learning a variety of practical skills. Those in primary relationships were able to develop resilience, which was vital in turning around their lives. Freedman found that elders had a special empathy for the young people, which he argues derives from a shared marginal status in society. A particularly striking finding was that the most effective mentors were not those who had led conventionally successful lives. Those that had survived and overcome adversity seemed able to make highly effective bonds with their mentees. He concludes that intergenerational relationships offer a 'distinct paradigm for youth development' through intense personal relationships, which are often absent from standard programmes for at-risk young people.

Evaluation of Across Ages

Between 1991 and 1998 approximately 90 students each year participated in all elements of the programme. The evaluation used a quasi-experimental design with a programme group of 90 students who did not have a mentor, but who participated in all other elements, and a control group of 180 students who had no interventions. Monitoring data, surveys and interviews were used in the evaluation.

The evaluation showed greater impact on students with mentors than on those without, in particular on attitudes to school, to the future and to their elders. They reported less substance use. Students who had more contact time with their mentors showed greater changes, for example in days absent from school, than those having less contact. The key to a successful relationship for mentees and mentors was when mentors 'nurture, coach, and encourage... engage in mutual problem solving, and work cooperatively with family members whenever possible'. Another predictor of a successful mentoring relationship was when mentors were able to help the students set realistic, attainable goals.

ISSUES

Social capital

Social capital can be defined as the resources in the community – such as social trust, networks, associations and norms – that can be drawn upon to solve common problems (Coleman, 1990). Networks of civic engagement, such as neighbourhood associations, parent-teacher associations and cooperatives are essential forms of social capital, as they make it more likely that members of the community will cooperate for mutual benefit. A theme of social capital theory is that it has been declining in the United States at least since the 1970s largely as a product of television (Putnam, 1995). Community mentoring programmes, including those that involve senior citizens and younger people, can play an important role in helping to rebuild social capital. Communities high in social capital will also tend to have a range of mentoring programmes that involve community and business leaders in mentoring young people. The programmes we have examined have created new networks of older people, reciprocal ties between young and old, and stronger linkages between schools and members of the local community. The development of intergenerational mentoring programmes is one way in which schools and voluntary mentoring organizations can help to rebuild social capital.

Separate or integrated

A key issue for mentoring programme organizers is whether to establish an intergenerational mentoring programme as a separate entity. The advantage of doing this is that it facilitates partnerships with community organizations supporting senior citizens. It makes it more likely that the mutual benefits for mentors will be a major feature of the programme. However, there may be some people coming forward for whom one-to-one mentoring may be unsuitable. For this reason it is desirable to see mentoring as one of a series of volunteering opportunities for older people who wish to work in schools. In other words, it may be better to establish an intergenerational programme that offers alternatives such as classroom support, out-of-school study support or involvement in oral history projects. A further option, one taken by the Salford Generations in Action programme, was to integrate older mentors into the general business-and-community mentoring programme. This has the advantage of mixing retired people and those of working age in mentor training and support sessions. The main disadvantage is that it can become more difficult to provide targeted support for the older mentors.

Stereotyping

There are a number of reasons why intergenerational programmes can sometimes fail. First, projects, which are one-off or ad hoc can increase rather than reduce the stereotypes that young people may hold of the old. It is important, therefore, for the school to make a longer-term commitment to intergenerational programmes. Second, the starting point in the thinking of the organizers needs to be 'what can we do with the older generation' not 'what can we do for them'. Third, the needs of both generations must be taken into account when preparing the programme. Finally, the people who are organizing the programme from the middle generation should be aware of their own stereotypes.

Objectives and targeting

Schools use a wide range of criteria when selecting students who may need a mentor. Students who are at risk of underachieving may be appropriate matches for older people where they lack basic skills or need general support and encouragement. It may be less appropriate to ask senior mentors to take on students with emotional and behavioural difficulties, especially when addressing the needs of this client group has not featured in the preparation of the mentors. Indeed some of the UK programmes target primary age pupils who are in need of support with their reading as the primary role of senior mentors.

SETTING UP INTERGENERATIONAL MENTORING PROGRAMMES

Intergenerational mentoring programmes have the dual goal of developing the mentee and including the mentor. It is important, therefore, that such schemes are based on partnerships between schools or education brokerage agencies and organizations that represent and understand the needs of older citizens. In the UK, for example, Age Concern's

Intergenerational Network is encouraging a range of local programmes for older people to work with younger people. These include: working with refugee families; involvement in after-school clubs; working with children in hospital; and undertaking information technology training with young people. The following good practice points aim to help schools and mentoring providers to set up and run effective intergenerational mentoring programmes.

Planning

- Decide whether to develop a stand-alone intergenerational mentoring programme, or a wider intergenerational programme that offers a range of options to volunteers. Decide whether to integrate older mentors within a general business and/or community mentoring programme.
- Make sure that the roles and responsibilities of school coordinators are well defined and understood, particularly in relation to customer care for older mentors.
- Encourage schools to allow the project coordinator to talk to the staff as a whole about the mentoring programme, so that they are all aware of its objectives and the processes involving mentors and mentees.
- Draw up a 'community map' that identifies those places and times when community groups meet, so they can be targeted for recruitment to the programme.
- Try to identify stereotypes that staff and students hold about older people and prepare to challenge them.
- Try to involve experienced older mentors in giving talks to prospective mentors.
- Draft a contract for mentors to sign up to, including ground rules on attendance, training, support and withdrawal or resignation from the programme.
- Prepare an information pack for project staff to use in making presentations to prospective mentors.
- Involve older mentors as ambassadors for the programme to recruit a friend.

Implementing

- Make sure that the training takes into account the considerable life experience and many skills of older mentors.
- Include a slot in training on the differences between schooling 'then and now'.
- Try to involve experienced older mentors as trainers of 'new' older mentors.

- Offer training for school coordinators and teachers on how to support mentors.
- Allow school coordinators to interview mentors prior to matching.
- Monitor the situation to ensure that the mentors are not being used as unpaid classroom assistants.
- Consider inviting all the mentors to visit the school at the same time each week to foster links and friendships between them.
- Provide tea and refreshments for visiting mentors.
- Try to allocate a hall or large space where mentors and students can meet.
- Have the project coordinator accompany the mentor into school for the initial meeting with the school coordinator or classroom teacher.
- Schedule support meetings for older mentors so that they feel part of a team and can engage peer support.
- Provide information and advice on further lifelong-learning opportunities that arise from their mentoring experiences.
- Consider using older mentors as witnesses during oral history projects.

FUTURE TRENDS

At the moment, intergenerational mentoring programmes are at the earliest stages of development in the UK. The baby-boomer generation of elder citizens is likely to want to be more actively involved in volunteering and mentoring young people than previous generations. Mentoring will be seen as one means of overcoming social isolation through building personal networks involving young people in schools, teachers and other mentors. Mentoring and befriending of young people by older people will develop as an alternative to the traditional family roles of grandparents. Highly skilled, active older citizens will want to play a bigger role in the management and governance of mentoring programmes.

5

Minority ethnic mentoring

INTRODUCTION

Minority ethnic mentoring schemes have been established to meet the needs of minority students who face particular disadvantages and barriers to their educational and career progression. In this chapter we begin by discussing the focus and targeting of minority ethnic programmes and their aims and objectives. Three case studies from different parts of inner London illustrate practices in 'Black' mentoring programmes targeting primary, secondary and college students. The rather limited research and evaluation evidence on minority ethnic programmes is discussed, together with some issues arising from the case studies. A checklist of good practice points on planning and implementing minority ethnic programmes is then provided. We conclude with the identification of possible future trends in minority ethnic mentoring programmes.

Context

Mentoring programmes targeting 'aboriginal youth' in Canada and Australia, and Native Americans, Hispanics and African-American youth in the United States are increasingly common. This chapter focuses on minority ethnic programmes that have developed in the last few years in the United Kingdom, although it draws on American experience. Mentoring for minority students in the UK has developed in part through the establishment of programmes by voluntary organizations set up to address the needs of these communities. More recently, government policy has supported the development of minority ethnic mentoring programmes. Following unrest in Brixton during 1995, a key recommendation of the report by the Runnymede Trust was the implementation of mentoring programmes for Black youth by local members of the Black community who could act as positive role models (Sewell, 1997). The National Mentoring Network Bursary Scheme in 1999–2000 was in part targeted at supporting minority ethnic mentoring programmes in inner cities (see Chapter 2). In 2000, the influential Social Exclusion Unit's Schools Plus report on combating social exclusion in education recommended that there should be 'an expanded programme of mentoring for pupils from ethnic minority backgrounds, offering qualifications through accreditation for mentors taking part in the programme' (DfEE, 2000d: 51).

It is important not to view mentoring as a panacea for underachieving students from minority ethnic backgrounds. In UK schools some students from minority ethnic communities have problems of underachievement, in part as a result of low self-esteem and issues of identity. However, it is wrong to think that there is a hierarchy of achievement between different ethnic groups. For example, a recent review of Ethnic Minority Achievement Grant applications from local education authorities in England revealed a complex picture (Gillborn and Mirza, 2000). Of six minority ethnic communities analysed, each one was the highest attaining in at least one local education authority. Nevertheless, there is clearly a problem of underachievement by students in all minorities, as well as in the majority ethnic group, in some schools in some areas that could be tackled through mentoring.

In other cases students may suffer from low aspirations for their educational and working lives. Mentoring schemes that target students from minority ethnic communities, therefore, frequently aim to raise self-esteem and aspirations through the use of role models from the wider minority ethnic community. One of the key purposes is to demonstrate to young people that barriers can be overcome through determination and particular strategies. Role-model mentors have had the experience of succeeding in overcoming barriers of racism and discrimination under difficult circumstances. Through mentoring they can pass on to the young valuable insights in terms of coping strategies and practical support. Same 'ethnicity' mentorships can also cut through problems of cultural understanding allowing underlying issues to be addressed more rapidly.

AIMS AND OBJECTIVES

Mentoring schemes for minority ethnic youths can be targeted at those young people who are at risk of social and school exclusion. In these circumstances there tends to be a 'holistic' approach to mentoring that includes developmental, work-related and academic aims. Some mentoring coordinators highlight the importance of dealing with identity issues as a key part of minority ethnic mentoring programmes. The aims of such programmes for at-risk youths include reducing those risk factors that can lead to school exclusions. They also include strategies for resisting peer pressure and developing self-discipline and greater motivation to succeed in school.

The ASELU mentoring programme aims at preventing drop-out from primary schools. Other programmes do not target at-risk youths, but rather those minority ethnic young people who, with added support, could aspire to higher education and successful careers. These are programmes, such as the Southwark Black Mentor Scheme and the North London Mentor Trust, that stress the aspirational objective. It could be argued that mentoring programmes are often based on either a deficit model or a positive model of minority ethnic youth. However, the case studies illustrate that whatever the context for the mentoring every attempt is made by the organizers to make it a positive experience for students.

Case Study 5.1 ASELU Black mentoring programme (UK)

ASELU was the name given to this Black mentoring programme by one of the mentors from Ghana; the name means 'cooperation' in the Yoruba language. The name of the programme was important in creating a Black identity and fully involving the mentors. In 2000–01 the programme involved 12 pupils aged between 10 and 11 at a primary school on a deprived housing estate in west London. The school was experiencing difficulties in maintaining standards and at the time of writing was under 'special measures'. The one Black teacher at the school had only recently been recruited and there were no Black parents on the parent-teachers' association. The school has had problems retaining staff and the class involved in the programme had a high turnover of 'substitute' teachers during the year.

Origins

The stimulus for establishing the programme was partly provided by 15- and 16-year-old students taking part in the business mentoring programme involving two local secondary schools on the same estate. Most of the students were from minority ethnic groups, but the majority of their mentors were white British. When completing their matching forms, several of the students expressed preferences for mentors from their own ethnic group. The reasons given were that they would find it easier to talk to same-ethnicity mentors and they would be likely to share similar experiences of schooling. The schools in the area also had high rates for permanent and temporary exclusions of students from ethnic minorities. This fact was coupled with the underachievement of minority ethnic students and the exaggerated drop in achievement at age 11 on transfer to secondary school. It was decided, therefore, to focus the mentoring intervention on primary pupils to try to prevent disaffection and the resulting underachievement during and after this transition.

Aims

The aims of the programme were to raise motivation and achievement, and to improve pupils' behaviour. An important aim in 'selling' the programme to pupils and their parents was developing leadership skills. This was also important in achieving the other aims, because it addressed the need to raise the self-esteem of the pupils. The school saw ASELU as a means of involving members of the local community in the school. The aims for mentors were to gain experience of working with children, to develop motivation and to explore alternative career paths.

A project worker was recruited to manage the programme, which initially involved visiting local voluntary groups and delivering leaflets to many locations where potential mentors might pick them up. Positive Black role models were sought regardless of their employment status, so that employed, part-time workers and the unwaged were targeted. References and police checks were conducted and all mentors had individual interviews with the project worker. A small number of those coming forward were deemed to be unsuitable for working with the age group in question. Recruitment proved difficult and after seven months only eleven mentors had been recruited, although there were twelve pupils requiring mentors.

Training

In addition to a general introduction to mentoring, training included sessions on: Black identity; racism in education; reflecting on their own experience of racism; and Black role models. This included discussing the causes of the underachievement of Black pupils, including the relative contribution of an absence of positive Black role models beyond the sports and music sectors and of institutionalized racism. It was important that mentors should have a constructive approach to handling racism, rather than putting across the negative messages that either 'nothing could be done about racism by individuals' or that an aggressive response was always appropriate.

The pupils chosen by the school represented a mix in terms of their behaviour and achievement. Some of the boys had presented behavioural problems and been excluded from the school. All were deemed to lack self-esteem and it was felt that they would benefit from the mentoring programme. The pupils also received significant preparation for the programme. A key focus was on leadership skills: What are the skills that leaders have? Which role models do they admire and why? A key aim of the programme was to raise self-esteem and, therefore, it was important to make the pupils feel that they had been specially chosen as potential leaders.

Activities

The process of recruiting mentors was slower than expected, so during the first term of the programme mentors came in each week and took it in turns to run 'workshops' on topics where they had expertise or interest. For example, a Black scientist ran a session on famous Black scientists and a musician ran an afternoon on the development of Black music. The mentoring sessions lasted about one hour a week and were held on Wednesday afternoons during the 'activities' period, so that pupils did not miss important lesson time. During the summer holiday period several trips were organized for mentors and mentees by the project worker. These included visits to:

- a mock-up African village in Hertfordshire;
- a walk around Westminster focusing upon 500 years of Black Britain;
- Queen's Park Rangers Football Club Study Support Centre to practise IT skills.

The project worker had a key role in structuring and focusing sessions as she met with mentors immediately before each session to brief them. Sessions included 'getting to know each other', managing behaviour, communication skills and leadership. The mentors and mentees began each session together and then divided into pairs. Every pair had time at the end of the session to discuss general issues. Mentors often brought in resources to help pupils with particular projects. For example, a mentor who was a trained therapist introduced some of these techniques to their mentee to help him with problems of poor concentration.

Endings

The Deputy Head evaluated the programme by asking the form teacher to complete a termly pro forma on each pupil. Mentors completed a self-rating sheet at the beginning of the programme and identified what they wanted from the mentoring. This was used as a baseline to measure the impact of the programme on mentors. One problem had been the difficulties over when the programme should end. The school wanted it to continue until pupils left school in the summer. On the other hand, mentors wanted to end the programme at Christmas, two terms before the end of the school year. The main reason for this was the once-a-week commitment was found to be heavy, given that some of them were employed and others were involved in different voluntary projects. Nevertheless most mentors did continue until the end of the school year and they attended an award ceremony with their mentees at the local college.

Case Study 5.2 Southwark Black Mentor Scheme (UK)

Funding

In 1992, the Southwark Black Mentor Scheme began as a pilot when two schools and thirty mentoring pairs were involved. Initially, the local council wholly funded it, but in 1995 £80,000 funding was received from the Single

Regeneration Budget Peckham Partnership, which enabled expansion to a peak of 120 pairs in 1997–98. In 2000–01, funding stood at £50,000 per annum, which paid for a project manager, assistant project worker and an administrative assistant. Each year assistant project workers have been recruited for six or twelve-month placements; they are drawn from among students taking sandwich courses at one of London's many universities. These student recruits must be culturally aware and sensitive to the needs of minority ethnic students, many of whom live on run-down, inner city estates. Schools received between £1,000 and £1,500 per annum, which included £250 per quarter for administration costs and the attendance of a designated scheme coordinator at meetings and events.

Aims

The aims of the Southwark Black Mentor Scheme are to highlight the value of education to students, to encourage them to continue with their education beyond 16, and to inspire students with confidence. The scheme targeted Black students aged 14–15 years from the eight secondary schools in the designated regeneration area. Although the majority of pupils were African or Black Caribbean, students from other minority ethnic groups were included in the scheme if they constituted a 'visible' minority. Thus Chinese, Cypriot, Turkish and Vietnamese students, together with others from other cultural backgrounds, had been included in the scheme over the years.

The mentors

The project philosophy was based on involving mentors who were 'successful Black adults' with whom students could identify both physically and culturally. According to the project manager:

> If mentors do not feel that they themselves are successful in some way, then how can they pass on a positive message to young people? Being an effective role model is more to do with someone's personal qualities rather than job, position or social status. Good role models are people who are: good listeners, positive in their approach to life, non-judgemental, honest and open, motivated or driven, able to set and achieve goals, and clear thinking.

Mentors were recruited through national and local community newspapers, such as *The Voice* and *Pride* magazine, with advertisements appearing in April for a September start. In response to inquiries, potential mentors were sent an information pack that included a magazine about the scheme and a leaflet. About 70 per cent of mentors were women and 30 per cent were men. On average 55–60 per cent were Black African, 40 per cent were Black Caribbean, and 2 per cent were of mixed heritage. Mentors tended to be between 25 and 40 years of age, but higher education students were accepted if they demonstrated sufficient maturity during an initial interview. Mentors with counselling or psychology backgrounds who wanted to develop their 'case experience' were often screened out. Men were harder to recruit than women, but they typically tended to stay for two or three years, compared with one or two years for women mentors.

Mentors were invited to an initial information session, which explained the aims of the scheme and how it operated. Sessions were held on one evening a week over a six-week period. Mentor application forms and the police check forms were distributed. A follow-up induction session used role-plays and case studies to train mentors in working with young people, building relationships with parents, ensuring confidentiality, and health and safety.

The mentees

Mentees were recruited during the summer term of Y9 when the project team visited the schools to give presentations at parents' evenings, option evenings and Personal Social and Health Education (PSHE) lessons. Students from minority ethnic communities were encouraged to volunteer, and then permission was sought from their parents. The main criterion for acceptance onto the scheme was that the students were failing to realize their potential. During the end of the summer term and towards the end of the summer vacation students were invited to attend briefing sessions at the headquarters of the scheme, which is located in the local council's education building. These sessions aimed to manage students' expectations of their mentors and about 40 per cent of students attended.

Matching

Mentors were matched with mentees from across the six schools using various criteria including gender, cultural background, career interests, hobbies and future aspirations. Mentors were invited to a pre-matching session at which they were encouraged to air any concerns about the match, and to the matching evening, when they had their first meeting with their mentees and their parents or guardians. Because gender is a key matching criterion, the gender balance of mentees matches that of the mentors; there is thus a 70–30 per cent split between girls and boys. There were occasional problems with religion in matching; for example, Rastafarian mentors with Muslim mentees tended to be a match to avoid according to the project worker. The matching evening provided an opportunity for mentors to arrange their first visit to the school, which took place during a lunch hour so that they could gain a 'mentee's eye view' of the school and understand what it was like to attend school in Southwark. Mentors were also encouraged to make a home visit to meet the mentee's family. This might be either formal and short or a more informal meeting, but it enabled mentors and parents to strike an agreement on how they proposed to communicate with each other about the mentoring meetings.

Processes

Minimum contact time was six hours per month during Year 10, which could be half a day or regular, shorter sessions. No independent meetings were allowed without police checks having been completed. Most pairs communicated more regularly on the telephone. The main aim of mentoring sessions was for mentees to set, achieve and review their own goals, which could be personal and social, academic or career-related. The project team visited mentees once a month to discuss how the mentoring was progressing, and mentors were asked to complete a simple, monthly evaluation form. Mentee workshops were held every six weeks for two hours at the scheme offices. These provided an opportunity to talk about how the mentoring was going without parents, mentors or school coordinators being present. There were also mentor networking sessions every six weeks, where they received additional training and met in small groups to discuss common issues.

There was a high-profile graduation event with keynote speeches from the Director of Education and a well-known, minority ethnic figure from the media. Certificates were presented to mentors and the young people. The scheme ended at the close of Year 10, as the final year tended to be the most full with examination and revision commitments. However, pairs were told that they could continue to meet, if both parties wanted to and the parents were supportive.

Case Study 5.3 North London Mentor Trust (UK)

The Trust managed a mentor programme for Black students at City & Islington College in north London. The college was housed on 11 sites and had over 18,000 full- and part-time students enrolled on over 1,500 courses. Sixty per cent of full-time students were Black and a third did not speak English as their first language. The mentor programme aimed to improve the achievements, expectations and life chances of Black students taking full-time courses by providing a programme of academic, social and vocational counselling, and intensive paired mentoring with role-model mentors. 'Black' students were defined as comprising Black-Africans, Black-Caribbeans and Asians from the Indian sub-Continent (Indians, Pakistanis, and Bangladeshis). The programme has been running since 1992 and was established by Howard Jeffrey following a year's secondment to the United States where he researched mentoring programmes. In comparing US and UK programmes he described the two big differences as funding levels, with UK mentoring programmes running on a shoestring budget, and the greater emphasis on measurement of outcomes in the United States.

Leadership Centre

The mentoring programme was an activity of the Leadership Centre, an impressive IT-and-personal-development suite, located within the College. In the first year of two-year courses students were offered a personal development programme to develop their confidence and skills. In the second year, Black students volunteered to join the mentoring programme. The mentoring coordinator visited tutor groups to introduce the programme and to distribute information leaflets and application forms. There was generally an enthusiastic response from the students and, in 2001, 60 students were signed up for the scheme, the majority from African-Caribbean backgrounds.

Mentor database

Students were matched with an extensive database of mentors that has been built up over the seven years in which the programme has been running. Mentors were contacted by letter each year to see if they wished to participate in that year's programme. Mentors have brought along other mentors to join the scheme and 'word-of-mouth' has been the most effective means of recruitment. Many of the mentors were past mentees from the college who were now successfully involved in a career. New mentors were offered a two-hour induction session during which they were briefed on mentoring, the college and student life today (many of the students had part-time jobs and busy social lives). About 60 per cent of mentors were African-Caribbean and most worked in the private sector, with a predominance in the IT or finance sectors; others had a teaching or medical background. The programme was aspirational, matching Black mentors from the world of work with students who aspired to careers in a similar field. Student and mentor wishes were taken into account when considering cross-ethnic or cross-gender matching.

Work-related dimension

There was a strong career-development strand to the mentoring programme and mentors were expected to pass on their experience in overcoming barriers to success in their area of work. Mentors were encouraged to take mentees to their place of work and 'work area-career interest' was a key matching criterion. Role modelling was an important dimension of the mentoring programme according to Howard Jeffrey:

> It's about Black people telling other Black people how you survive in corporate Britain. It's not be like me, it's this is how I have done it. One mentee asked his mentor how do you get on in BP with all those white people. He said this is why BP appointed me; they do welcome Black people and this is how I operate in BP. You don't lose your culture, your ways of living, but you give and take with the culture of BP. That is a good role model; he can make students feel happy about going to BP; now the student would apply to BP.

If the mentors cannot arrange work experience (internship), then at least they should arrange a workplace visit.

Meetings

Mentors and mentees had their initial meeting at an evening session in the Leadership Centre and they were then expected to have approximately three contact hours per month. How this was organized was at the discretion of the pairs, although the proliferation of e-mail and mobile phones has made keeping in contact much easier than in the very recent past. They usually meet in a public place to go for a coffee and work through one of the activities in the handbook, but social events such as going to the theatre were also encouraged. The programme lasted for the academic year, and there was a closing celebratory evening when certificates were presented to students; however some pairs chose to carry on and many remained friends after the student had left the College.

RESEARCH AND EVALUATION EVIDENCE

UK research

There is a paucity of research and evaluation into the outcomes and processes of minority ethnic mentoring in the United Kingdom. However, a small-scale research project sought to establish whether young people from minority ethnic groups can be mentored successfully by people from the white community (Howells, 1998). The research was based on the Dalston Youth Project, a socially excluded mentoring programme operating in the London Borough of Hackney, where 80 per cent of mentees are Black (see Chapter 6).

The overall conclusions were that mentors and young people did not have to be from the same racial and cultural background to benefit from mentoring, unless there was a special need for the cultural development of the mentee. Factors that were more important were the practical skills of the mentor in helping to build on the aspirations of the mentee, the networks to which they belonged and the ability of the mentor to support the mentee. The mentee must, however, feel comfortable with the mentor in order for rapport to develop, and with less confident young people a mentor of the same race was more important.

Cross-cultural mentorships can also help mentees and mentors to recognize diversity and to value and respect differences. There may also be benefits for local communities in the formation of cross-cultural links through interracial mentoring. Interestingly in the survey (which involved 57 mentors and 51 mentees), discussions about race and culture were ranked 17th by mentees and 12th by mentors in a list of 20 discussion topics. Practical issues such as college, work, friends and the police were more commonly discussed.

US research

Cross-cultural research in the United States reports that African-American males can perceive themselves as 'involuntary minorities' and in response they may adopt 'secondary cultural differences' that make it difficult to achieve in school and work settings (Weiner and Mincy, 1993).

Mentoring programmes designed to tackle this issue require mentors who appreciate cultural differences, can demonstrate the rewards arising from educational achievement, and can clarify the link between school performance and employment opportunities. So-called bi-cultural competence can be promoted by mentoring that allows the students to operate with ease in two social contexts while maintaining pride in their distinctive identity. Bi-cultural competence enables the youth 'to use street-wise communications at home and in the neighbourhood, and middle-class communication at school (and later at work)' (Powell, 1999: 57).

ASELU evaluation

The evaluation of the ASELU programme was based on ratings made by the form teacher for each child each term. The rating scale ranged from one (low) to five (high) against nine categories of school performance:

- the ability to concentrate on a given task;
- the ability to communicate appropriately and to listen to others;
- the ability to follow instructions;
- the ability to share with other pupils;
- the ability to express anger and frustration in an appropriate way;
- motivation;
- attendance at school;
- punctuality;
- returning homework.

Ratings at the end of the programme were compared to the baseline ratings at the start of the programme. The results showed that the areas of greatest improvement were in the ability to concentrate, the ability to express anger, and motivation. Least change occurred in the ability to share with others, and in punctuality and attendance. Clearly, the modest improvements in the programme could also result from better parenting or teaching or from the Hawthorne effect. In spite of the modest impact of the programme, none of the pupils had been excluded and in that sense the programme did achieve wider goals.

North London Mentor Trust evaluation

The North London Mentor Trust has an internal evaluation every year. In the first year of the programme (1994), when the Queen's Anniversary Award for Higher and Further Education was given, the inspection team conducted an evaluation and 96 per cent of mentored students finished their courses, while only 70 per cent of other college students completed. This impact of mentoring on the retention rate has continued over the life of the programme. Other long-term benefits have been the introduction of students to networks of Black professionals who can support them in their careers. In a recent example, a group of eight mentees (over three years) who have gone on to study pharmacy at the same university have formed their own group to support each other through the course. The mentoring coordinator regarded this as a natural, group-mentoring extension of the planned mentoring programme in the College.

ISSUES

Exclusivity

Minority ethnic mentoring programmes often raise equal-opportunities issues within educational institutions. Some teachers and parents might ask 'Why should there be a mentoring scheme for pupils from a particular minority ethnic community?' There are other options, for example, Black pupils and mentors could be included within a broader mentoring programme. Some programmes, particularly those in inner cities, target young people with 'risk' factors such as low motivation, poor attendance or disruptive behaviour. They often include high proportions of students from ethnic minorities. The benefit of this is that it would not appear to discriminate in favour of a particular group. The drawbacks are that the mentor training and mentee preparation might not reflect the particular interests and needs of minority students and mentors. It might also be harder to recruit mentors from minority communities to a general programme. This is because many Black mentors say that they are keen to help young people from their own community. Other schools have distinct minority ethnic schemes as well as general mentoring programmes that are open to all students, to overcome any objections from parents.

Institutionalized racism

It may be the case that voluntary organizations are invited by schools to help set up a minority ethnic mentoring programme. The programme may be considered necessary as a response to behavioural problems presented by minority youth. It is important before 'parachuting' in mentors as role models to motivate or raise the aspirations of the young people and to evaluate the context in which the behaviour is occurring. Following the racially motivated murder of Black teenager Stephen Lawrence in South East London, the MacPherson Report produced a new definition of institutionalized racism:

The collective failure of an organization to provide an appropriate and professional service to people because of their colour, culture or ethnic origin. It can be seen or detected in processes, attitudes and behaviour which amount to discrimination through unwitting prejudice, ignorance, thoughtlessness and racist stereotyping which disadvantage minority ethnic people.

(MacPherson Report, 1999: 321)

Mentors from minority ethnic communities will want to know that schools where they are serving as mentors have reviewed their policies and curriculum practices to eliminate institutionalized racism. This is important, because it may be one of the factors contributing to students' problems in school, and it will be one of the areas that mentees and mentors will discuss. Opening up the school in this way can also act as a catalyst to stimulate debate and change in addressing the needs of minority students.

'Black' or 'mixed' minorities

A further issue for people setting up minority ethnic mentoring programmes is to decide which minorities should be included. Some schemes are identified as 'Black' mentoring programmes and they then generally include a list of minorities catered for by the programme. Often there will be a mix of minorities recruited from among students and mentors, for example, Black-African, Black-Caribbean, Indian, Pakistani and Bangladeshi. Matching often needs to be handled sensitively because of cultural and religious differences between minorities, which can result in difficulties with some pairings. Parents can sometimes raise objections to particular pairings and this can create problems for scheme organizers.

Cultural matching

There are strong arguments both for and against matching on the basis of race or ethnicity, founded on deeply held beliefs about the nature of race and ethnic relations. However, the decision to exclude cross-race and cross-ethnic matches means that the task of recruiting an adequate number of mentors is made more difficult. Experience in the United States suggests that the consequences of this policy are to leave a large number of disadvantaged young people without mentors.

Benefits of same-ethnicity matching

The arguments advanced in favour of racial or ethnic matching are:

- The level of trust demanded in an effective mentoring relationship can best or only be achieved in same race or ethnicity mentorships.

- Situations where white majority ethnic adults mentor minority youths carry the risks of imposing dominant white cultural values upon the mentees and devaluing their own cultural identity and heritage.
- Adults who have not suffered the disadvantages faced by minorities are unable to understand the problems mentees encounter and are poorly placed to offer coping strategies.
- Mentoring programmes offer an excellent way of building solidarity in ethnic communities and promoting self-help.
- The message to the mentee and to the wider society when a minority youth is paired with a majority ethnic adult is that white rather than Black society is the appropriate source of role models

Benefits of cross-ethnicity matching

Programmes that have used cross-racial and cross-ethnic matching generally do not deny the potential drawbacks listed above. However, they point to the positive benefits of such matching, which have been supported by research (Tierney *et al*, 1995). The arguments in support of cross-racial and cross-gender matching are as follows:

- Same race or ethnicity matching can promote trust but does not guarantee a good match. It is more important to match minority students with skilled mentors who have emotional intelligence and cultural sensitivity.
- Mentors can be trained in intercultural sensitivity, which includes being aware of their own 'cultural baggage', as well being prepared to engage in activities to enhance the mentee's own cultural identity.
- Cross-cultural matching can be turned from a negative into a positive by helping to break down barriers between the individuals and their respective communities.

Mentor supply

In the United Kingdom there has been a difficulty in recruiting male Black mentors for schemes. However, this is a reflection of a general problem with male recruitment (see Chapter 11) rather than a minority cultural issue per se. It is also the case that 'successful' members of minority communities are often much in demand to become involved with worthwhile community projects. In some cases this may result in 'mentoring fatigue' or a feeling that they have made their contribution and it is now time for others to shoulder the burden. It may also be that school staffs are unrepresentative of their local communities and that there is no project worker, teacher or learning mentor from the minority community, which may constitute an additional barrier to minority participation in mentoring. In the long term one of the most promising sources of minority mentors is likely to be from among students who have themselves been mentees. Indeed it can be argued that the responsibilities associated with becoming a mentor can act as an apprenticeship in being a good father (Weiner and Mincy, 1993).

Project workers

The ethnicity of project staff can be important in encouraging mentor and mentee volunteering. US research for Big Brothers, Big Sisters indicated a strong correlation between the ethnicity of outreach staff and minority mentor recruitment (Furano *et al*, 1993). It showed that where minority staff were responsible for recruitment there were twice as many minority volunteers as in other projects. The same may also be true of mentee volunteering although there is a need for research. However, a recent consultation by the Connexions Service with Black and minority ethnic organizations in the United Kingdom found that delegates believed that White staff, who were conscious of Black issues, could be just as effective (Crime Concern/Youth Justice Board, 2001). The predominant view was that the most crucial factor was the capacity to perform the role to a high standard. It is also essential that projects have at least some staff who are able to communicate in the first language of mentees. This is vital for discussing the nuances of mentoring relationships and building partnerships with parents. The ability to build relationships with families is also a way of challenging racial and domestic stereotypes regarding the background of the mentees.

SETTING UP A MINORITY ETHNIC MENTORING PROGRAMME

It is essential that schools and voluntary organizations, when considering establishing mentoring schemes aimed at young people from minority ethnic communities, build partnerships with people from those communities. There are a greater range of issues and sensitivities raised by minority ethnic programmes than other forms of mentoring we have discussed. It is important, therefore, that careful thought is given to the issues raised in this chapter before new programmes are launched. The following good practice points are based on the experience of people managing minority ethnic mentoring programmes.

Planning

- Ensure that individuals and representatives of the minority group targeted are represented on the project steering group.

- Identify any specific issues of identity, race and racism facing the minority ethnic mentee target group.
- Ensure that the educational institution has reviewed its policies and practices to counteract institutionalized racism.
- Ensure that participating schools have an overall strategy for tackling underachievement by students from the target group. It is important that the mentoring scheme is not seen as a token, bolt-on solution that involves no change on the part of the school. Where there is no overall strategy for raising the achievement of minority ethic pupils, calculate whether the introduction of a mentoring programme is likely to act as catalyst for change.
- Decide whether to target minority ethnic students within a general programme or to have an identified minority ethnic programme. Write down the rationale for your programme.
- Consider the need to offer other forms of educational and social support alongside the mentoring. These may include basic skills, residential experience and group mentoring.
- Recruit a project worker who is from the minority ethnic community and can draw on personal experience to help young people and their mentors tackle issues of behaviour management, identity and racism.
- Ensure that at least one of the project workers can speak the first language of the mentees and their families.
- Review mentor recruitment and screening policies and practices to see if they unintentionally exclude potentially valuable mentors.
- Consider inviting mentors and mentees to choose a name for the programme in order to increase the feeling of ownership.
- Draw up a community map showing where members of the target community gather so that recruitment literature and briefings can be carefully targeted.
- Allow for the reproduction of recruitment and other scheme literature in the appropriate community language(s). Consult with minority youth about the content and style of proposed marketing literature.
- Target community media – newspapers, magazines and local radio – in any mentor recruitment drives.

Implementing

- Make sure that students are clear about the aims of the mentoring programme and can understand the relevance of it to their school career and their life beyond school.
- Ensure that students are able to raise difficult questions of race, racism and identity in training and review sessions. Make sure that trainers are able to handle these subjects with sensitivity and clarity.

- Include a discussion of expectations in student preparation covering what they expect from the scheme and what the scheme organizers expect of them.
- Encourage mentors to think through their personal philosophy for addressing questions of minority underachievement and to consider what it means to be a role model for young people.
- Make sure that mentor training includes discussion of mentees' culture and religion. It might also include: experiences of racism; barriers to education, training and employment; media stereotyping; and valuing diversity
- Be aware of potential cultural and historical issues in cross-gender and cross-minority ethnic group matching. Ask mentors and mentees about any preferences they might have in cross-cultural matching.
- Include parents in early meetings between mentees and mentors in order to build positive relationships, confidence and trust.
- Ensure that the project worker or scheme coordinator provides close support for mentees and mentors.
- Try to offer some form of accreditation for mentors as people from minority ethnic communities often face additional barriers in their own careers.
- Bring mentors and mentees together for group cultural experiences.

FUTURE TRENDS

The continuing difficulties in recruiting mentors will limit the expansion of minority ethnic mentoring programmes. However, students passing through the school system who have been helped by mentoring will often volunteer to become mentors as they enter higher education and work. Most schools will tend to avoid setting up exclusive minority ethnic programmes, because of the controversy and questions of equal opportunities that they can raise with parents. However, minority ethnic organizations will offer more community-based programmes for their young people outside the school setting where they have more control over the aims and processes of the scheme.

6

Mentoring for students 'at risk' of exclusion

INTRODUCTION

Social exclusion is a process that leads to individuals and groups being shut out from the full benefits of being a citizen (Walker, 1997). Exclusion is often the product of multiple disadvantages that certain families experience, including lack of income, lack of basic skills, homelessness and unemployment. It is not simply a question of poverty, but rather of a lack of integration and power that reduces the opportunity to be active citizens. The term social exclusion has replaced poverty in the discussions of disadvantage (Lee and Murie, 1999).

We begin this chapter with a discussion of 'at-risk' students and the issue of exclusion from school within a UK context. This is followed by a brief outline of mentoring within the UK youth-justice system. Two case studies from mentoring programmes in London illustrate some of the issues involved in running programmes for young people with a high number of risk factors. The Chance project for primary pupils and the Dalston Youth Project for secondary students have both attracted the interest of UK government ministers and officials interested in possible replication. The Juvenile Mentoring Program (JUMP) in the United States is an example of a mass mentoring scheme targeted at young people at risk of delinquency, gang involvement, educational failure or dropping out of school. Several issues for organizations intending to target at-risk students are raised, including the cost-effectiveness and problems of labelling. This is followed by a summary of good practice points to consider when developing a programme for students 'at risk' of exclusion and possible future developments. We conclude with speculation on future trends in mentoring for students at risk of exclusion.

AT-RISK STUDENTS

Social inclusion strategies attempt to remove the barriers which block the excluded from participating in society. In schools, there are certain groups that are at high risk of school – and subsequent social – exclusion:

- those with special educational needs;
- 'looked-after' children;
- minority ethnic children;
- travellers;
- young carers;
- those from families under stress;
- pregnant schoolgirls and teenage mothers.

In school settings the phrase 'at risk' is used in a variety of ways. In its mildest sense, teachers often describe students as being 'at risk of under-achievement'. In this sense most students referred to the mentoring schemes described in this book are 'at risk'. A second meaning is the preferred American term of being 'at risk of dropping out' and either becoming a persistent and long-term truant during compulsory schooling or failing to complete the course in post-compulsory education. A third use of the term refers to students who are 'at risk of school or college exclusion', which means a curtailment of their education. The final use concerns students who are 'at risk of offending', where they will engage in criminal behaviour and risk entering the youth-justice system. For each risk factor, there are also protective factors that can help prevent negative outcomes. Mentoring may help at-risk youth by ameliorating the risk factors and accentuating the protective factors.

EXCLUSION FROM SCHOOL

Many school-based mentoring schemes have been established to support students who may be at risk of being excluded from school. Exclusion in a school context can be permanent or temporary. Permanent exclusion in England is small in relation to the total school population, but it rose rapidly during the 1990s. The first survey figures for 1990–01 indicated 3,000 permanent exclusions, which rose to 11,100 in 1994–95 and an estimated 13,500 in 1996–97 (Social Exclusion Unit, 1998). A recent estimate is that 34 children are excluded from UK schools every day (Slaven, 2001). Most excluded pupils are white, male (83 per cent) young teenagers (80 per cent are aged 12–15). However, some groups are much more likely than others to be excluded:

- Children with special educational needs are six times more likely than others to be excluded.
- African-Caribbean children are more than six times more likely.
- Children in care are ten times more likely.

Excluded students generally experience serious disadvantage, including high levels of family stress involving unemployment, low income and family disruption. OFSTED research (1999) highlighted poor acquisition of basic skills, particularly literacy, limited aspirations and opportunities, poverty, and poor relationships with peers, parents or teachers. Students who are permanently excluded are generally offered 'education otherwise', which is usually not full time, in a pupil referral unit, or college or home tuition. Those excluded from school are at risk of offending and 77 per cent come to the attention of the police (Slaven, 2001). Mentoring is an intervention, which is seen as a way of reducing exclusions among high-risk groups and also of supporting students being educated 'otherwise'. 'A mentor, perhaps a university student, someone from the local community or business, or someone who has overcome earlier school difficulties, can help to remotivate young people and turn them away from antisocial behaviour' (Social Exclusion Unit, 1998: 14)

MENTORING FOR YOUNG OFFENDERS

In the UK the courts now have mentoring as an option for young people presented to them, following the Crime and Disorder Act (1998). Mentoring can form part of a reparation order, action plan order, or be used for those most at risk of offending or re-offending (Tilley, 2000). The compulsory nature of these mentoring relationships can lead them to be described as a form of pseudo-mentoring, as for many practitioners the essence of mentoring is its voluntary nature. Young people at risk of serious or repeat offending tend to exhibit multiple-risk factors as described above. Local Youth Offending Teams can contract with voluntary-sector mentoring programmes to offer mentors to the young people they are asked to deal with. Mentors can provide these at-risk young people with an adult role model from the community whom they can trust. This is in contrast to their relationships with other adults, such as social workers, probation officers, police, teachers and parents, which may be fraught.

Although a mentoring scheme for a young offender may be a stand-alone intervention, common sense suggests that mentoring by an adult from the community is more likely to be successful when combined with other activities (Benioff, 1997). Such complementary activities include: residential experiences, education and parenting groups, training, basic skills, work to address offending behaviour, drug use and family relationships. This so-called 'mentoring plus' approach has been developed in the UK by Crime Concern and is illustrated in the case study of the Dalston Youth Project. The Mentoring Plus programme developed by Crime Concern is for young offenders and young people excluded from school. It aims to reduce youth crime and to help young people aged 15–19 back into education, training or employment. Each project recruits 30 young people on a six-monthly cycle to join in a one-year programme of support and development. The programme consists of residential experience to build confidence, trust and personal skills, as well as goal setting, one-to-one mentoring, and an education and training programme that includes college tasters, basic skills and pre-employment training.

AIMS AND OBJECTIVES

Mentoring programmes for 'at-risk' young people can involve 'school-based' mentoring programmes aimed at preventing permanent exclusion, truancy and drop-out. They may also be 'community based' in response to offending behaviour or because the young person has been excluded from mainstream schooling and is being educated 'otherwise'. Mentoring for excluded young people is most likely to have the characteristics of what we have called holistic mentoring. There is likely to be a range of objectives covering developmental, work-related and subject aims, longer and more rigorous training for mentors, and a more intensive, highly structured programme. The main aim of mentoring for at-risk young people is usually developmental. The precise objectives tend to vary with the analysis of the young person's problems by the mentoring programme managers. In some school-based, preventative schemes the focus tends to be on the self-esteem, motivational and personal and social skills objectives.

In programmes addressing the needs of excluded students who may also be in trouble with the youth-justice system, then the focus also includes attitudinal and behavioural change objectives. Planned outcomes can include a reduction in offending behaviour, and an increase in young people's awareness of their motivation for offending and the impact of their offending on others. The academic objective also features when at-risk students exhibit poor basic skills and mentors aim to develop literacy skills. However, these may also be developed through parallel basic-skills provision as part of a 'mentoring plus' approach.

Case Study 6.1 Chance primary programme (UK)

Chance UK is a voluntary organization that runs mentoring programmes for vulnerable children aged 5–11 who are most at risk of school and social exclusion, and of developing anti-social and criminal behaviour in later life. The children referred to the programme exceed the UK 80th centile for problem behaviour on the Goodman Stengths and Difficulties Questionnaire (SDQ). They were typically the most disruptive and isolated primary-aged pupils with poor school attainment. They tended to be hyperactive, exhibiting emotional problems, having difficulties in building peer relationships and demonstrating poor social skills. The aims of the mentoring scheme were to:

- provide increased stability and consistency;
- reduce isolation;
- support children to find motivation, insight and life skills;
- divert disruptive and challenging behaviour into creative projects;
- support learning by encouraging a sense of discovery;
- support parents in developing 'good enough' parenting practices.

Selection and training

Schools were briefed about the mentoring programme and were given referral information, criteria and questionnaires. Head teachers, teachers and special needs coordinators referred pupils to the programme. Children who met the referral criteria then received a home visit at which a comprehensive assessment was carried out with the parents present. If both parents and child were motivated to join the programme, then they were offered a mentor.

Mentors underwent careful screening and a detailed interview; references were taken up and there were police checks. They also took a three-day intensive training programme that included: communication and interpersonal skills; group interaction; concept of family; personal values; solution-focused intervention; the components of the Chance programme; the role and responsibilities of mentors; child protection guidelines; and the nature of the commitment required. Those selected to be mentors were then carefully matched with a child and a meeting was arranged between the child, parent(s), mentor and Chance programme manager prior to the start of mentoring.

Processes

The mentoring lasted for one year, with weekly one-to-one sessions of two to four hours on average. Each child was offered a tailored programme that took into account the individual's interests, needs and personal circumstances. The mentoring took place in a variety of settings including the child's home, the Chance Resource Centre, public libraries and community centres. Mentoring sessions were as varied as the needs of the child, ranging from one-to-one discussions, art and craft projects, literacy and reading activities, visits to museums and libraries, sports and other outdoor activities. They also undertook educational projects, for example, researching and collecting information about a country or culture related to the child's heritage, and keeping a journal of major news events.

The first three months of the mentoring was the 'engagement' phase, in which the mentor and child established rapport and trust. Towards the end of this phase they agreed specific goals, with the support of the parent(s) and the Chance programme manager, and then worked towards achieving these. These goals generally focused on: behavioural and cognitive skills; building on existing skills, abilities and interests; creating new solutions; and supporting the child in achieving competence in the usage of new skills. Progress towards these goals was reviewed on a quarterly basis at a meeting involving all parties, and new goals were identified where appropriate. At the end of the mentorship, a graduation ceremony marked the progress and achievements of the child and the contribution of the mentor. In some cases it was necessary to provide continued support for a further three or four months. Chance also worked closely with parents and teachers to refer children with continuing needs at the end of the programme to other agencies. This included referrals to mentoring programmes for older children, befriending schemes, play schemes, educational and child psychology services, and youth projects.

Management

Programmes were managed and delivered by Chance programme managers, who supported up to 20 mentoring pairs each, with oversight, guidance and supervision from the Senior Programme Manager and Chief Executive. Programme managers maintained close liaison with the primary school throughout the mentoring programme. This included: facilitating meetings between mentors and class teachers to share information about classroom behaviour and performance; any needs identified during the early stages of the mentoring; and the progress and impact of the mentoring on the child's behaviour and educational attainment. Schools also provided agreed information on teacher assessments and grades in national tests. Programme managers supervised and supported mentors through monthly meetings at which progress was reviewed, mentoring sessions were planned, and problems and possible solutions were discussed.

There was a comprehensive monitoring and evaluation strategy, which included:

- the tracking of all referrals, volunteers and mentorships;
- monitoring of educational attainment, including teacher and national test grades, improvements in the reading age, and attendance and exclusion records;
- baseline and outcome assessment involving the SDQ;

- interviews with all parties focusing on different issues: child (perspective and impact); parent (behavioural changes at home and relationships with other people); teacher (progress at school and interaction with peers); and mentor (cognitive-and-emotional development, and social skills);
- documented supervision sessions, mentoring session plans and reviews;
- long-term follow-up of the mentees.

Case Study 6.2 Dalston Youth Project (UK)

The Dalston Youth Project (DYP) began life as a three-year, Home Office initiative operating in three secondary schools in inner-city Hackney, London (Clarke and Tarling, 1998). It is part of the national charity, Crime Concern, which runs a series of programmes for young people who are at risk of offending. The original programme focused on after-school literacy and numeracy classes for 11–14 year olds at risk of exclusion from school. During 2000–01 DYP was working with 30 pupils, all aged 13, from the three schools. The project was based in a renovated chapel that houses two classrooms where the after-school clubs are held. The project team comprised the manager, full- and part-time education coordinators and a part-time mentoring coordinator.

There were three components to DYP:

- a residential course at the start of each programme;
- one-to-one mentoring by volunteers from a wide range of backgrounds with meetings once a week;
- education programmes, which focused on developing basic skills and personal development: self-assessment, behavioural target-setting and the development of cooperative skills.

The residential period at the start of each programme cost around £7–8,000. This meant that the total cost of the programme for 30 student beneficiaries was around £120,000 in total, or £4,000 per beneficiary (at 2000 prices).

Mentoring was a core element of the programme and key aims included: improving self-esteem, anger management and improving mentees' attitudes towards school. Schools used a referral form to inform DYP about potential mentees. This included:

- a rating of the potential for dropping out of school;
- behaviours of concern;
- other agencies involved with the student;
- relevant family information;
- a record of exclusions;
- potential areas of benefit from DYP.

Recruitment and matching

Mentors were recruited from a variety of sources: advertisements in 'minority' community newspapers and the *Guardian* 'volunteering' section, and flyers left in local colleges and churches. People expressing an interest were interviewed and, if accepted onto the programme, they attended three weekends of training. There tended to be a shortage of younger Black males volunteering to become mentors. Other problems have been the mentors' own literacy problems that have prevented them from supporting their mentee, lack of maturity, and the occasional tendency of mentors from the churches to want to 'push' their religion by using the mentoring scheme. Mentors and mentees attended an outdoor residential centre for a weekend of teambuilding and to enable the project team to identify suitable matches. Female mentees were only matched with female mentors, and there were some problems involved when taking into account the interracial tensions in the area when matching. Accreditation was offered to mentors through a university.

Processes

There were two sessions per week, each lasting three hours. Mentors became involved in project work with their mentees. Mentors also attended monthly in-house training sessions on a variety of relevant topics, for example, working effectively with schools and learning mentors (see Chapter 1). DYP project staff worked intensively with the schools and attended regularly to support students who were withdrawn from lessons to work on themes such as emotional support, development of key skills, counselling and dealing with conflict. When exclusions occurred the project workers sought to support young people in re-integrating them back into school, and they also became involved in multi-agency work to address truancy and exclusions. Attendance at the after-school clubs was high and most students were aware that they wanted something about their lives at school to change. Recent activities included watching the modern (Baz Luhrmann) version of Shakespeare's *Romeo and Juliet*, which was a set text in English at school. Another workshop introduced the students to the skills of photography. Each young person on the programme had an individual development plan and a half-yearly report.

Role of parents

Parents attended the DYP centre on a regular basis, and a recent innovation has been the start of a parenting course aimed primarily but not exclusively at the parents of mentees. The parenting programme included: English as an Additional Language (EAL); helping support their child's learning; and how to work effectively with schools. A parenting programme based on a US model involved twelve sessions aimed at enhancing family relationships and developing positive discipline (Steele with Marigna, 2000) Staff also supported parents by interacting with various agencies and on occasions acting in the role of advocate. There was also a parent representative on the steering group, which met monthly.

Some mentors were experienced, as they had been through the DYP programme more than once, and a number wanted to pursue a career in mentoring, for example, by applying to become learning mentors. Some mentors had asked to 'shadow' their mentee at school, so that they could gain a better understanding of their experience. A further development of DYP was the peer-mentoring scheme, where young people who had been through the programme were encouraged to become advocates for the scheme by talking to groups of potential mentees in their schools. DYP had also purchased a Webcam system to enable virtual meetings to occur. One successful innovation this year was the project diary for mentees to communicate issues to their mentors and the project team. Students had used these diaries, which were kept at the project and were open for the mentors and the project team to read, to communicate thoughts that they might have had problems expressing face-to-face.

The main criterion for success was keeping the mentees in school, and only one member of that year's group had been excluded. There were also regular tests to gauge improvements in literacy and numeracy. A problem for the project has been what happens to 'graduates' when they are 14 and about to embark on their examination programmes. It was clear that some students needed ongoing support to keep them from getting into trouble at school.

Case Study 6.3 Juvenile Mentoring Program (USA)

The Office of Juvenile Justice and Delinquency Prevention established the Juvenile Mentoring Program (JUMP) following the passage of Part G of the Juvenile Justice and Delinquency Prevention Act of 1974, as amended in 1992. The programme provides one-to-one mentoring for youth at risk of delinquency, gang involvement, educational failure or dropping out of school (Novotney *et al*, 2000). Between JUMP's implementation in 1996 and September 2000, federal funding had been awarded to 164 projects in 41 states. A number of guidelines were issued to projects, including a focus on schools or communities where 60 per cent or more of young people were eligible for free or reduced-price lunches. Projects were required to submit management information using an automated system, and data was available for 7,515 young people, 6,163 mentors and 6,362 matches. The JUMP national evaluation, therefore, provides an excellent overview of mentoring for at-risk youth across the United States.

Risk domains

Overall the projects served a roughly equal balance of boys (48.4 per cent) and girls (51.3 per cent). At the time of enrolment mentees were on average just under 12 years of age, but there is a normal distribution curve in ages from four-and-a-half through to twenty-and-a-half years. A range of minorities were served by JUMP: although 51 per cent of mentees were African-

American, 18.5 per cent were Hispanic and 6.9 per cent were American-Indian. More than half of all projects either served minority young people exclusively or had below 10 per cent of white children. Less than one in five lived in 'intact' two-parent households. Table 6.1 shows the risk domains of JUMP youth who are usually exposed to some of these risk factors. They also tended to lack protective factors such as clear standards and consistent discipline at home, a sense of social belonging or realistic parental expectations for achievement at school.

JUMP mentors were 63 per cent female; 55 per cent were white, 31 per cent African-American and 9 per cent Hispanic. Mentors were mainly well educated, with 83 per cent having completed college. In the evaluation of the projects youth and mentors were asked whether they believed the mentoring relationship had helped in respect of the following behaviours:

Table 6.1 *Risk domains of JUMP youth*

	Percentage of enrolled youth	
Risk domain	**Male** (n = 3,592)	**Female** (n = 3,807)
School Problems	74.6%	63%
School behaviour	39.5	23.5
Poor grades	53.6	45.9
Truancy	10.4	9.1
Social/Family Problems	51.7	56.4
Delinquency	17.5	8.5
Fighting	12.8	6.3
Property crime	2.8	0.5
Gang activity	3.0	1.0
Weapons	1.1	0.4
Alcohol Use	3.2	1.5
Drug Use	4.0	1.8
Tobacco Use	2.3	1.9
Pregnancy/Early Parenting	0.2	1.5

- getting better grades and attending all classes;
- staying away from alcohol and drugs;
- avoiding fights;
- staying away from gangs and not using knives or guns;
- avoiding friends who start trouble;
- getting along with family.

RESEARCH AND EVALUATION EVIDENCE

Chance primary mentoring evaluation

An evaluation of the Chance primary mentoring project was carried out for the Home Office using semi-structured interviews with mentors, mentees, teachers and mothers (St James Roberts and Singh, 1999). The findings included a 60 per cent drop-out rate among mentors between initial contact and the end of training. However, this occurred before mentoring began and only 10 per cent of actual mentoring relationships broke down. The behavioural problems of children on the scheme were severe and multiple:

- 80 per cent were hyperactive;
- 82 per cent had conduct problems;
- 62 per cent had social problems;
- 59 per cent had peer problems;
- 44 per cent had emotional problems.

The children were 97 per cent male, 50 per cent White and 50 per cent excluded from school.

All the mentors said they felt affection for their mentees and were satisfied with the relationship. The children were very positive about their mentors. Three-quarters of mothers interviewed said that mentors were having a positive effect on the children's behaviour and that their own relationship with their children had improved. Teachers reported improvements in behaviour, ability to communicate, willingness to cooperate and the ability to talk about feelings.

Dalston Youth Project

The 11–14 Dalston Youth Project was based on the successful 15-to-18 programme, which has consistently showed positive results with young offenders. Two-thirds of participants on the first three 15–18 programmes had previously been arrested and four in ten had been excluded from school. Self-reported offending and arrest rates were substantially lower than the previous year among active participants. In the first programme, the number of arrests was 40 per cent lower than in the year preceding involvement and the total number of arrests was halved (Webb, 1997). Programme 7 of the 15-to-18 programme included 21 young people, of whom 81 per cent were male, 71 per cent were Black and all but two had been excluded from school (Webb, 2000). Almost a third of mentors dropped out, but only two mentees left the programme early. Self-reported offending fell in all but one case, and arrests fell by 17 per cent compared to the previous year. As in previous programmes young people admitted that starting college was the greatest incentive to reducing their offending behaviour. By the end of the programme, 85 per cent were in education, training or employment.

The 11–14 DYP was evaluated as part of the Home Office pilot (Clarke and Tarling, 1998). The evaluators hoped to establish a control-group methodology, but were unable to find one in the schools because of the criteria set for mentees, which was at the extreme on all measures of behaviour and achievement. In its first year the project experienced the problems of start-up, which can particularly afflict projects aimed at this target group. Although 26 young people started the programme, only 15 engaged with the educational and mentoring programme. When interviewed, teachers judged that between six and eight students had benefited from the programme, whereas project staff felt the number to be between 11 and 13. According to project workers, the main areas of improvement were reductions in aggressive and disruptive behaviour that resulted from greater confidence and self-esteem.

JUMP national evaluation

Analysis of data on 463 matches raised a number of interesting issues concerning perceived satisfaction and benefits of mentoring (Novotney *et al*, 2000). It seemed that boys differed in their perceptions of the benefits of mentoring depending on whether they were matched with male or female mentors. Boys with female mentors liked them as much and felt understood by them as much as boys with male mentors. However, those with male mentors reported greater benefits in avoiding drugs and gangs. Female mentors who were paired with boys reported significantly less progress than male mentors by their mentees in the following areas:

- staying away from drugs and alcohol;
- avoiding fights and friends who start trouble;
- staying away from gangs and not using knives or guns.

When mentors and youths were matched across races or ethnicity, then the mentors perceived significantly less improvement in the areas listed above, and the same applied to class attendance. Mentors paired with youths of the same race or ethnicity reported that they understood them better than did mentors in cross-race matches. The issues of cross-race and cross-gender matching are important areas for further research in the national evaluation of JUMP.

US resilience research

Resilience is the capacity of young people who face particular risk factors to overcome those risks and to avoid long-term negative outcomes such as school exclusion or arrests (Rak and Patterson, 1996). Resilience research in the United States suggests that the additional guidance and supervision deriving from a mentor can play a key role in developing resilience. Resilient young people often had at least one significant person (not necessarily in the family) who accepted them unconditionally (Werner and Smith, 1992). Other researchers identify adult role models outside the family as buffers who help children to resist negative influences. Resilient young people often had a number of significant adults who acted as mentors through their development (Rhodes, Gingiss and Smith, 1994). The strength of mentoring with at-risk young people may, therefore, derive from the fact that it can impact on a range of risk factors and support several protective factors at the same time.

ISSUES

Community-based versus school-based mentoring

An issue for schools in considering whether to offer mentoring to at-risk students is where the programme should be located, together with how it should be managed. Mentoring for students who have a number of risk factors requires a rigorous approach that often involves holistic mentoring and elaborate procedures for screening and training mentors. The costs associated with mentoring for students at risk of exclusion are, therefore, higher than say for business-and-community programmes targeting underachieving students. There may also be only a relatively small number of students in many schools who meet the referral criteria. It is generally more cost-effective for schools to work in partnership with a mentoring organization such as Crime Concern in the UK that specializes in work with at-risk students. As in the case of the Dalston Youth Project, the mentoring can take place away from the school – where the roots of a student's disaffection may lie – and be set in the community, where students may feel that they can make a fresh start without adults making assumptions about their attitudes and behaviour.

Use of labels

A further issue concerns the use of labels to describe the at-risk young people, and the thinking that lies behind them. Not everyone agrees that mentoring is an appropriate method of combating disaffection and exclusion in young people (Piper and Piper, 2000). Pupils who are at risk of permanent exclusion are also frequently described as 'disaffected', a term that is widely used but ill-defined and judgemental. It can be argued that applying the label 'disaffected' to a young person is essentially blaming the victim and not taking into account the range of factors that have contributed to the situation. The term 'disengaged' is also employed to suggest that perhaps schools and the curriculum carry part of the blame for a lack of motivation among some pupils. 'At risk' is a non-pejorative term, but as we observed earlier in the chapter it is open to various interpretations. It needs to be qualified, so that students are seen as specifically at risk of underachieving, of school exclusion, of social exclusion, or of offending.

Behaviour modification

Piper and Piper (2000) argue that there is a big difference between a mentorship where values and goals are shared, and the mentee is committed to following their mentor as a role model, and one where the mentee is pressured to take part and has other priorities. This is likely to be the case when mentoring is part of a court order or when schools prescribe mentoring for students who are not volunteers. As Piper and Piper note, mentoring can become in practice a programme for behaviour modification compounded by 'prior prejudicial stereotyping, the deficit model of the young person, and the significant status differences between the mentor and mentee' (2000: 86). They suggest that mentors should not only discuss what the mentees can do to improve their chances, but also how such situations came about and their rights, as well as their responsibilities. Indeed, it might be argued that behaviour-modification techniques are incompatible with mentoring and that what is being offered is yet another form of pseudo-mentoring.

Mentoring plus

One of the characteristics of this target groups is that these young people will tend to have multiple problems. Often behavioural problems in school can be traced back to inadequate basic skills that make it impossible for students to access the curriculum. Students may have poor social and interpersonal skills. Problems manifesting themselves in school may also originate within the family. For these reasons mentoring schemes for students at risk of exclusion generally use a 'mentoring plus' approach.

This means that in addition to one-to-one mentoring by an adult there is a range of other support and learning opportunities. These can include parenting skills, family learning, basic skills, cultural experiences, counselling, group work, residential experiences and classroom support. These additional opportunities add to the cost and complexity of mentoring aimed at this target group.

SETTING UP AT-RISK MENTORING SCHEMES

There are differences between school-based and community-based mentoring programmes. School-based programmes are generally preventative, and mentoring meetings take place within the school. Community-based programmes can involve young people who have already been excluded from school and whose difficulties are likely to be more severe. The level of structure imposed on the programme by the organizers in terms of mentor training, monitoring and supervision will tend to be greater. The good practice points that follow are largely based upon the *Quality Framework for Mentoring with Socially Excluded Young People* published by the National Mentoring Network (Skinner and Fleming, 1999). For mentoring schemes aimed at young offenders there are particular issues that need to be addressed and specialist advice should be sought.

Planning

- Clarify the rationale for the mentoring scheme and think through by what mechanisms mentoring will help to prevent at-risk young people from being excluded. Define, as precisely as possible, the target group.
- Develop and adopt policies and procedures that cover child protection, health and safety, insurance, complaints and monitoring policies and procedures.
- Consider what aspects of school life, family circumstances and the individual are contributing to behaviours that result in teachers defining the student as being 'at risk'.
- Ensure that referral criteria and selection procedures are clear and are communicated to everyone who may be making referrals. Enable self-referrals through leaflets, posters, open events and presentations.
- Develop a referrals form to capture all relevant information.
- Make sure that selection criteria use positive characteristics of young people such as potential for motivation, leadership and determination, and enthusiasm to join the project.

- Involve successful mentees in talking to future potential mentees about their experience and the value of the mentoring programme.
- Ensure that there are sufficient resources to allow for proper supervision of mentors by programme organizers.
- Think about ways in which the young people can be included in making decisions about the programme (for example, social events involving mentors and mentees, or the location of meetings).
- Identify the characteristics, qualities and experience of mentors that the scheme wants to attract and any negative features that would be a criterion for screening out a volunteer.
- Make sure that any marketing literature or messages about the mentoring programme are positive and non-stigmatizing in the eyes of the peer group.
- Develop screening and selection procedures for mentors that reflect the desired levels of commitment and skill.
- Consider and agree the involvement of parents and carers in the mentoring process, but allow older mentees the option of keeping the relationship separate if there are special circumstances involved.
- Make sure that there is a clear policy for dealing with offending behaviour during the mentoring programme.
- Agree success indicators and how the project will be monitored and evaluated.

Implementing

- Plan an induction programme for the mentees that includes an explanation of how the process will work, confidentiality issues, support processes, the nature of the relationship and how it will end.
- Allow young people to specify in broad terms the kind of mentor they would like, but ensure that they are aware that an exact match may not be possible.
- Make sure that both mentors and mentees have a clear understanding of the boundaries of acceptable behaviour within the relationship and the consequences of infringement.
- Ensure that there is an opportunity for the young person to be involved in the matching process and that, at a minimum, the project worker or programme manager is present at the first meeting.
- Develop an action plan procedure that can be used to guide the content of sessions and to gauge progress over the course of the mentorship.
- Allow for the length and location of meetings to be negotiable within the project rules, and responsive to the needs of the young person.
- Consider the level of budget required to meet an agreed level of costs incurred by mentors and mentees during the mentoring relationship.

- Insist that mentors keep a written record of the content of mentoring sessions. This should be shared and agreed with the mentee, and in a form that can be monitored by the project worker.
- Allocate a project worker or supervisor to monitor regularly the welfare of the mentees and the progress and concerns of mentors.
- When working with a school, make sure that teachers and managers are familiar with the aims and processes of the mentoring scheme and that the project worker meets regularly with the school contact to monitor students' progress in school.
- Collect baseline information and record changes in key indicators written into the action plan.

FUTURE TRENDS

The expansion of programmes for at-risk students will be constrained by continuing shortages of suitable mentors with the skills, experience and time to be effective holistic mentors. Concerns over child protection and the need for evidence of effectiveness will limit the use of community mentoring for vulnerable younger children. Reductions in school drop-out rates will ease demand for at-risk mentoring programmes as a range of strategies are employed to address the needs of the 'hard to help' young people. Similarly the mentoring plus approach will be increasingly used in community-based schemes where mentoring is seen as one part of an armoury of strategies to deal with young people's problems, rather than as a stand-alone intervention. In a youth-justice context, mentoring will be increasingly seen as the preserve of a cadre of experienced, professional mentors.

7

Peer mentoring

INTRODUCTION

Peer mentoring is when people of similar age and/or status take on the roles of mentor and mentee. However, the simplicity of the definition masks a diversity of practice. The majority of programmes of this sort have been peer tutoring where the emphasis is often upon learning support in the areas of basic skills or subject learning. Peer tutoring 'involves educational support through meetings between advanced learners and less advanced learners' (Saunders and Gibson, 1998). However, programme titles can be variations on a theme – peer mentoring, peer teaching, peer tutoring, peer facilitation, peer counselling, peer coaching – but often describe very similar activities. Some argue that 'peer helping' is a convenient umbrella term that includes all these activities (Rosenroll, 1994). Most of the research has focused on peer tutoring rather than peer mentoring. Whereas peer tutoring is often undertaken in small groups, peer mentoring is more likely to be one-to-one.

We begin this chapter with a discussion about the various types of peer mentoring and the aims, objectives and benefits of peer mentoring programmes for students. The case study of McGavrock High School in Tennessee's peer-buddy programme shows the overlap between mentoring and buddying, and how peer relationships can support the social inclusion of students with special needs. The case study of the Coca-Cola Valued Youth Program provides an example of a US peer-tutoring programme that has been replicated in the UK. The case study of South Wigston High School illustrates an attempt to introduce a whole-school approach to mentoring involving tiered peer mentoring. The research and evaluation section provides an overview of much of the US evidence on peer mentoring. We then discuss some of the issues facing schools when establishing peer mentoring, and offer a checklist of good practice points to consider when setting up and running peer mentoring programmes. The chapter concludes with speculation on possible future trends in peer mentoring for young people.

TYPES OF PEER MENTORING

There are a number of variables that distinguish between peer mentoring schemes (Topping, 1994):

- age of mentors and mentees;
- ability of mentors and mentees;
- role continuity – one-way or two-way mentoring;
- cross-institutional or intra-institutional programmes.

Age

Mentors in peer mentoring programmes can be of the same-age, near-age (1–3 years age difference) or cross-age (4 years or more age difference) in relation to their mentees. Same-age peer mentoring is probably more common in further or higher education than in schools, as there is more likely to be student resistance in school to someone in the same year group acting as their mentor. The McGavrock High School peer-buddy scheme is an example of a same-age peer programme. Same-age mentoring is more likely to be acceptable when there is a reciprocal element to the pairings. The Coca-Cola Valued Youth Program is an example of a near-age tutoring scheme, while the next chapter on higher education students mentoring school students provides case studies of cross-age peer mentoring.

Ability

The second variable in peer mentoring programmes is ability. Students can be matched with someone of a broadly similar level of academic ability, or the mentor's ability may be relatively high compared to their mentee. The use of relatively high-ability students to help their less able peers is based on the assumption that they are likely to be more effective tutors or mentors. Peer tutoring has been defined as more-able students helping less-able students in cooperative working arrangements organized by the teacher. If this were applied to peer mentoring, then mentors would always be more able than their mentees. When mentors are three or four years older than their mentees, however, innate ability is probably less important than knowledge, skills, experience and the ability to communicate.

Role continuity

Role continuity refers to the extent to which mentors and mentees remain in their roles throughout the mentorship. Peer mentoring generally involves one student as mentor and the other as mentee, but roles can be alternating in so-called 'reciprocal peer mentoring'. This is a way of making both students more comfortable since each takes on the role of learner or mentee at different times. Reciprocal peer mentoring is probably most appropriate in same-age programmes.

Cross-institutional

Peer mentoring programmes can be intra-institutional, as in the South Wigston example where mentees and mentors are drawn from the same school. In contrast, cross-institutional programmes involve mentors and mentees from different institutions. The Coca-Cola Valued Youth Program is an example of a cross-institutional, near-age peer mentoring scheme where 14-year-old high-school students mentor 10-year-old primary pupils. Cross-institutional and cross-age peer mentoring often occurs where university students mentor primary pupils or high-school students. An example of near-age, peer mentoring programmes in the UK is when sixth-form students (17–18-year-olds) mentor students taking their examinations at age 16.

AIMS AND OBJECTIVES

The main aim of peer mentoring has been subject learning, and it is often used as an alternative term for peer tutoring where the mentor acts as a surrogate teacher imparting knowledge and skills. Many peer mentoring programmes, for example, are essentially 'reading partnerships' where an older, more experienced reader listens to a younger child read and offers general encouragement (see Case Study 7.3). Although many peer mentoring programmes are concerned with supporting basic skills, they also include the development of high-order knowledge and skills in higher education or in a professional development context. These kinds of programmes are beyond the scope of this book.

Peer mentoring schemes often also have a maturational objective, because the mentee is about to embark on an educational transition. Thus high-school students will mentor elementary pupils about to move into the high school. Sixth-form students mentor pupils undertaking their GCSE examinations. University students mentor high-school students to support and encourage them to progress into higher education.

However, a prime aim of peer mentoring is also to develop the mentor. The Coca-Cola Valued Youth Program is primarily about changing the attitude and behaviour of the mentors who are at-risk students from the high schools. The self-esteem objective is also very important within this scheme. Indeed there is some evidence that peer mentoring schemes may be more successful in this objective than in helping the mentee (see the section below on the evaluation of the Coca-Cola scheme). Education for citizenship has become an increasingly important part of the curriculum, and peer mentoring provides one obvious way in which schools can generate service learning opportunities.

BENEFITS

Peer mentoring has a number of advantages for educational institutions compared with other forms of mentoring. Most obviously there is a large supply of potential mentors, which reduces the costs and problems associated with the recruitment of external mentors. Greater numbers of students can receive mentoring support than is often possible with other forms of mentoring, so that a broader range of students can be helped. Extensive peer mentoring in a school may also serve to improve the atmosphere in classrooms and the school as a whole by reducing competition between students.

There are a number of benefits claimed for mentees from peer mentoring. Mentees may:

- learn more from peer mentors as they find it easier to ask questions and tend to resist less when working with peers than with teachers or other adults;
- find that what is being communicated is more interesting when taught by peer mentors;
- discover that what is being learned is easier when a peer mentor is involved;
- learn to concentrate harder for longer periods of time.

It is also argued that mentors who have struggled academically will show more patience and understanding with their mentees, as they can empathize from their own experience (Gaustad, 1992).

Unlike most other forms of student mentoring, in peer mentoring the benefits to the mentors are likely to be just as important to the institution as gains for the mentees. There are a number of potential benefits for mentors (Goodlad, 1995). They can:

- develop and demonstrate personal qualities that are important in life and to future employers, including commitment, responsibility and self-confidence;

- reinforce their knowledge of the subject matter being communicated;
- develop communication, interpersonal, tutoring, counselling and mentoring skills;
- gain credit for their work as mentors, for example as part of community service learning.

Case Study 7.1 The peer-buddy programme at McGavrock High School, Tennessee (USA)

McGavrock High School is the largest high school in Tennessee with around 3,000 students, including 300 with special education needs (Hughes and Guth, 2001). The support of the Department of Special Education at Vanderbilt University was important in the development of the peer-buddy programme during the 1994–95 school year. The main aim of the programme was to help overcome the social barriers faced by students with severe learning difficulties when integrating into high school.

Guidance counsellors informed students of the opportunity to become a peer buddy and identified strong candidates to the special education teachers. Following this referral, and the completion of an application form, the teacher and students of the special education class interviewed the would-be buddies. The teachers felt that this screening process was essential to ensure a good match. Once a week the peer buddies met their teacher supervisors for help in setting goals with their partners and to devise ways of meeting their partner's special needs.

The programme involved a range of joint activities including:

- attending a regular education class at least once a day, for example in restaurant trades, bodyshop or cosmetology;
- interacting in the special education class;
- visiting the library;
- attending the Student Council;
- going to clubs, social events or extra-curricular activities.

Peer buddies helped their partners complete class projects and introduced them to their own friends in order to enlarge each student's 'circle of friends'. All peer buddies and their partners met once a week to have lunch together in the canteen.

Case Study 7.2 Coca-Cola Valued Youth Program (UK/USA)

The Intercultural Development Research Association developed the Coca-Cola Valued Youth Program (VYP) in the 1980s as a cross-age, peer-tutoring scheme aimed at reducing high school drop-out rates in Texas. It has since expanded across the United States and the world, including the United

Kingdom where there are programmes in Birmingham and London. The scheme identifies at-risk students in high schools and pairs them with tutees in elementary schools (Cardenas *et al*, 1991). Training promotes higher-order and critical-thinking skills. The basic assumption behind VYP is that the development of self-esteem and self-discipline involved in being a tutor will lead to improvements in their academic performance, school attendance and progression into higher education. The VYP offers students positive recognition, instruction and support. The underlying philosophy of VYP is that through being valued as part of the school community doing an important job, under-performing and at-risk students will flourish. 'Coca Cola valued youth are an inspiration to the children they tutor, positive leaders among their peers, motivated learners to their teachers, a source of pride to their parents, and contributors to their community' (Second City, Second Chance, Birmingham, England).

Over the first 12 years of VYP the drop-out rate for tutors was 2 per cent, compared with 14 per cent annual drop-out rate for students across the United States. However, unlike many peer mentoring schemes tutors are paid for their time.

The Greenwich Programme

In 1999–2000, 120 secondary age students from six schools and 360 primary aged pupils from 15 schools in the London Borough of Greenwich were involved with the VYP (Maras and Bingham, 2000; Maras *et al*, 2001). The programme was based on the American original, and Dr Rogelio Lopez del Bosque from the US VYP acted as a consultant to ensure that the original ethos of the scheme was transferred to the United Kingdom. Primary and secondary schools in the programme each appointed a teacher as link coordinator. Secondary schools received £2,500 each for their participation, but the primary schools had no additional funding.

At the start of the 1999–2000 programme 67 tutors were identified, with an even split of males and females. Tutors were identified as being at risk of underachievement rather than school drop-out and they received training from the school coordinator. The training focused on interpersonal skills, communication and tasks in which they would engage their tutees. A number of the tutors had adult mentors from business or the community, as part of other mentoring schemes run by Greenwich. Once trained the tutors worked with primary pupils, under the supervision of the class teacher.

Case Study 7.3 Peer mentoring at South Wigston High School (UK)

South Wigston is a high school for 10–14-year-olds, with a predominantly white, working-class population drawn from estates on the fringe of the city of Leicester. On entry to the school about half of the 10-year-olds were at least one year behind academically. A whole-school approach to mentoring was developed involving all year groups, in order to raise standards through improving self-esteem and developing the 'learning ethos' (Toward, 2000). The mentoring scheme contributed to the school's strategy for raising the quality of teaching and learning. There were links to school policies for student target setting, and the monitoring of assessment and effort across the curriculum. The school 'organizer' (filofax/diary) played a key role in the mentoring process, and it was stressed that teachers should attach high importance to its completion and make regular checks. Staff training sessions highlighted the need for monitoring progress on targets using the school organizer.

The target audience for mentoring was pupils, of any ability, who were underachieving. Students were selected based on performance data provided by subject departments and individual teachers. The target group was refined down to a viable size by the mentoring coordinators and the heads of year, who ensured that the whole ability range was included. Early in the mentoring year, pairs of mentors and mentees attended a residential experience over a weekend for the purposes of teambuilding.

Tiered mentoring

There were three tiers of mentoring in the school. The first tier, the student-assisted learning scheme, involved Y8 and Y9 students mentoring Y6 and Y7 underachievers. Mentors were chosen by heads of year for their empathic qualities, communication skills and ability to work with other people. There were weekly meetings lasting half an hour during lunchtime, when the mentors listened to their mentees read, assisted with their homework, and discussed targets and how they could be achieved. Meetings took place in the English department rooms and everyone was given a free snack on arrival, which was paid for from business sponsorship. This was designed to act as an additional incentive to encourage attendance and participation.

The school organizer played an important part in mentoring meetings as it contained students' targets, and effort-and-achievement grades. The outcomes of meetings were recorded in the school organizer, so that parents could see their children's targets and progress. Mentors also recorded outcomes in a special sheet that was then inserted into the their own school organizer. The most common problem cited by mentors was of mentees being uncooperative and not bringing their organizers to meetings.

Cross-institutional mentoring

The second tier of mentoring involved a partnership with the local sixth-form college, which provided mentors for Y8 students. The main aim was to focus students on what they needed to do in order to improve the quality of their learning. Pairs met every three weeks to set and discuss targets. There were progress sheets, individual targets and reports from *Assessment Manager* (a software package), which informed mentoring meetings. Mentors and mentees all met at the same time in the same place: after school in the dining hall. Tea, coffee and soft drinks were made available through business sponsorship in order to make meetings more relaxed and informal. Parents and classroom teachers monitored the outcomes of mentoring meetings through the records in the school organizer. Again, the most common problem identified by mentors was the failure of mentees to complete their tracking sheets prior to meetings.

The third tier of mentoring for Y9 students involved community mentoring by parents, school governors and business people. Apart from police vetting procedures, the mentoring processes were similar to the second-tier model. At the end of the school year, all student mentors and mentees received a certificate confirming their successful participation in the scheme. Older students included these certificates in their records of achievement. All pupils with over 85 per cent attendance took part in a school trip as a reward.

RESEARCH AND EVALUATION EVIDENCE

US research

There has been more research into peer tutoring than on most other forms of student mentoring. A meta-analysis of 65 tutoring programmes (Cohen *et al*, 1982) found peer tutoring to be 'moderately effective' at raising academic achievement, as tutored students outperformed controls in examinations and were more positive about the subjects in which they were being tutored. Peer tutoring was particularly effective for children from disadvantaged backgrounds with learners demonstrating better than average gains in reading and mathematics, and improved attendance. Peer tutors also developed more positive attitudes to the subjects they were teaching and a better understanding of those subjects. However, there was no evidence that peer tutoring improved the self-concept of tutor or tutee.

A national US study of academic tutoring and mentoring (Pringle *et al*, 1993) found that cross-age tutoring and mentoring seemed to foster bonds, so that mentors and mentees came to regard each other as surrogate siblings or extended family members. Peer tutoring and mentoring helped new students or those with limited proficiency in English to socialize successfully into mainstream schooling through being supported by an older peer. Mentors helped them to understand rules, schedules and activities, and fostered academic achievement. Six major characteristics of successful peer tutoring and mentoring programmes were identified:

- Recruiting at-risk students and training them to serve as mentors reduced the stigma associated with receiving help.

- Providing incentives encouraged tutors to view their mentoring responsibilities as important and productive.
- Training was provided for both peer tutors and classroom teachers.
- There was ongoing support for peer tutors through debriefing, problem-solving sessions and reflective journaling.
- The matching of mentors-mentees or tutors-tutees was based on inter-personal bonds.
- Collaborating with local universities brought new ideas and research capabilities into mentoring projects.

Evaluation of the McGavrock High School peer-buddy programme

Staff from the Department of Special Education at Vanderbilt University evaluated the scheme (Hughes and Guth, 2001). The programme led to a dramatic increase in the number of social interactions among students with severe disabilities and other students. Peers and teachers observed that previously isolated students now initiated conversations frequently and felt comfortable in 'hanging out' with regular students. The programme was also been successful in building public awareness and greater sensitivity towards young people with disabilities at the school. Peer buddies reported that the programme had improved their own communication skills, and had developed their sensitivity and emotional intelligence.

Evaluation of the Coca-Cola Valued Youth Program

Research in the United States on the VYP used a quasi-experimental design to examine outcomes for tutors compared to controls (Cardenas *et al*, 1992). Over the two years of the scheme, positive outcomes for tutors included: lower drop-out rates; higher reading scores; higher self-concept scores (Piers-Harris Self-Concept Scale); and better attitudes toward school (Quality of School Life Scale). A four-year tracking study of VYP in San Antonio showed that 100 per cent of VYP tutors graduated and 56 per cent went into higher education, compared with 6 per cent of the school population.

An evaluation of the Greenwich VYP obtained a variety of data from questionnaires to students, school coordinators, parents and primary school teachers and interviews with students (Maras and Bingham, 2000). Various psychological measures were used to profile gains to tutors, including academic competence (Gresham and Elliott, 1990); Strengths and Difficulties Questionnaire (SDQ) (Goodman, Meltzer and Bailey, 1998) and self-concept (Harter, 1990).

During the course of the year a quarter of tutors dropped out of the scheme. The evaluation showed a number of positive outcomes for mentors who completed the scheme: improved self-awareness; increased maturity; enhanced communication skills; and improved academic performance. There were significant differences between schools on all measures, which suggested that the extent of preparation and support for students by the link teacher were important factors. Students who were taking their GCSE examinations thought that participating in the scheme had had a negative effect on their work. One particular area of success was improved attendance, although many students with improved attendance also had adult mentors. Although the attendance of some students with poor behaviour improved, this was sometimes accompanied by an increase in the reported incidence of poor behaviour. All students had more positive attitudes to the school at the end of the scheme than at the beginning. Students also became more confident and considered themselves to be 'good company', one measure of high self-esteem.

Evaluation of the South Wigston programme

South Wigston High School conducted an internal evaluation of their mentoring programmes that included an examination of various indicators of performance against a control group (Toward, 2000). One particular measure used was the effort grade in the core subjects of English, maths and science. Monitoring data showed the percentage of mentees where effort had increased, been maintained or decreased during the year. It showed greater evidence of impact in English than in the other subjects, possibly because this was the subject where peer mentors can be most helpful. It also indicated that the apparent impact of mentoring on effort increased with the age of pupils. This may be because the cross-age mentoring by sixth formers and adults had greater impact than near-age mentoring by peers, or because of increasing maturity on the part of mentees. The average attendance of mentees had improved and stood at 93 per cent. Mentees, mentors and parents completed a questionnaire. Three-quarters of mentors, and four-fifths of parents and mentees thought that mentees' school work had improved as a result of the mentoring. Four-fifths of mentees felt more positive about school and two-thirds of parents observed positive changes in work and behaviour.

ISSUES

Focus

Clarity of purpose is the first issue for schools to consider when deciding whether to introduce peer mentoring. The focus of the programme can be on easing transition or on supporting academic performance, and it could be designed to benefit the mentors as much as the mentees. Some research findings suggest that gains to mentors may outweigh benefits to mentees, and schools will want to ensure that benefits are balanced. Some schools may feel that cross-age mentoring is likely to be more fruitful for mentees than same-age or near-age mentoring. For many schools peer mentoring will be viewed as part of a learning support strategy to help raise standards of achievement. The idea of tiered mentoring is a good strategy for developing a whole-school approach and a mentoring culture. In tiered-mentoring programmes, students who act as mentors to their peers also have a mentor, in some cases someone from business, the community or a teacher.

Cross-institutional programmes

One central issue is whether the peer mentoring is to be cross-institutional, as in the Coca-Cola Valued Youth Program. Such schemes involve significantly higher costs and logistical issues than when just one school or college is involved. The VYP scheme did allocate funding for secondary schools to pay for the time of mentors and school coordinators. However, universities and colleges may have resources to set up and run mentoring programmes in schools, which may mean such schemes are relatively low cost for the school. However, there will still be significant tasks that need to be undertaken by the school coordinator (see Chapters 9 and 10). It may be advisable to gain experience of peer mentoring and tutoring within the institution before embarking on cross-institutional programmes.

Mentor selection and training

There are a number of potential pitfalls and drawbacks that can be avoided through careful programme planning and monitoring. There may be particular difficulties when at-risk students are targeted to be mentors. Insufficient training and supervision can result in the use of inappropriate behaviours, such as the threats of punishment or 'verbal put-downs' of their mentees. A further problem is that tutors or mentors may have insufficient grasp of the content of what they are trying to put across or may lack the skills to help their mentees to learn. In cross-age mentoring, however, mentees tend to be operating at a much lower level than their mentors and this tends to be less of a problem.

SETTING UP A PEER MENTORING SCHEME

Unlike the other mentoring programmes that we have discussed so far, all the resources required to operate a peer mentoring programme can be found within any school. It is generally prudent to begin with a modest pilot programme within the school involving no more than about 15 pairs. Once the inevitable start-up problems have been tackled, then the programme can be widened to include greater numbers. A further development of peer mentoring can then be to explore cross-institutional programmes. These might involve secondary or high schools providing mentors to junior high or primary schools. Alternatively, the high school may look to the local college or university to provide near-age mentors to its students. The following good practice points are designed to act as a checklist for teams to consider when discussing the introduction of peer mentoring programmes.

Planning

- Consider the aims of the peer mentoring programme in terms of the problems that it is designed to address, for example, transition, academic performance, bullying and family problems.
- Chose the kind of peer helping scheme that is most appropriate: peer mentoring, peer tutoring, peer buddying or peer counselling.
- Investigate opportunities for cross-institutional peer mentoring with neighbouring institutions.
- Involve a local university in the evaluation of the programme.
- Approach local businesses to sponsor elements of the programme, such as a school organizer or refreshments for mentoring sessions.
- Decide whether the priority of the programme is to develop the tutor/mentor or the tutee/mentee or both.
- Consider involving at-risk students as mentors to reduce the stigma attached to having a peer mentor and to include these students in the school through making them feel valued.
- Determine whether the primary aim is subject learning or developmental.
- Consider the relationship between the peer mentoring programme and the school's overall policies for raising standards and school improvement.
- Examine the linkages and overlaps between the peer mentoring programme, teacher mentoring and external mentoring.
- Articulate the relationship between peer mentoring and the school's strategy for developing basic skills.
- Sell the programme as an opportunity for service learning for the mentors.
- Identify the target group of students for mentoring and the criteria for selection.
- Decide whether peer mentors should be same age, near age or cross age.
- Identify key performance indicators to assess the success of the programme and tools for recording and monitoring mentee progress.

Implementing

- Use interpersonal bonds between students as a key criterion in matching.
- Consider the use of residential experiences or other teambuilding activities to help in the development of mentors, and in the matching and development of effective pairs.
- Consider using school organizers or other methods as a way of tracking the process and impact of mentoring meetings.
- Provide training for classroom teachers so that they understand what peer tutors or mentors are trying to achieve.
- Use experienced peer mentors in mentor training and recruitment.
- Where mentoring involves tutoring, consider the need to include sessions on learning and teaching in mentor training sessions.
- Build generic mentoring skills into the training, together with specific knowledge and skills linked to the aims of the scheme, such as anti-bullying procedures.
- Use the training process to build the mentors into a cohesive, supportive group.
- Offer incentives to mentors to increase their level of commitment to the programme.
- Offer mentor support sessions at least once a month to discuss common issues, while maintaining confidentiality.

FUTURE TRENDS

It is important that research is carried out to investigate what are the most appropriate peer helping strategies for tackling different kinds of need. It may be that peer counselling or buddying schemes are seen as more effective than peer mentoring at addressing issues to do with personal development, bullying or other student problems. Similarly, more research is needed into how benefits for mentees can be maximized from peer mentoring programmes. The increased demand for service learning or citizenship opportunities in education will lead to many schools viewing peer mentoring schemes as a way of providing these opportunities, while at the same time gaining wider benefits for the schools in terms of improved relationships, ethos and raised standards. Schools will experiment with tiered mentoring, so that peer mentors have the benefit of an older or experienced peer or community mentor to support them.

8

Telementoring

INTRODUCTION

Telementoring involves the use of distance technology to develop the mentoring relationship. Telementoring can use e-mail, text, audio or video conferencing technology, or a combination of these varied means of communication. It has been defined as the 'use of e-mail or computer conferencing systems to support a mentoring relationship when a face-to-face relationship is impractical' (O'Neill, Wagner and Gomez, 1996: 39). This suggests that it is a poorer alternative to traditional mentoring, but there are many people who advocate telementoring as an effective means of achieving a range of educational goals. As with traditional mentoring relationships it may occur naturally or be part of a structured programme (Single and Muller, 1999).

In this chapter we begin with a discussion of the origins of telementoring and the various forms that it can take. This is followed by an analysis of the aims and objectives of telementoring, and its advantages over conventional face-to-face models of mentoring. Case studies feature two large-scale telementoring programmes from the United States, the Electronic Emissary Project and the Hewlett-Packard E-Mail Mentoring Project. The UK case study features a pilot e-mentoring project between City of Leeds School and the University of Leeds. The evaluation evidence emerging from these programmes is discussed to highlight the strengths and weaknesses of telementoring. Various issues and problems are described before good practice points are provided on setting up and running telementoring programmes. Finally, we conclude with some possible future trends in telementoring programmes for young people.

Origins

Telementoring was first used for the professional development of teachers in the curriculum use of new technologies. This can be traced backed to the early 1990s in British Columbia, where a cadre of teachers who were experienced in using computers provided online support to novice users. In 1993 the University of Texas launched probably the first, and most ambitious, telementoring programme for students. The Electronic Emissary Project matched telementors from around the world with schools. The Hewlett-Packard E-Mail Mentoring Project to match company staff with student mentees began in 1995. In 1998 the International Telementor Center was established to coordinate several company-sponsored telementoring schemes. It was projected that by 2003 the Center would be servicing 10,000 telementoring relationships world-wide. It was not until 1999 that the first telementoring programmes started appearing in the UK (Hughill, 2000; Field, 2000; Parsonage, 2000).

E-mentoring

E-mail mentoring (e-mentoring) is probably the most common form of telementoring, where a telementor is paired with a mentee. Such relations can be called 'telementorships' (Harris *et al*, 1996). The communication is characterized as asynchronous (that is, with a time gap between sending a message and it being received and read), primarily text-based and relatively fast. However, telementoring is also used with small and larger groups, often a sub-set of a school class or the whole class of students.

E-mail communication is often compared unfavourably with face-to-face communication and characterized as a 'lean media' (Harrington, 1999). Specifically, e-mail:

- makes immediate feedback difficult;
- filters out significant social cues;
- is impersonal and reduces the variety of language.

However, studies of the use of e-mail in a business context have shown that managers can overcome these challenges and often find special ways to bring greater 'richness' to e-mail communications (Clark and Brennan, 1991; Walther, 1992). Indeed it may be that willingness to offer honest feedback is increased when it does not have to be delivered face-to-face (Walther and Burgoon, 1992). The increasing use of Internet support groups dealing with personal problems indicates that e-mail can be used for deep personal communications. For example, the Samaritans began offering e-mail support in 1994 (Binik *et al*, 1997).

Uses of telementoring

Telementoring can also be used as an adjunct to traditional mentoring to facilitate communication between mentors, mentees and programme coordinators. There are mentoring schemes that exclusively involve tele-mentoring. However, some programme coordinators think that telementoring should be preceded by a face-to-face 'getting to know each other' encounter between mentor and mentee. This is clearly not possible in those telementoring schemes that operate over a wide geographical area.

Telementoring has the potential to be a key element of a school's links with its community (Nellen, nd). Schools in deprived neighbourhoods may be 'resource poor' in potential telementors, in part through problems in accessing the Internet. Telementoring gives the school access to a much wider 'virtual community' that can be brought in to enrich the curriculum.

There is a range of telementoring 'styles' that can be adopted by the mentor. These represent a spectrum of online behaviours from the 'responder', who only provides help when asked for it directly, to the 'initiator' who assumes full responsibility for initiating interactions, posing questions, identifying resources and providing support (Odell, 1990).

Teletutoring

There are related activities which often go under the label of telementoring, but which are very different in their scope, focus and outcomes (Riel, 1999). Organizations sometimes provide so-called 'expert mentors' who respond to questions sent to them over the Web. In practice, they are providing answers to single questions and are in essence a 'question-answering machine'. In telementorships an expert mentor is often paired with a group or whole class of learners. Generally there will be a clear focus on the subject or topic in which the mentor is an expert, for example, science, information technology, or teaching methods. When the primary aim is to impart knowledge to the group of learners, a more accurate term to describe this restricted form of telementorship would be 'teletutoring'.

Linked activities

Telementoring can also be effectively combined with other Web-based tools for learning. For example, the Telementoring Young Women in Science, Engineering and Computing Project aimed to encourage young women to pursue courses and careers in these 'non-traditional' areas (Center for Children and Technology, 1996). In addition to one-to-one telementoring with a female professional, discussion forums gave the mentees access to a broader range of perspectives on the difficulties women encountered in technical work environments, and the strategies they used to overcome them. Mentors acted as forum facilitators who prepared and moderated an online 'mini-seminar'. 'Lounges' were also made available to stimulate peer mentoring, and mentors, students and teachers could also raise issues and discuss strategies amongst themselves. The Hewlett-Packard E-Mail Mentoring Project encourages mentors to incorporate the Internet in the process by guiding mentees to useful sites linked to their learning interests.

AIMS AND OBJECTIVES

Telementoring can be used for instrumental mentoring, including work- and career-related programmes, as well as subject-focused mentoring. Probably the most common form of telementoring in the United States focuses on subject learning. Typically the mentor is a 'subject matter expert' (SME – a term coined by the Electronic Emissary Project) supporting an individual or groups of students as they work through a project or assignment.

Telementoring may be inappropriate for psychosocial or developmental mentoring, except as a tool to be used alongside traditional mentoring. In this case e-mail is used between face-to-face meetings to increase the number and frequency of mentor-mentee interactions and to arrange or re-arrange meetings, particularly when 'off-site' venues are used. However, although personal development may not be the prime function of telementoring, it is important to build the 'personal dimension' into e-mail communications within a subject-focused context. This is to avoid the mentor being cast as a kind of interactive encyclopaedia. The discussion above indicates how 'richness' can be brought into e-mail communication so that personal development issues can also be addressed.

TELEMENTORING VERSUS TRADITIONAL MENTORING

There are several possible advantages for telementoring over conventional face-to-face, one-to-one mentoring (Harrington, 1999):

- In principle, e-mail offers a means of connecting professionals with students on a much larger scale than would be practicable with traditional mentoring programmes. It also can enlarge the pool of potential mentors by encouraging busy people with heavy workloads or irregular work patterns to volunteer. The number of mentoring pairs can be much greater than in traditional programmes and the cost per pair can be greatly reduced in terms of time and financial cost of meetings, such as travelling expenses.

- There is no geographical limitation on the pairing of mentor with mentee. In theory, mentors could be operating on a national or even international stage. This advantage is particularly helpful for schools in rural locations or indeed, as is often the case, in inner-city locations where employed mentors are in relatively short supply or where they may be reluctant to travel because of concerns about personal security. It is particularly helpful for business people who may be interested but 'time poor', and for higher education students who often have irregular lifestyles with frequent examinations and holiday breaks.

- Telementoring reduces the problems of arranging and/or changing the dates and times of meetings that can beset traditional, external, mentoring programmes. In fact failure to meet has condemned more mentoring relationships than any other factor (Noe, 1988). E-mails can be sent at any time and they allow for convenient, frequent communication between mentors, mentees and programme coordinators.

- Potentially telementoring allows for a lot more interaction between mentor and mentee than in many conventional programmes. The need to operate in the written form can lead to greater clarity of communication than in face-to-face communication. Some argue that telementoring eliminates the personal bias or 'noise' that can result from face-to-face contact (Cardow, 1998). It can also be argued that electronic communications mask differences between higher- and lower-status groups that might otherwise hinder communication (Sproull and Kiesler, 1992). This also makes it safer than traditional mentoring, provided that all communications are monitored.

- It generates an archive of communication that can be used to evaluate the success of the programme and that can serve as a reference for all parties.

- A positive by-product can be an increase in communication between students and their parents via e-mail. This enables parents to study the work of their children and to become more engaged in their education (Nellen, nd).

- It can improve the quality of student learning through the regular sharing of knowledge and experience. Telementoring also increases opportunities for students to express their own ideas and to have feedback from an adult who is not their teacher. It may deepen students' understanding of lifelong learning and help them to appreciate that learning is something that goes on beyond the confines of the school.

- Finally, it can be easier for the mentors to perceive and understand the impact that they are having on their mentees when they can first read and later improve drafts of projects and assignments. It can give mentors instant access to students' work.

Case Study 8.1 The Hewlett-Packard E-Mail Mentoring Project (USA)

The Hewlett-Packard telementoring scheme began in 1995 with around 1,500 employees (from a world total of over 100,000 in 1997) linked by e-mail to students in grades 5–12 from across the United States. The aim of the scheme was to motivate students to excel in mathematics and science, while stressing the importance of good communication and problem-solving skills. The company was keen to promote improved proficiency and to provide increased opportunities for young women and minority ethnic students to gain experience and knowledge in these subjects from kindergarten to grade 12. Hewlett-Packard (HP) employees were given four hours per month for community service, which allowed them time for telementoring.

Schools must show how the programme will form an integral part of the maths and science curriculum, and they must designate a school link coordinator. Once a school was selected they were required to: provide information to potential student participants and teachers; select no more than 10 students per teacher coordinator; and assist students with their applications, which were used in matching.

Ground rules

Students and HP mentors were matched on the basis of several criteria, including shared interests, hobbies and skills. Pairs were encouraged to go through a 'getting to know each other' phase via e-mail and to develop mentees' familiarity with the medium and the technology tools available. The ground rules for the scheme were that pairs should communicate two or three times each week and that correct spelling and grammar must be used. Mentors were encouraged to motivate students to excel in maths and science, but also to make linkages between these subjects and the world of work.

The role of the school link coordinator was crucial in the success of the scheme. It included:

- monitoring mentor relationships to make sure that they were on track and successful;
- helping students and mentors resolve any communication problems;
- participating in evaluations of the programme.

The project Web site gives many examples of successful mentorships. For example, sixth-grade math students from Summit Elementary School in Cincinnati, Ohio, created robotic models using the Lego Dacta Robotics system. They sent pictures of themselves working on their project designs as e-mail attachments to their mentor. The teacher described the benefits of the telementoring element.

Mentors gave suggestions for model improvement and shared some of their interests and knowledge in robotics and Lego. This motivated the students to work on their designs and implement the modifications suggested by their mentors. Students were able to connect the use of a toy like Lego to the planning and designing of models for real-world problem solving.

(www.telementor.org)

Case Study 8.2 The Electronic Emissary Project (USA)

One of the largest US telementoring programmes is the Electronic Emissary Project, which was established in 1993 at the University of Texas. The Texas Centre for Educational Technology and the JC Penney Corporation funded the programme. The Project is described as a 'matching service' that helps teachers with access to e-mail link with people who are subject matter experts (SMEs) in different disciplines for the purposes of setting up curriculum-based, electronic exchanges among the teachers, their students and the experts. The Electronic Emissary is also a research project, which is exploring the nature of adult-child, text-based interaction in which students are active inquirers (Harris *et al*, 1996).

Example projects

There is a great diversity in the telementorships facilitated by the Project as the following two examples show.

Eight groups of four girls each, who were studying in an honours science program at a New England high school, communicated with a graduate student at the University of Minnesota about DNA and infantile leukaemia (the topic of the SME's thesis), cancer research and therapy, and professional careers for women in science. The teams discussed both scientific and ethical issues online with the university-based genetics expert.

A computer scientist at the State University of New York-Potsdam with interest and expertise in American history posed as a young Union soldier to help gifted and talented fifth-grade students in Omaha, Nebraska, learn about the Civil War. He answered the students' questions in character. The students used what they learned from his responses to write a play about the Civil War, which was performed at the school early in 1996.

(Harris *et al*, 1996: 2)

Start-up communications

Schools wanting to take part in the Project made contact and described the kind of SME they were looking for. Teachers were able to search a telementor database to see if a suitable SME was available. Once they had located one, three electronic conversations took place between the telementor and:

- students, about a curriculum-related topic in which the mentor had expertise;

- the teacher, in planning and implementing the learning activity;
- the teacher and the online facilitator, about the design, direction and evaluation of the project.

The mentorships were inquiry-based, which meant that students asked and responded to questions, and answers were discussed in depth. All online messages were copied to the overall project coordinators for the purposes of monitoring and research. Prospective telementors were required to complete an electronic consent form and to fill in an evaluation questionnaire at the end of the project. They were also asked to respond to questions and suggestions made by the online facilitator and to help the teacher complete a one-page summary for the project database at the end.

Each telementoring project was preceded by several weeks project planning by the teacher, telementor and online facilitator, using e-mail or desktop teleconferencing (if available to all team members). Projects lasted an average of between 12 and15 weeks.

Case Study 8.3 City of Leeds School (UK)

In 1999, a small-scale telementoring pilot project was set up for a group of 15-year-old students at City of Leeds School (Hughill, 2000). The school is located in a socially and economically deprived district of the inner city of Leeds, an industrial city in the north of England. The project was supported by Business in the Community, which was launching a new campaign called *com.unity* to engage local business support for information and communications technology (ICT) in the community. Information technology (IT) students at Leeds University were already engaged in support for local schools via IT clubs and running Internet trails. One of the aims of the pilot was to make comparisons between e-mentoring and conventional face-to-face mentoring schemes that were being established in the city at the same time.

Eleven mentors were drawn from the IT students at Leeds University and staff of an IT recruitment agency. There were four criteria for the selection of a broad range of students: underachievement, risk of school exclusion, talent in and/or enthusiasm for IT. A profile of students was written using comments from the form teacher, application forms completed by the students and interviews. They were given to mentors at the start of the pilot to help them build up an impression of their mentees.

The pilot was evaluated through questionnaires and the monitoring of school records of projected coursework grades, absenteeism, punctuality and disciplinary incidents. Qualitative data was collected through interviews with mentees and telementors, and focus groups. A video was made of the three most successful pairs.

RESEARCH AND EVALUATION EVIDENCE

US local evaluation

Nellen (nd) conducted a survey of students, parents and teachers involved in the telementoring scheme that he established at Murry Bergtraum High School in New York City. The findings showed that:

- Most students thought that telementoring was boosting their self-esteem and aiding their academic achievement.
- Parents were more comfortable than teachers with the idea of a tele-mentor for their children.
- Students believed that mentors had a more positive attitude towards their academic performance than did their teachers.
- The aspects of learning where mentors were helpful were in rank order: 'basic skills', 'multicultural education' and 'learning to learn for life'. Students viewed telementors as a way of learning about other cultures and life beyond their immediate environment.

Evaluation of the Electronic Emissary Project

Dimock (1998) found that students involved in the Electronic Emissary Project had increased interest in the subject. Their involvement with the content, the volume of content in their assignments and the depth of analysis all improved. A key factor in the success of projects was the flex-ibility of the teachers in modifying the scope of the learning in the light of experience. She describes the telementorships made through the Electronic Emissary Project as creating a new social environment for learning. The pilot programme showed how SMEs have easy and frequent access to telecomputing tools, whereas their students have much less frequent and less convenient access (Harris *et al*, 1996). This can create differing expectations that need to be effectively managed by the programme facilitator.

Evaluation of the Hewlett-Packard E-Mail Mentoring Project

A researcher from Colorado State University evaluated the Hewlett-Packard E-Mail Mentoring Project (Cobb, 1997). He conducted online surveys during 1996–97 that examined changing expectations and impact, and over 1,000 students and their mentors responded. Mentors and students both thought that the programme would benefit personal development, enhance career choices, and improve interest and perfor-mance in maths and science. Teachers reported that mentors often had unrealistic expectations of what students could achieve in their work. Students reported that they did not get as much direct help with completing homework and coursework as they had expected. Mentors often made the wrong assumptions about students' access to e-mail. Teachers and mentors alike underestimated the amount of time required to set up the programme.

Mentors reported good relationships with their students and positive impact on their interest and confidence in maths and science, ICT skills, personal development and career issues. The reasons why a limited number of mentors struggled to find rapport were predictable: lack of student interest, technological problems with e-mail, lack of support from the school and lack of mentor time.

There was no evidence that the programme had an impact on encouraging students to do better at school, to be more responsible for their own learning, to be more involved in class or to take more advanced maths or science courses. However, students did plan increased enrolment in other advanced courses. They also had greater understanding of the relevance of non-maths and science courses for their academic and personal futures. Their skills in use of the Internet and e-mail were greatly increased. Overall students were very positive about the programme, arguing that it was fun and helpful.

Evaluation of the City of Leeds e-mentoring programme

The evaluation strategy involved the collection of quantitative and qualitative baseline information on the mentees (Hughill, 2000). Students completed questionnaires and were interviewed, and school records of projected grades, absenteeism, punctuality and disciplinary incidents were monitored. A video was made to publicize the pilot programme, and three of the eleven pairs were working particularly effectively. The poor literacy and IT skills of some of the members of the target group presented a number of difficulties. E-mailing the mentor became a chore akin to letter writing for some mentees, that is, arduous and time consuming. A learning point was, therefore, to select students with better literacy standards for e-mentoring. Not all mentees grasped the concept of an e-mentor and an important lesson was the need for face-to-face meetings at the start of the project.

ISSUES

Focus and purpose

A key question to address is always the focus and desired outcomes of the telementoring scheme. The successful US programmes have a clear subject focus, with telementors cast in the role of expert bringing their knowledge, skills and experience to bear on student projects and assignments. They also play a key role in making the link between the school curriculum and both higher education and the world of work. The UK case study was less successful in achieving its objectives, arguably because these were primarily developmental and telementoring is less appropriate where development is the main aim of the programme. For most schools telementoring can provide an additional means of communication to supplement the main face-to-face interaction. In other words, it is an additional means of communication between mentors and their mentees, which supplements the primary face-to-face contact.

Resourcing

The case studies illustrate the range of practice in telementoring, from well-funded, global or national programmes to modestly resourced local schemes. Effective, well-managed telementoring programmes require a level of resourcing that is beyond the average school, but which might be possible for colleges or universities. The experience of the International Telementor Center also suggests that large companies may be willing to sponsor telementoring programmes as a comparatively low-cost way of supporting local communities, education and staff volunteering. The role of online facilitator is important in ensuring the quality of telementoring and, although this role can be undertaken by a teacher, it is probably most appropriate for someone outside the school, with the training, support and time to monitor interactions and to make regular interventions. Again this requires a level of funding that is often unavailable to small local schemes.

Problems

There are a number of potential problems associated with telementoring programmes, all of which can be overcome with proper resourcing and planning.

- There is a need for good technology infrastructure and support, for example, for the establishment and maintenance of online databases or the creation of special mail groups. The Leeds case study highlighted the problems of 'going live' before software problems were sorted out. Such infrastructure is more likely to be available when a scheme is organized for a number of schools in an area or on a wider basis.
- Students with poor basic skills can struggle with the task of communicating effectively in writing, which can become a chore. This is particularly because a general requirement of telementoring schemes is for the use of correct grammar and accurate spelling. This may limit

the use of telementoring for some at-risk students, and their behavioural and attitudinal problems may make telementoring a less effective intervention than traditional mentoring.

● Communication between mentor and mentee is generally limited to text, and this can tend to inhibit the development of trust, openness and commitment. This may affect students in different ways, but there are ways in which telementors can include the personal, as well as the academic, dimension in all their communications. Some would argue that local telementoring programmes should begin with a face-to-face meeting.

● There is a heavy reliance on the teacher supervisor and/or online facilitator to monitor communications. In well-managed schemes it is important to provide feedback once or twice a week to mentors about the programme, barriers, challenges and successes. This clearly has heavy resource implications.

SETTING UP A TELEMENTORING PROGRAMME

It should be clear from the above discussion that setting up a telementoring programme is not like creating an introductions service. Superficially matching a mentor and mentee, exchanging e-mail addresses and urging the two parties to communicate for the benefit of the student appears relatively unproblematic. However, one of the key lessons of the pilot programme of the Electronic Emissary scheme was that there were real challenges posed by time, the medium and differing expectations of mentors and mentees (Harris *et al*, 1996). This highlights the need for an online facilitator who has knowledge of both Internet-based communication and education. They need to engage in 'contextual translation' to adjust expectations concerning the amount, frequency and types of communications, so that expectations will fit the realities of both school and the mentors' environments. The following good practice points are based on the varied experience of the innovative and pioneering telementoring programmes described above (Wighton, 1993; Harris *et al*, 1996; Center for Children and Technology, 1996; Hughill, 2000). They also incorporate the main features of the model of structured e-mentoring set out in the paper by Single and Muller (1999).

Planning

● Consider whether telementoring is the right approach to deliver the desired outcomes.

● Contact existing 'matchmaking services' to see if they can meet your needs, or if their materials can guide you in setting up your own programme. Search the World Wide Web for existing telementoring projects to find out how they function.

- Develop clear learning goals and try to ensure that the programme is an integral part of the students' curriculum rather than extra-curricular.
- Ensure that software problems are sorted out before launching the programme.
- In a company or university, use the organizational Intranet to recruit mentors.
- Develop a Web site where guidelines can be posted along with mentor and mentee application forms. Consider setting up a Web-based training tutorial.
- Make sure that teachers, mentors and students all have e-mail addresses.
- Decide on a final project outcome that students will individually or collectively produce.
- Support teachers in thinking through the role that they and the telementors will play in the project and the learning of the students.
- Set a start and end date for the project. State realistic deadlines for response times to messages and parameters for the frequency of communications.
- Select mentees from one group or class, as it will be easier to offer them support during curriculum time.
- Select mentees who have sufficient literacy and ICT skills not to find writing e-mails a problem.
- Ask students and parents to sign an Acceptable Use Policy contract setting out the ground rules of the project. Ask students not to give out personal details, such as their phone numbers and addresses.
- Make sure that mentors are aware of any problems of access to computers that students may have and how this may affect response times to messages.
- Brief mentors on the level of communication that is appropriate to the age and educational level of the students.
- Consider using experienced telementors as online telementor trainers.
- In group mentoring, brief mentors to try to respond to all the questions asked, to avoid some students feeling neglected.
- In group mentoring, brief students to share the information they receive from the mentor rather than guarding it as private property.
- Include a 'netiquette' guide in the training of students about good manners and style in using e-mail.
- Include some 'sensitivity' training for mentors in their preparation, as issues of race, gender and class do not just disappear online.
- Allow mentors and mentees to view information about their potential match without giving contact information. Give them time to accept or reject the match in order to increase ownership.

- Ask students to prepare a short biography to share with their mentor at the start of the programme.

Implementing

- Ensure that the telementors and the link teacher establish a rapport at the outset and communicate regularly during the project.
- Brief mentors and mentees to balance both personal and academic information in their exchanges. Make suggestions as to how personal rapport can be established.
- Brief telementors and mentees to establish the most appropriate tele-mentoring 'style' for the mentor to adopt.
- Provide offline support for students to help them plan for communicating with their mentor. Consider sessions where mentees discuss questions and messages to their mentors before sending them.
- Make sure that students edit their communication by proof-reading, spell-checking and, possibly, peer review.
- Ask students to include their mentor's previous message when responding (as busy mentors may not remember all the questions they asked).
- Consider a number of face-to-face meetings at the start of the programme in local telementoring schemes.
- Try to maintain a regular frequency of communications and short turnaround times. Ask online facilitators to do some 'electronic sleeve tugging' to make sure that the habit of regular communication is established.
- Send regular 'coaching messages' to mentors and mentees to prompt activity, stimulate movement through the phases of the mentoring relationship, and direct attention to relevant Web sites.
- Encourage active, inquiry-based and student-centred communication, as it is easy for the adults to dominate the interactions.
- Invite telementors to communicate with each other to reduce isolation and to share experience of what approaches are most effective.
- Make sure that telementors provide regular progress reports to the online facilitator.
- Ask students to keep a telementoring journal in which they record expectations and things they have learnt.

FUTURE TRENDS

The rapid increase in the number of schools, students, businesses, universities and voluntary organizations going on online will facilitate the expansion of telementoring programmes. There is likely to be major funding to support large-scale pilot telementoring programmes with research and evaluation into the benefits for students. The Electronic Emissary Project will be replicated in other countries. The continued downsizing of larger businesses will create pressures for telementoring programmes to replace conventional face-to-face programmes. The monitoring requirements in telementoring coupled with continued concern over child protection issues and e-mail will inhibit the growth of telementoring for younger students. E-mentoring will be seen in many mentoring programmes as an additional means of communication to be used by mentors and mentees between meetings, rather than as the main means of communication.

9

Higher education student mentoring in schools

INTRODUCTION

We are defining higher education student mentoring as students from colleges and universities mentoring students in schools. It can be described as a form of cross-age, cross-institutional mentoring, but the distinctive features of these programmes warrant a separate chapter. Mentoring in higher education includes peer mentoring programmes and programmes where academic staff mentor students. These schemes are outside the scope of this book. This chapter focuses on programmes where college and university students mentor school students. These schemes are increasingly popular as a form of voluntary service, community service learning or citizenship education. They also enable higher education institutions to build links with local schools, and to encourage widening participation, that is, progression into higher education from under-represented groups.

The chapter begins with an overview of college–school mentoring and tutoring in the United States that establishes some of the key variables of these programmes and illustrates their proliferation across the country. An overview of developments in the United Kingdom is followed by three case studies. The National Mentoring Pilot Project is a national programme supported by the UK government, which is based on the *Perach* model in Israel (see Chapter 1). The Middlesex University scheme illustrates a local volunteering programme in North London schools. The GEAR UP Program is an example of US mass mentoring based on local strategic partnerships. A review of research and evaluation evidence is followed by a discussion of the issues arising from the case studies. A good practice checklist provides points to consider when setting up and running mentoring programmes with colleges and universities. We conclude by speculating on future trends in higher education student mentoring.

US COLLEGE-SCHOOL MENTORING

A US study commissioned by the Department of Education investigated 1,700 programmes in nearly a third of all two- and four-year colleges (Cahalan and Farris, 1990). Four out of ten students mentored were in elementary schools, a third were in middle schools and a third were in high schools.

The main aims of the tutoring and mentoring were improving basic skills (61 per cent), improving self-esteem (12 per cent), providing role models (8 per cent) and preventing school drop-out (5 per cent). Most programmes were relatively small in size, involving a median of 20 college students and 60 school students during the course of a year. Data on student motivation showed that 40 per cent volunteered, 29 per cent received payment and 28 per cent gained course credits. The main goals for tutors and mentors were to gain practical experience in their professional field (77 per cent), to develop a commitment to public service (71 per cent) and to have non-campus experience (54 per cent). Two-thirds of mentors and tutors were female and a quarter came from minority groups. In contrast, half the mentees were female and three-quarters were from minorities.

The operations of the programmes tended to last for half an academic year. Nearly all college students (96 per cent) fulfilled their commitment to the programme. Around half the schemes based the tutoring and mentoring at the college, but four out of ten programmes were based at the school. One-to-one sessions were the most common form of interaction (61 per cent), followed by small group sessions (22 per cent) and large group sessions (17 per cent). College students spent a median of three hours per week on mentoring or tutoring, with an average of three tutees or mentees each. In four out of five programmes, staff met weekly with the student tutors or mentors, and in half the programmes they were required to write a report. The most significant problems cited by programmes were transport (41 per cent), physical space to conduct meetings (32 per cent) and coordination with parents (31 per cent).

There were interesting differences between programmes with tutoring or mentoring as the primary focus. In programmes described as tutoring, most of the tutors' time was spent on helping with basic skills (60 per cent) and homework support (28 per cent) rather than on recreational activities or cultural activities (12 per cent). In mentoring programmes the bulk of the time was spent on recreational and cultural (39 per cent) or other activities (30 per cent). Support with basic skills (21 per cent) and homework (10 per cent) took up relatively less time.

GEAR UP

In 1998, federal funding was provided to support partnerships of high-poverty middle schools, colleges and universities, community organizations and businesses to work with entire grades of students starting in the 7th grade or earlier. Around 22 per cent of college-qualified high school graduates from low-income families did not go to college, compared to only 4 per cent of high-income graduates. Gaining Early Awareness & Readiness for Undergraduate Programs (GEAR UP) was based on research that showed that students taking more challenging courses in their middle years were much more likely to go on to college. In its first year over 1,000 partners were involved in supporting 450,000 students through tutoring, mentoring, information on college preparation and financial aid, an emphasis on core academic preparation and, in some cases, scholarships. It is a requirement for federal dollars to be matched locally on a one-for-one basis. The programme lasts for a period of six or more years, so it provides sustained support to raise standards and aspirations. The partnerships focus not only on the students, but also on the teachers through the provision of enhanced professional development. In the programme's second year, President Clinton announced 185 new grants, totalling $120 million to assist 200,000 students.

UK UNIVERSITY AND COLLEGE VOLUNTEERING

During the 1999–2000 academic year, there were 181 student volunteering schemes in universities and colleges across the United Kingdom (Community Service Volunteers, 2000). A survey of schemes found that there were 8,405 student volunteers from 77 institutions. Over the years the vast majority of student volunteers have been female (between two-thirds and three-quarters of the total). Many volunteering schemes target second-year undergraduates. Volunteering schemes can be broken down into three broad categories. Mentoring and tutoring generally involve working with schools, but other project schemes involve students working in wider community settings. The statistics show that tutoring is much more prevalent than mentoring, largely because of the national programmes on offer that institutions can link into, such as CSV Learning Together and its literacy equivalent, CSV Reading Together. Such national programmes have only just become available through the National Mentoring Pilot Project (see Case Study 9.1). The majority of institutions benefiting from student volunteer tutors and mentors were primary schools (55 per cent), with secondary schools making up the next largest group (35 per cent).

AIMS AND OBJECTIVES

The primary aims for schools involving higher education students tend to be academic and career-related. Higher education students have reached a higher level of academic attainment than school students and can help them to improve their grades and study skills. In some schemes there is an emphasis on the higher education students developing the basic skills of literacy and numeracy with younger students. The National Mentoring Pilot Project in the UK illustrates the close link between higher education mentoring and the government's 'raising standards' agenda. In this programme universities are paired with Education Action Zones with the aim of helping to raise standards of achievement in primary and secondary schools.

The career-related aim of higher education student mentoring is also important in most schemes. By exposing younger students to university and college students it is hoped that they will aspire to succeed in school and progress into further and higher education. The university students act as role models and show what can be achieved through application at school. These schemes often involve briefings on going to university and visits to experience campus life.

KEY SKILLS

There are also benefits to mentors from working with school students. Student tutors or mentors have the opportunity to demonstrate key skills and personal qualities through mentoring in schools. For example, the Tyneside and Northumberland Students into Schools Project asked teachers to assess students' performance in four areas (Wood, 2000):

- reliability, which includes punctuality and attendance;
- communication, which means speaking and listening effectively with teachers and students;
- working with others, which involves negotiation skills and building effective working relationships with teachers and school students;
- initiative, which means taking independent action where appropriate and assuming personal responsibility for completing agreed activities.

Citizenship

In most American colleges, mentoring and tutoring in schools is viewed as a form of service learning, community service or citizenship. In some programmes high-school and college students undertake community service learning projects jointly as an additional element in the mentoring programme. Thus, the mentoring-plus element of programmes means that both mentors and mentees can achieve broader citizenship objectives, such as developing positive attitudes towards public service.

Case Study 9.1 The National Mentoring Pilot Project at South Bank University (UK)

The University is one of the largest in London with 19,000 full- and part-time students, including 2,500 international students; over half the total students are mature, many with family responsibilities. There is a high proportion of minority ethnic students, including many from the local inner London boroughs of Southwark and Lambeth. The University is a member of the National Mentoring Consortium, which places minority ethnic students with successful Black mentors from business, industry and the public sector. The Access Links Unit, which is part of the Department of Academic Affairs, manages the community mentoring programmes.

National Mentoring Pilot Project

The University was one of the original members of the National Mentoring Pilot Project (NMPP) operated by the University of Wales, Cardiff, and funded by the Department for Education and Skills. The aims of the NMPP were to pay university students to act as mentors in order to raise the academic achievement of students aged 12–17 in local Education Action Zone (EAZ) schools and to encourage progression into higher education. By October 2001, the NMPP involved 16 universities, 21 EAZs, around 860 mentors and 65 schools. Students tended to be those on the C/D borderline who, with mentor support, could achieve five higher grade GCSEs. The reasons for the University's involvement were, first, that the Chair of the EAZ was a member of the Academic Affairs department; second, the University wished to demonstrate work with the local community on widening access and participation in higher education; and, third, it would help public relations.

The University received £45,000 per annum for the project, which funded the post of Project Director, a part-time administrator and several coordinators, academic staff who took responsibility for supervising 10 student mentors. Additional funding to cover the £5 per hour payment to mentors came from the Higher Education Funding Council for England and the two local EAZs. The target number of student mentor pairs over the two years of the pilot scheme was 100, although the numbers achieved were 24 in the first year and 52 in the second. The pilot had just been extended for a further three years from 2001–2004.

Recruiting mentors

The ground rules were that students should make a commitment to four hours per week, giving four mentees an hour each. Mentors had to be full-time students, which meant that many South Bank students were ineligible. A big issue in London was the time students spent travelling to the schools; they had to attend on two or three different days, at times that had been set by the project to avoid a clash with lesson times, for example 8–9 am, 12 am–1 pm or 3.30–4.30 pm. Various methods were used to recruit students including a project poster, advertisements in the student magazine, the careers shop and the University Web site. However, the best results were achieved when two student mentors staffed a stand in the entrance hall to the main building, handing out leaflets and talking to fellow students, and then addressing groups of students in their classes with the permission of their lecturers. Major selling points included the contribution of the mentoring experience to their employability, as well as the earnings potential.

Mentor preparation

In order to standardize practice, members of the central project team conducted the initial awareness-raising session with mentors that spelt out the required level of commitment and enabled application forms to be distributed. Students were interviewed by the University coordinators and then attended a two-day interactive training session. Police checks then took a further six weeks, which meant that some students dropped out of the programme. In order to circumvent this, students were able to meet pairs of pupils at the school until they were able to meet their mentees individually. Matching criteria included interests and subjects studied, although ethnicity and religion were particularly important. Students from minority ethnic communities often expressed a preference for mentoring a student with the same background. In the first year the bulk of mentors were of African or African-Caribbean background and there was an even gender balance, but in the second year there was a greater diversity; more international students were involved and 70 per cent of mentors were female. These students did not have knowledge of the UK education system and so briefing on curriculum matters was particularly important.

Processes

There was a detailed mentor's handbook with action-planning and progress sheets to facilitate monitoring and evaluation. At each meeting mentors were encouraged to review targets, to record proposed action in pursuit of targets and to list progress to date. On progress sheets they listed main discussion points and targets set for the next meeting, as well as reviewing long-term targets. Although it was not part of the NMPP, the scheme coordinator encouraged pairs of mentors to host a visit to the University by their eight mentees.

As part of a separately funded Student Focus programme eight of the mentors acted as ambassadors who visited the schools in the area to run sessions on going to university. The total time commitment for mentors was 120 hours per year (4 hours per week over 30 weeks). The model that was emerging was a year-long scheme running from February in Year 10 to February in Year 11, when students were embarking on their final revision programmes for their GCSEs.

Monitoring

Academic staff monitored mentors through group meetings held once a term, as well as their termly meetings with individual mentors. University coordinators were paid £1,000 per annum for undertaking this role. Students tended to be critical of the prevailing chaos and the poor revision methods in some of the schools they were visiting, which they felt hindered their mentees' progress.

Case Study 9.2 Mentoring at Middlesex University (UK)

Middlesex University is situated in the north-east margins of Greater London and has campuses in several outer London boroughs. In 1998 the University set up a unit to coordinate service learning in local communities. There was demand from local boroughs and schools for mentoring programmes, involving Middlesex students working in local high schools. Mentees were drawn from Year 10 and the scheme lasted for four terms in the run-up to GCSE exams.

Initially, the schools viewed the higher education students as role models to work with four categories of student:

- underachievers in general;
- those with the potential to achieve the benchmark of five good GCSEs;
- high achievers who did not see higher education as an option;
- students with poor social and communication skills.

However, this was broadened to include an aspirational programme in one school, where the focus was on progression into higher education for students who might not have seen this as a realistic or desirable option. In another school, mentors were working with able pupils with problems who needed extra support. In the first year of the scheme, 1998–99, there were 76 mentors working in 6 schools. By 1999–2000, the number of mentors rose to 88 in 7 schools, but the number declined in 2000–01 to 50 mentors in 11 schools.

Mentor recruitment

There was a mentoring coordinator, who managed the Voluntary Community Service Learning Programme (Iremonger, 1999 and 2000). She was responsible for recruiting mentors and a wide variety of methods had been used. Posters and notices were widely distributed throughout the campuses and in halls of residence. Students received e-mail notices and leaflets in their in-trays. The scheme was advertised in the monthly newsletter and at the Freshers' Fair. A database was used for regular mailouts to students and experienced mentors were invited to write articles about their experiences. Social events were planned where active mentors were encouraged to bring a friend who could sign up to join the programme.

Mentor training and matching

Student volunteers attended an initial briefing session where they met teachers from local schools and active mentors. The coordinator then inter-viewed interested students, and this was followed by police checks and the taking up of references. Volunteers were provided with mentoring guidelines during two three-hour training sessions, which covered the following topics: fears, anxieties and expectations; the first mentoring session; building self-esteem; school information; child protection; listening skills; and diversity issues. Undergraduates gained credits for mentoring by choosing mentoring as a Placement in the Community Module. They also signed up to a Mentor's Code of Practice. Matching forms were completed and these were sent to the school link teacher for matches to be finalized. After a school induction session, mentors met their mentees for around one hour every week or two weeks.

Mentors used a range of strategies to engage their mentees. Some of these involved raising awareness of higher education through visits to the campus and sharing their own experiences of student life. Other strategies involved direct support for academic work through help with project work, identifying sources of information for coursework and support with exam revision. Mentors provided feedback to the scheme coordinator each month using an e-mail monitoring form. There was also a termly mentor support-group meeting, which was compulsory. In 2001, the coordinator called in all mentors for one-to-one supervision after the initial three meetings. At the end of the programme there was a celebratory party for mentors and mentees and certificates were formally presented.

Case Study 9.3 Local GEAR UP Programs (USA)

In 1999, the New Jersey Commission on Higher Education received a $1.4 million grant for the first year of GEAR UP, which rose to $10 million over the five years of the programme. GEAR UP built on existing state-funded College Bound programmes, which had been modified to meet national criteria. The programme targeted ten middle and seven high schools in New Jersey. Eligibility rules for the programme were that students must:

- be in the seventh or eighth grade;
- meet family income requirements;
- attend a target school.

Local partnerships were a key element of GEAR UP, as was a comprehensive range of activities. Mentoring was just one aspect of the programme, but there were many other components provided by the school, college, private sector and community partners:

- a six-week summer educational programme;
- academic lessons on Saturday mornings during the school year;
- after-school tutoring during the school year;
- a 21st Century Scholar Certificate;
- college visits and tours;
- assistance with college applications;
- financial aid and information workshops;
- academic and personal counseling;
- examination and test preparation classes;
- cultural and educational field trips.

Rutgers University programme

There were a number of local projects within the New Jersey GEAR UP Program. The Rutgers/LEAP GEAR UP project provided a college-awareness and college-readiness programme to students at LEAP Academy and University High Charter School, starting in the fifth grade and continuing throughout high school. Rutgers University was the lead organization, working in partnership with the Delaware River Port Authority, the New Jersey State Aquarium, First Union Bank, I Have A Dream Foundation and ASPIRA of New Jersey Inc.

The specific activities fell into three categories:

- Academic development: development of a pre-college curriculum; tutoring; test preparation; academic counselling; financial aid workshops; college application and essay workshops; company tours; job shadowing; internships; career awareness; curriculum vitae and interview workshops.
- Social development: community service; mentoring; cultural outings.
- Strengthening support systems: home visits; parent workshops; professional development for project staff.

A key component of the programme was the introduction of age-appropriate curricula for grades 5–12, to include issues of college awareness and preparation for college. Each of these curriculum modules lasted a semester and, in keeping with the holistic approach, involved the participation of various project partners.

RESEARCH AND EVALUATION EVIDENCE

Evaluation of the National Mentoring Pilot Project

South Bank University's mentoring scheme was included as one of the case studies in the national evaluation of NMPP (Huddleston, 2001). The evaluation used a mixture of quantitative and qualitative methods. The findings described here are from all the projects. Two-thirds of student mentors were female and three-quarters were aged 18–21. Motivations for volunteering were a balance of the altruistic (nine out of ten wanted to help young people), and self-developmental (four out of five thought it would help their career development). The bulk of mentees were drawn from Years 10 and 11 and perceived the main purpose of the programme as helping their study skills and GCSE examination results. The emphasis placed on target setting in mentor training and the NMPP's mentor manual was reflected in the most frequently discussed topics at meetings, which were progress in GCSE subjects and general school progress. The key issue affecting the success of a local NMPP programme was the effectiveness of the school coordinator. Poor communication between schools and universities was a further cause of difficulty, as was the plethora of initiatives involving EAZ schools.

Local evaluation of the Middlesex University programme

The University's mentoring coordinator has evaluated the programme in a formative sense (see Chapter 13). There have been three main sets of problems. First, problems with mentors included some not attending supervision and support meetings, failing to respond to e-mails or letters, and ending their mentorships without informing the mentoring programme. It also proved difficult to assess properly the skills developed by undergraduates through the mentoring scheme.

Second, there have been particular communication problems with schools, such as lack of response to messages from mentors, failure to reschedule meetings when mentees had missed appointments, and difficulties over rooms for meetings. Some schools wanted mentors, but were unable to put systems in place to run an effective mentoring programme. Others did not allow school coordinators enough time to undertake the tasks associated with operating the scheme. Increasingly, schools have identified a wider range of students for whom they want mentors, whereas higher education students primarily want to work with underachievers.

Third, and most important, was the problem of non-attendance by mentees, which may reflect the fact that they had not genuinely volunteered for the programme. A related problem was the lack of good preparation and training for mentees, so that they could make the most of the experience. The effects of non-attendance on mentors were that they felt frustrated, lost confidence and became annoyed. The problem was generally caused by not having a school coordinator who could monitor and follow up missed appointments. This was exacerbated by not including school reception staff in briefings about the mentoring programme, as they were often a first point of contact but were often unsympathetic towards mentors' enquiries. These findings are in line with recent evaluations of school-based mentoring in England (Miller, 1998; Golden and Sims, 1999).

US evaluation

An evaluation by Public/Private Ventures of six programmes involving college students mentoring at-risk youth (Tierney and Branch, 1996) aimed to shed more light on findings of the earlier study of 1,700 US programmes discussed above (Reisner *et al*, 1989). They examined six of the 12 Campus Partners in Learning (CPIL) programmes sponsored by the Education Commission of the States. The programmes were at Boston University, Connecticut College, Georgetown University, Porterville Community College, West Virginia Wesleyan College and Xavier University. The programmes varied widely, but all involved tutoring and mentoring by college students and at-risk youth. Although the small size of the sample limited the usefulness of the generalizations emerging, there were some useful lessons.

The main finding was that such programmes required much greater administrative and other support than ones targeting students who were not at risk. No programmes had solved the problem of how to recruit more students. Programmes with rigorous selection and screening procedures had much higher rates of attendance. Tierney and Branch (1996: 39) provide a number of useful lessons about the messages that should be communicated through mentor training:

- The nature of the youths' neighbourhood and the background of the mentee are important.
- There should be, clear programme rules, especially about what is expected of mentors and mentees in terms of attendance and behaviour.
- The mentoring scheme alone cannot be expected to change their lives.
- An authoritarian approach by the mentor will harm the development of a relationship with the mentee.
- Special patience is required at the start of the relationship.
- Expressing interest in their mentees' preferences is a good way of gaining their trust.
- Recreational activities are enriching for mentees, who may not otherwise gain access to them

Mentee preparation benefited from a discussion of the structure of college life (eg breaks and exams) and its likely impact on the mentorship. Programmes that simplified logistical problems had higher attendance rates and a greater number of mentor-mentee interactions. The most important factor was establishing set meeting times. The research found that 45 per cent of relationships were successful. The criteria for success were the mentee's satisfaction with the relationship, its duration, and the mentee's desire that it continue. Successful mentors exhibited the flexibility to switch roles from being in a peer or older sibling role to becoming a coach or teacher.

GEAR UP evaluation

The GEAR UP Program is an example of evidence-based policy making in that it is based on research into the need for and value of similar predecessor programmes. The Chicago I Have A Dream programme provided entire grades of low-income students with intensive mentoring, academic support and a promise of public and private financial support for college tuition. Of the I Have A Dream students in the class of 1996, 75 per cent graduated from school compared with just over one-third of the control group. Project GRAD was a Texas-based college-school-community partnership to improve standards in inner-city schools. Students received curriculum, counselling and scholarship opportunities to encourage college attendance. The results of Project GRAD were dramatic. The percentage of middle-school students passing the statewide maths test tripled from 21 per cent in 1995 to 63 per cent in 1998. In one Project GRAD high school, the number of students graduating increased by 64 per cent between 1988 and 1998, during which time the overall district number fell by 7 per cent. GEAR UP adopted a similar rigorous approach to project evaluation. This included the setting of benchmark performance indicators against which to monitor progress. GEAR UP was a five-year programme, and the national evaluation is not yet available.

ISSUES

Ambition and targeting

The UK examples show two main roles for higher education students in mentoring school students. One is to use their academic skills to support the achievement of school students and to motivate them to succeed academically. The other is to encourage them to aspire to higher education. Students targeted are often aged 15–16, while others may be in the 16–19 age group. Generally a minority of students are being targeted in each school. The US examples from the GEAR UP Program illustrate how mentoring by higher education students is part of a much more ambitious, long-term and broader partnership to transform the educational opportunities for students in low-income schools. Mentoring is seen as one element within an overall package designed to raise standards and promote college attendance. Students targeted are in the seventh grade or below, much younger than those typically targeted in the United Kingdom. Clearly, the US programme has been based on research into what works, and supported by large amounts of federal funding to support statewide and local partnerships. There is a risk that when higher education mentoring programmes are isolated, under-resourced initiatives involving hard-pressed inner-city high schools they may be unsuccessful.

Alternative models

There are a variety of programmes termed 'mentoring' that involve students from colleges and universities working in schools. A creative partnership between schools and a university can result in innovative mentoring programmes. One interesting Australian example involved 25 Year-10 students from Hamilton Senior High School and students from Murdoch University (Silburn and Box, 1999). The school was chosen because of the low levels of progression into higher education, and various 'equity groups' were targeted: recently arrived migrants, refugees, aboriginal students, students with disabilities and students from low income families.

The high school students were paired with university student mentors, and provided with a video and stills camera with which to make a video and photo-journal of a week spent on campus. They were asked to work with their mentor to organize and film a number of interviews with people on campus. They were given a video-making skills workshop. The project was designed to empower these students and to give them a fun experience in the University. In the second year of the project the mentoring was extended through telementoring by academic staff and student mentors. Staff provided career and study advice, and undergraduate mentors offered on-going academic support and general encouragement.

Coordination

The success of higher education mentoring programmes depends on effective coordination at both the university and school. Evaluations of the higher education programmes in the UK and of business-and-community mentoring consistently show that school coordination is often weak and that this can undermine the effectiveness of programmes

(Miller, 1998; Golden and Sims, 1999). It is important that universities and colleges build partnerships with schools that are sufficiently committed to make available the resources that are needed to make the programme work. This may involve securing funding for school as well as university coordinators. Universities and colleges may want to sign partnership agreements with schools, setting out formally what each party will provide to make the programme a success. Coordinators need job descriptions setting out their roles and responsibilities, and there should be regular review meetings to iron out any teething troubles.

Matching

The selection of higher education education students and their matching to school students can be problematic. An action-research approach to managing a student tutoring scheme over a number of years at the University of Newcastle concluded that there were negative outcomes associated with particular student 'risk' factors (Wood, 2000). These factors, which would apply equally to student mentors working in schools, were unreliability, poor communication skills, inability to develop an effective working relationship in a short period of time and lack of initiative. A number of positive or 'low-risk' characteristics were identified. When students exhibited a number of these, then they were more likely to be successful tutors or mentors; they were often female, tutoring for credit, in their final year, having a preference for difficult or special school environments, willing to travel, possessed of significant previous experience, intending to become a teacher and not an only child. Students with a number of opposite characteristics would fall into the high risk group, where the mentoring and tutoring would have a high chance of being unsuccessful.

When matching students to schools it is important to avoid matching high risk students with high risk schools (Wood, 2000). School 'risk factors' include the following characteristics:

- There is previous experience of 'weak' students placed at the school.
- The school is new to the project.
- The key member of staff is sick or there is a new link teacher.
- The school is a long way from the university or where the student lives.
- The school has an imminent external inspection or is under pressure, for example through being in 'special measures'.

SETTING UP A HIGHER EDUCATION STUDENT MENTORING PROGRAMME

It will be clear from the above discussion that there are considerable resource implications in higher education mentoring programmes. This is especially the case where student mentors are being paid for their time, which is an increasing feature of such programmes. However, universities often have sources of funding to enable them to establish and manage these programmes as part of general enrichment or as a service-learning scheme. The case studies illustrate that it is not sufficient for the university to manage the programme for the scheme to be successful. The role of the school coordinator is also critical in ensuring that the programme is effective. The following good practice tips are written from the perspective of the university or college and are based on the experience of the University of Westminster in operating the Student Focus programme (Amis and Marsh, 2001).

Planning

- Be clear about the type of mentoring or tutoring that the programme will offer.
- Decide whether mentoring will be a voluntary or paid activity.
- Consider combining mentoring with other activities such as higher education awareness talks and visits to the university.
- Identify credits that students can gain through mentoring.
- Ensure that the school is committed to the mentoring programme and is prepared to put some resources into making it work.
- Consider designing a partnership agreement which both school and the university can sign. This will set out the roles and responsibilities of each to make the programme a success.
- Make sure that there is a named link teacher in the school and that they have sufficient status to iron out any problems that may arise.
- Identify the precise times of the week when university students will be able to make regular commitment. Also eliminate on the mentoring calendar those times when university and school students will be involved in preparation for or sitting examinations.
- Make sure that students are clear about what they have been contracted to do in terms of providing feedback on meetings, completing evaluation forms and attending review meetings.
- Arrange a meeting at the school with the link teacher to address any logistical problems that may arise. During your visit make an appointment to talk to the head teacher or member of the senior management team.
- Ensure that the criteria for referring school students to the scheme are realistic and appropriate.

- Identify 'risk factors' in students and schools when matching students to schools; avoid matching high-risk students to 'high-risk' placements.
- Clarify the times when meetings will take place before, during or after the school day.
- Check the suitability of rooms that are to be used, whether they are left open, and if not who holds keys.
- If a university visit is part of the scheme, then plan the date to make sure that there will be plenty of things to see.

Implementing

- Training for mentors must take into account the target group and the purposes of the mentoring programme to avoid mismatches between the school's selection of mentees and the university's choice of mentors.
- If several mentors are going to one school, then bring them together and talk through any materials that you want them to use. Encourage them to exchange contact details so that they can support each other and share lifts to the school.
- Set up a session when mentors can meet mentees for the first time. Schedule this so that you can accompany them and introduce them to the school link coordinator.
- Provide mentors with plenty of paper materials to help structure early sessions as this will give them more confidence.
- Ensure that they have a schedule of meetings and provide a location map.
- Make sure that they have considered how much travelling time to allow in order to arrive promptly at appointments.
- Arrange a debriefing session after the first mentoring meeting and one later on when the programme has been running for some time.
- Telephone students to offer advice, support, additional ideas and materials.
- Keep evaluation forms short so that they are completed properly.

FUTURE TRENDS

The future growth of higher education student mentoring in schools is a likely by-product of the continuing trend towards mass higher education. However, the need to attract non-traditional students to higher education will increase the number of widening participation programmes. One-to-one and small-group mentoring are generally a key feature of widening participation as university students act as role models to their near-age mentees. The desire to engage students with local schools, as a form of service learning, will continue with renewed interest in education for citizenship and building social capital. There will be a tension between involving students lower down the school to support under-achieving students and using them to encourage post-16 students to go to university. The introduction of paid mentoring will tend to force out voluntary schemes as economic necessity forces students to generate income to compensate for fees and the cost of living. Universities will increasingly be seen as local partners which can provide not only student mentors but also research, evaluation and staff development experience to support mentoring programmes for young people.

Part III

Guide to effective mentoring

10

Planning and managing mentoring programmes for young people

INTRODUCTION

The purpose of this chapter is to discuss some of the issues involved in planning and managing mentoring programmes for students and young people. It begins by giving an overview, breaking down a standard programme into its constituent elements. These elements form the substance of Chapters 11–13, which focus on mentors, mentoring processes and evaluation. This chapter identifies some of the first steps that need to be taken when setting up a new programme. These include especially identifying the needs of the target group. There is a discussion about the supporting documentation that needs to be produced. The chapter highlights one important aspect of project management, namely the clarification of roles and responsibilities between the programme manager and the school coordinator. It also identifies the main resource needs associated with mentoring programmes and provides a sample budget. This is followed by a discussion of a whole-school approach to mentoring and a case study example of a UK school that is developing a mentoring culture. The next section examines the need for leadership in running successful mentoring programmes. We conclude with a summary of good practice points and speculation about future trends in management of mentoring programmes.

A MODEL MENTORING PROGRAMME

One way of thinking about a mentoring programme is as a discrete project with a beginning, middle and end. Most mentoring programmes for reasons of efficiency operate in cycles, and therefore they tend to follow similar stages. RPS Rainer, a voluntary organization operating mentoring programmes for young people at risk of social exclusion in the United Kingdom, has developed a flow chart illustrating the interrelationships between the different elements of a mentoring programme cycle (see Figure 10.1). Although the model was developed for socially excluded mentoring programmes, it is broadly applicable and adaptable to most forms of mentoring for students and young people (Skinner and Fleming, 1999). This is because programmes for young people at risk tend to be more rigorous than other forms of student mentoring. The model is particularly helpful in identifying possible monitoring and evaluation points.

Stages of a mentoring programme

The principal stages in running a mentoring programme are as follows:

1. *Pre-planning*: can involve setting up a steering group, recruiting staff to manage the project and establishing the basic parameters of the scheme.
2. *Mentor and mentee recruitment and selection*: involves setting referral criteria for mentees (see Chapters 6 and 12), marketing the programme to mentors, police checking and selection procedures such as interviews (see Chapter 11).
3. *Preparation of mentees and mentors*: includes briefings, induction and training (see Chapters 11 and 12).
4. *Matching*: may be a 'paper and pencil' exercise or a more sophisticated activity, for example involving residential experience for mentors and mentees (see Chapter 12).
5. *Mentoring meetings*: also involves ongoing support for mentors, monitoring of meetings and mentee achievements, and mentor supervision (see Chapter 12).
6. *Endings*: includes preparation for closure, celebratory events and possible future involvement of mentors and mentees (see Chapter 12).
7. *Evaluation and quality review*: includes gathering data on the outcomes of the project against its objectives, assessing the quality of the programme and how it can be improved (see Chapter 13).

PRE-PLANNING

The pre-planning process often involves the following tasks (RPS Rainer, 1999):

- recruiting programme staff or persuading teachers to take on the responsibility for mentoring;
- undertaking research on the rationale for a mentoring programme in the locality or institution;
- agreeing on the form of mentoring, objectives, outcomes and duration of the programme;
- fundraising or budgeting to ensure adequate levels of financial support for the programme;
- liaising and joint training with partner agencies (mentoring programme and schools or schools and voluntary groups/businesses providing mentors);
- making a commitment to a high-quality service by building in certain agreed national, state/regional or local quality standards into the mentoring programme;
- developing an evaluation strategy by which the programme's success can be measured and judged;
- creating a mentoring policy statement that includes equal opportunities, health and safety, insurance, child protection and confidentiality policies.

FIRST STEPS

The first issue to consider before setting up a new mentoring programme is whether it is the right solution to the problem that has been identified. There is a sense in which mentoring is regarded as the 'new panacea' for addressing many of the problems facing students and young people. In the United Kingdom there is a strong 'bandwagon effect', with schools being urged to set up mentoring schemes or to work with external mentoring agencies. The danger is that such schemes are poorly thought through and are 'bolted on' to the curriculum. The result is that the mentoring schemes have disappointing outcomes, because of a lack of commitment from the school and an absence of synergy with existing school strategies, policies and systems for pastoral care and academic standards.

Need for research

It is important to do some background research prior to accepting or

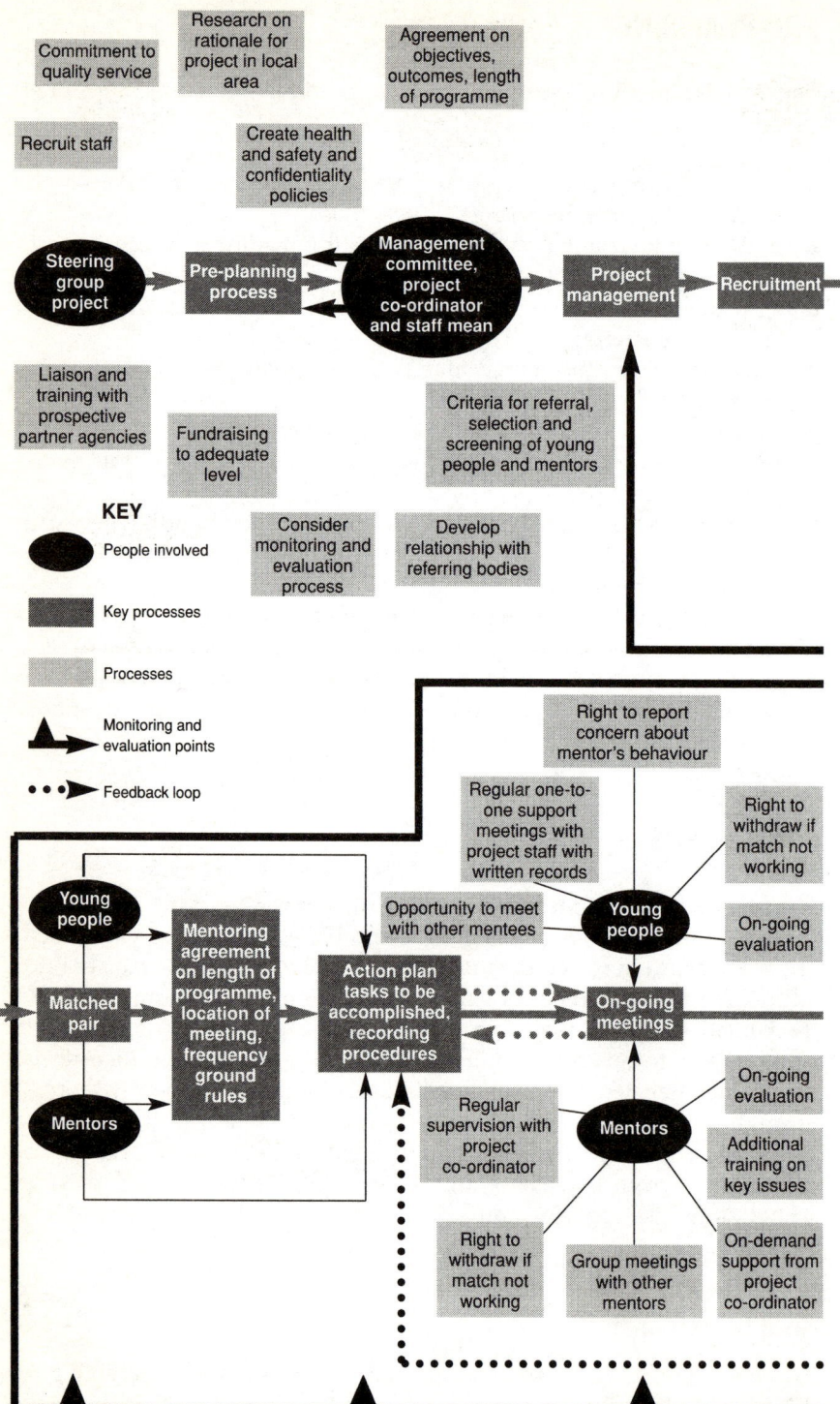

KEY

People involved

Key processes

Processes

Monitoring and evaluation points

Feedback loop

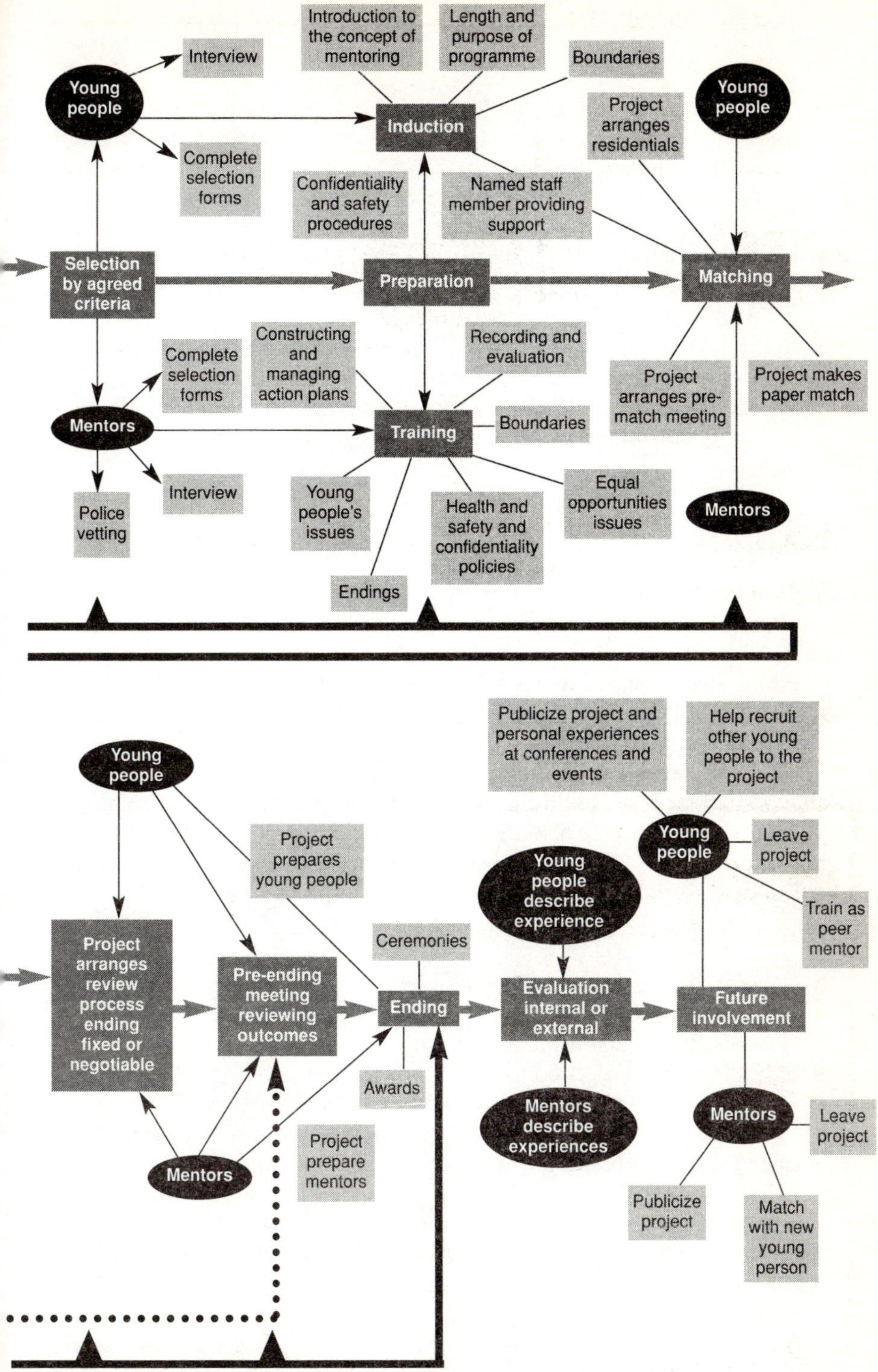

Figure 10.1 *Model mentoring programme*
(reproduced with permission of RPS Rainer)

establishing a mentoring programme. This research can take a number of forms:

- Desk research involves visiting appropriate Web sites to gather information about mentoring and the forms of mentoring under consideration (see the Web guide, pp 275–77). There are also publications setting out good practice, quality standards and the findings of national and local evaluations.
- Visits can be made to local mentoring schemes to discuss some of the issues involved in setting up a scheme and to see what help can be offered by mentoring organizations.
- It can help to join a mentoring networking organization, such as those that have been set up in the United States, Canada, Australia and the United Kingdom. Such networks offer guidance, helpful Web sites, training information and contacts to help establish the mentoring scheme.

Partnerships

It is most important to find out what programmes are being offered by voluntary sector organizations in your locality. Such organizations may share objectives with the school and may be looking for partners and clients to help them to deliver their own targets. A partnership between the school and a mentoring organization can help enormously in sharing the burden of setting up a new mentoring programme. Clearly, organizations already operating mentoring programmes across an area have valuable experience of building in successful practices when planning programmes. There are also likely to be economies of scale for the school in cutting the costs of mentor recruitment and training.

The case studies in Part II offer many examples of mentoring partnerships between:

- schools and businesses (Case Studies 3.1–3, 8.1);
- schools and voluntary organizations (Case Studies 4.1–3, 6.1–2, 7.2);
- schools and local education authorities (Case Studies 5.1–2, 7.1);
- schools and other schools (Case Studies 7.2–3);
- schools and universities (Case Studies 8.2–3, 9.1–2);
- complex partnerships between schools, universities, voluntary organizations; faith-based groups, local government and the private sector (Case Study 9.3).

As we have discussed, a major issue is whether mentoring is seen as a stand-alone initiative or is combined with a range of other strategies to tackle the problem. The GEAR UP Program in the United States was a good illustration of a long-term holistic approach to the problem of youth underachievement involving complex partnerships (see Chapter 9).

OBJECTIVES AND FORMS OF MENTORING

Mentoring is generally viewed as a possible solution to a particular set of problems facing young people. There is a range of other programmes that have similar objectives and represent alternative methods of achieving similar outcomes. However, there is an absence of research examining the relative effectiveness of mentoring and other forms of intervention. This book has outlined various forms of student mentoring that are open to schools and colleges. In Chapter 2, 11 objectives of mentoring programmes were identified and each chapter on the forms of mentoring contains a discussion of key aims and objectives. Guidance on setting up mentoring programmes often recommends involving a focus group of students drawn from the target group to discuss the proposed mentoring programme. This is in order to ensure that the programme takes their expressed needs into account.

Table 10.1 maps the main objectives against the main forms of student mentoring. This should enable schools, colleges and other organizations to select the forms that provide a 'best fit' with aims and objectives. Many mentoring programmes identify a long list of aims and objectives, while others tend to focus on one or two objectives (Miller, 1998). Clearly it is easier to evaluate the effectiveness of the programme when the number of objectives is limited. Table 10.1 aims to be illustrative rather than prescriptive. It is possible for most forms of mentoring to address most of the objectives, but the table shows the main objectives associated with each form as a general guide. Thus, for example, if the *learning skills* objective is paramount, then teacher or higher education student mentoring is probably most appropriate. The *employability* objective is most likely to be achieved through business mentoring or telementoring by people from business. *Self-esteem* and *motivational* objectives are associated with most forms of mentoring, although there is a need for more research to find which forms are most effective in achieving these goals.

MENTORING DOCUMENTATION

It is important when establishing a mentoring programme to develop a mentoring policy statement. Policy statements provide a rationale for the use of mentoring within a school or college. They include a statement of overall aims and specific objectives, and links can be made to related policies such as those for raising achievement, student retention, teaching-

Table 10.1 *The main objectives associated with the different forms of mentoring*

Objectives	Business	Inter-generational	Minority ethnic	At risk	Peer	Tele-mentoring	HE student
Self-esteem	●		●	●		●	
Personal-and-social skills	●	●		●			
Motivational	●		●				●
Maturational		●			●		
Attitudinal				●			
Behavioural				●			
Aspirational			●				●
Employability	●					●	
Vocational	●					●	
Academic		●		●	●	●	●
Learning skills						●	●

and-learning styles, business-and-community links, and student support. Such policy statements often also explain roles and responsibilities of mentoring coordinators and arrangements for management, which may involve steering groups and staff appraisal arrangements. When there is more than one mentoring scheme in the school or college, then the policy should explain the relationship between the various programmes.

Mentoring organizations working in partnership with educational institutions also produce a variety of other documents in support of their mentoring schemes. These can include:

- *Mentoring project handbooks*: these provide programme managers with guidance on the procedures and practices of the project (see, for example, Divert, 1999). Handbooks generally cover all aspects of the programme from identifying the target group to ending the mentoring relationship and evaluation. They also tend to include samples of all the forms used by the project.
- *Mentor training manuals*: these manuals are usually developed by long-running projects that undertake regular mentor training (see, for example, Jucovy, 2000b). They contain guidance for the trainer, materials for use with participants and course evaluation materials.
- *Mentor handbooks*: these handbooks are produced to accompany mentor training, but they also contain ideas for mentoring sessions and forms to be used, for example, in target setting with mentees (see, for example, National Mentoring Pilot Project, 2000).

INFORMATION FOR MENTORS

When would-be mentors are making decisions about whether or not to put themselves forward, there are several details about the programme that they need to know. MacCallum and Beltman (1999) note that information for mentors should include the following issues:

- the age and characteristics of the students in the programme;
- a description of the length, location, timing and duration of mentor training;
- the number of 'contact' hours per week or month and the suggested frequency and duration of meetings;
- the length of time mentors are expected to commit themselves to the programme;
- the boundaries between what can be discussed with students, and what should not;
- guidance on the relationship and communications with parents and carers;

- places where mentors and students can meet;
- guidance on the means by which mentors and mentees can communicate with each other;
- guidance on what to do if the relationship seems not to be working;
- information on how the mentoring relationship will be evaluated;
- details of any funding available for transport or other incidental costs;
- the skills required of mentors and the activities to be undertaken with students individually or as a group;
- who is in overall charge of the programme, who is the mentor's supervisor, and when and how the mentor reports to the supervisor;
- what to do if serious issues arise during mentoring;
- the person(s) that the mentor should consult if further guidance is needed during the relationship;
- guidance on the requirement for confidentiality and the ethics of being a mentor;
- information on accreditation available for mentors.

ROLES AND RESPONSIBILITIES

Many of the mentoring programmes described in this book involve a local project manager or programme coordinator working across institutions, and a school or college coordinator. This can be described as a 'centrally coordinated model'. This generally involves the programme manager or coordinator undertaking the following tasks (Golden and Sims, 1999):

- developing documentation;
- recruiting mentors;
- arranging police vetting of mentors;
- selecting and training mentors;
- matching mentors and mentees (with the school);
- liaising with schools and mentors;
- arranging supervision of mentors and support for school coordinators;
- monitoring, evaluating and reviewing the programme.

However, in the United Kingdom there is also evidence of a 'devolved model', where programme managers take on a more strategic role and pass on more of the responsibility for the operational tasks listed above to the school coordinators. Fundamental to the success of either approach is having someone with the time to devote to ongoing support for mentors and mentees.

Role of the school coordinator

The role of the school coordinator is crucial to the success of school-based mentoring programmes, whether in the centrally coordinated or the devolved model (Miller, 1998; Golden and Sims, 1999). There are several tasks, which the effective school coordinator typically undertakes (Golden and Sims, 1999):

- ensuring that the mentoring scheme fits in with other relevant school policies such as equal opportunities, raising achievement and inclusion;
- identifying the target group of students, selecting and briefing students in consultation with other staff;
- seeking parental permission and possible involvement;
- informing stakeholders about the programme;
- keeping senior staff and all other staff informed about the programme;
- establishing, collecting and recording monitoring data on students, and keeping the programme manager and others informed of student progress;
- progress chasing with mentees about their appointments, making sure rooms are available for meetings and following up missed meetings;
- welcoming mentors to the school and liaising with them;
- setting up in-school mentor and mentee review meetings and social events;
- providing support for mentees and dealing with any problems raised.

According to a study of 20 mentoring schemes in the United Kingdom, school coordinators spend between 15 minutes and 2.5 hours per week on their mentoring duties (Golden and Sims, 1999). School coordinators often have senior- or middle-management roles and the coordination of mentoring is generally added to an already busy workload. As Golden and Sims (1999; see also Sims *et al*, 2000) note, the main problems facing school coordinators are often very practical ones:

- recruiting mentors and ensuring their commitment and retention;
- timetabling mentoring meetings and finding out whether or not they have taken place;
- taking action when mentors or mentees have missed meetings;
- acting as an advocate for mentoring to sceptical colleagues who question whether 'undeserving' students should be rewarded with a mentor;
- coping with the unrealistic expectations of colleagues about the impact of mentoring on student behaviour and performance;

- dealing with issues raised by mentors who are unprepared for the problems presented by students from very different socio-economic or cultural backgrounds;
- responding to requests for mentors from students, or to the disappointment of students who could not be allocated a mentor;
- finding rooms for mentoring meetings in schools where space is often limited.

Service level agreements

There is scope for confusion if the roles of school and programme coordinators are not clearly defined. One helpful approach to building successful mentoring partnerships between schools and external mentoring organizations is the service level agreement. The service level agreement sets out what the mentoring programme and the school are committed to in order to make the programme effective. The agreement is signed by both parties and used as a basis for the regular review of the relationship (see Box 10.1).

Box 10.1 Mentoring service level agreement

The student mentoring programme makes the following commitment to the school to:

- recruit mentors and ensure that they complete application forms and are police checked;
- provide relevant training and support to mentors, for example on child protection, confidentiality and the role of mentors;
- facilitate mentor-student matching;
- work in partnership with the school in the selection of appropriate students by relevant means, including interviews;
- coordinate regular group meetings in line with school timetables and ensure that mentors and the school have a programme of events for the academic year;
- provide training, advice and updates on mentoring issues for school coordinators;
- inform the school with two days' notice when a mentor is unable to attend a meeting;
- provide feedback from mentors to the school;
- coordinate an effective evaluation of the scheme.

The school makes the following commitment to the mentoring programme to:

- appoint a school mentoring coordinator;

- ensure that the senior management team and wider staff are aware of, committed to and updated on the mentoring programme;
- work in partnership with the programme manager in briefing businesses/universities about the programme;
- identify students, brief them and collect application forms;
- complete a baseline assessment on each student at the start of the programme and a final assessment at its end;
- obtain parental/carers' consent for students to participate in the programme and attend out-of-school events;
- keep students informed about their mentoring meetings and inform the programme manager if students are unable to attend;
- ensure that mentors are made welcome in the school and invited to school events;
- ensure that the school coordinator attends mentoring group meetings, training sessions and conferences;
- assist in the evaluation and monitoring of the project;
- provide an end-of-programme report from a school perspective outlining successes and recommendations.

(Adapted with permission from Service Level Agreement, Education Business Section, London Borough of Hammersmith & Fulham)

RESOURCING

One of the main questions to be asked when setting up a new mentoring programme is how much it will cost. There is a tendency to underestimate the costs of mentoring programmes because in most cases the prime resource, the mentors' time, is given free of charge. After initial set-up costs, so runs this argument, mentoring pairs manage themselves and additional costs are modest. However, many programmes find that they have inadequate resources but are faced with the pressure to produce 'miraculous results' (Struchen and Porta, 1997). Resources are often used largely for marketing, recruitment and training and there are insufficient resources allocated to ongoing support, monitoring and evaluation (MacCallum and Beltman, 1999).

There are, however, considerable differences in costs involved in different mentoring programmes. Community-based programmes involving at-risk young people are probably the most heavy on resources, as standards of training, selection, support and monitoring have to be much higher (see Chapter 6). In contrast, relatively cheaper schemes would include academic mentoring by teachers, as this is seen as an evolution of the teacher's existing role, or peer mentoring. Peer mentoring schemes within institutions are less expensive than cross-institutional programmes. Business mentoring can also bring in additional resources in the form of company sponsorship to partially offset the costs.

Box 10.2 Student mentoring budget

£/$

Income

In-kind (staff time)
In-kind (mentors' time)
Public and voluntary grants
Fund raising schemes
Corporate donations and grants
Charges levied on participating institutions

Total income

Expenditure

Marketing and promotional materials
Design and printing of project handbooks and certificates
Project manager salary and on-costs
School coordinators' honoraria
Staff development
Mentor trainer's fees
Training venue
Police check charges
Insurance premium
Mentor travel expenses
Accreditation of mentors
Mentee travel expenses
Residential centre costs
Social events and outings
Telephone costs

Total expenditure

Mentoring programmes operating across institutions will have considerably greater resourcing needs than programmes set up and run by staff within an educational institution. In-kind contributions, which involve allocating a notional financial value to the time given by staff and volunteer mentors, often provide a form of matched funding to set against grant income from public sources. The usual funding opportunities are open to educational mentoring programmes, including fund-raising events, donations, and grants from the private sector. In the United Kingdom, central government has increased the levels of funding available to the voluntary sector to provide mentoring for young people, as well as supporting various national schemes (see Chapter 1). Mentoring programmes may make a charge 'per mentoring pair' for the service provided to schools to cover all or part of their costs.

Mentoring costs

The main costs involved in running mentoring programmes are those associated with staffing (see Box 10.2). Mentoring programmes, in common with many other educational programmes, are often subsidized by educational institutions and are seen as part of their normal business. The costs of teacher involvement are, therefore, frequently absorbed by the institution. As has been observed, however, school mentoring coordinators are more likely to be effective when they receive some allowance for undertaking the role and when they are allocated some time to carry out the role properly. Mentoring organizations operating in partnership with educational institutions find that staffing is the main cost. In order for the programme to appear professional there is a need to spend money on materials, which might include: a programme handbook, posters, marketing flyers, certificates, training materials, assessment materials, mentor handbooks and mentee handbooks. There is also a set of costs associated with police checking, and training and accreditation of mentors. There are costs incurred in providing activities for mentees, including travel expenses, residential costs and the costs of social events.

WHOLE-SCHOOL APPROACHES

It is easy for mentoring schemes that are organized by external agencies to be 'bolted on' to the curriculum of a school. Schools have become accustomed to working on a range of short-term, 'sunburst' initiatives that shine brightly for a while and fade rapidly when the funding dries up. External mentoring schemes can be 'bolted on' without being integrated into the main policies and strategies of the school. In these circumstances mentoring may be an initiative associated with one enthusiastic teacher or department working with the outside mentoring project. As the practice of mentoring spreads throughout educational institutions, it is important that programmes are managed and coordinated. A whole-school approach to mentoring can involve the development of a mentoring ethos or culture, which embraces mentoring as a key element in learning for staff, students and support staff. Table 10.2 shows four, non-sequential stages of development towards a mentoring culture. The case study of Pershore High School in Hereford and Worcester offers an example of a school that has a whole-school approach and is moving towards a mentoring culture.

Table 10.2 *Typology of mentoring development in a school*

Type of programme	Description of school-based mentoring programmes
1. School-managed single programme	The school has set up its own external or internal mentoring programme for a limited number of students. The school mentoring coordinator manages the programme in its entirety.
2. Mentoring programme/ school partnership programme	The school has a partnership with an external mentoring programme that coordinates mentoring schemes in schools. The school coordinator links with the local programme manager, who manages recruitment and training of mentors.
3. Uncoordinated multiple mentoring programmes	The school has two or more mentoring programmes run by different departments, but these are uncoordinated. Mentoring schemes have grown incrementally, focusing on different aims and objectives and different year groups. There may be a number of school coordinators and links with local programme coordinators.
4. Mentoring culture coordinated, multiple mentoring	The school has embraced a mentoring culture. Staff are involved in mentoring other staff, senior staff may have external mentors. There is a variety of peer, business and community and higher education student mentoring programmes with individual coordinators reporting to a member of the senior management team.

Case Study 10.1 Pershore High School: towards a whole-school approach (UK)

Pershore High School is an example of a school that is developing a whole-school mentoring culture with coordinated multiple mentoring programmes. It is an 11–18 comprehensive of 1,050 pupils with a sixth form of some 250 students, and is located in rural Worcestershire. The GCSE results were 52 per cent A–Cs in 2000, which was a small improvement on 1999. The last OFSTED Report was in September 1999 and the school received a special commendation, the gold star, as one of 281 outstanding schools inspected out of 4,700 inspected during the year.

Multiple programmes

The forms of mentoring used in the school included: teacher mentoring, business mentoring, peer mentoring (sixth form mentors to Y10 mentees), peer counselling/mentoring by Y11 students of younger students, senior teacher mentoring of newly qualified teachers, and mentoring for all new members of staff (including support staff). Mentoring programmes have grown in their range and size over the past few years. During 1997–98, 30 students had academic mentors and this grew to 35 in the following year, and to 50 young people involving 16 teachers in 2000–01. Some 12 of these were Y13 students who were in need of additional support from teachers. The head teacher had also acted as a mentor to students. There were 22 pupils with industrial mentors in 1997–98, which expanded to 32 in the following year. In 2000–01 there were 20 business mentors working with 44 mentees. Mentor retention was good with external mentors staying on average 3–4 years with the programme. Y12 students were able to choose peer mentoring of Y8 students as an option within the community service enrichment module in the sixth form. There were six Y11 mentors in the current year. The peer counselling scheme involved twelve Y11 counsellors with a drop-in service and appointments system.

Management

Mentoring programmes were well managed and there was strong support from the senior management team for the programmes. The roles and responsibilities of key staff were set out in the mentoring policy document. The mentoring policy was complemented by related school policies, notably on teaching and learning, pastoral care, staff development, equal opportunities and the home-school agreement. The policy statement set out how mentoring fitted in with the overall ethos of the school. The aims of mentoring in the school were to:

- provide guidance to all mentees so that they feel better supported during their time at Pershore High School;
- help students to maintain high standards of behaviour, attendance and commitment to their school work so that they are given every opportunity to reach their full potential; it is hoped that involvement in the programme will help to combat disaffection and reduce the likelihood of exclusion;
- help staff to better understand their roles and responsibilities, and their contribution to the school's ongoing development;
- fully involve business people, community members, parents and governors in the work of the school and the achievements of its students.

The mentoring policy document clarified the roles and responsibilities of each mentoring coordinator. For example, the deputy head teacher's role was to coordinate all programmes, and to review and appraise the work of the individual mentoring coordinators. He took an active role in promoting the mentoring schemes, for example through annual presentation evenings. Scheme coordinators were appointed for business mentoring, Post-Graduate Certificate in Education (Initial Teacher Training) mentoring and staff/academic mentoring. Staff commitment was built, in part, through the experience of having a mentor on joining the school as a newly qualified teacher or new member of staff. This programme developed from the school's work on Investors in People, an award achieved in 1997.

Links to school development plan

Mentoring was integrated into the school's management systems. The school development plan for 1998–99 included the objective to 'improve mentoring system by recruiting more business/teacher mentors and to use Y12 mentors for Y8 pupils'. The 1999–2000 development plan identified peer/sixth-form mentoring as a priority for development. Academic mentoring formed part of the school's Raising Achievement Policy. A staff-development workshop was held on mentoring covering benefits, expectations, good practice, listening skills, identifying their interests, overcoming barriers to communication and monitoring.

(Adapted from Miller, 2001)

LEADERSHIP AND MANAGEMENT OF STAFF

It has been argued that any mentoring programme that lacks good leadership and coordination will fail (Lauland, 1998). Successful mentoring programmes are likely to have leaders who exhibit some of the following attributes. They:

- have the respect of the community and an established base of support;
- understand the issues involved in dealing with schools, voluntary sector organizations, businesses and local government;
- are sensitive to the problems facing the target group;
- have excellent organizational and coordinating skills;
- have access to the leaders in partners' organizations;
- have the authority to commit resources and make decisions on behalf of the project.

Leadership is also an important factor in the success of student mentoring programmes in schools. Miller (1999a) outlines how senior managers in schools can show leadership in the mentoring programmes by:

- modelling the mentoring philosophy by becoming mentors themselves to staff and students;
- offering visible and active support in promoting the scheme to students, parents, governors and potential mentors from the community;
- taking an active role in building partnerships with businesses and other organizations that can provide mentors;

- recognizing and celebrating the successes and achievements of staff, students and mentors;
- making sure that other staff fully support the mentoring coordinator(s);
- focusing on continuous improvement and the development of the programme(s) over time;
- advocating and supporting the development of a mentoring culture to students and staff.

Schools and colleges that have external mentoring programmes often find it valuable to form an advisory or steering group. This provides a forum for interested parties to review policy and practice, and to ensure accountability for programme expenditure and decisions made by the coordinators. Steering groups might also commission external evaluators to report on the programme. They provide a forum for schools and their partners to share decision making and ownership of the mentoring programme.

Senior managers in several of the case study schools, in particular at Deptford Green School (Case Study 3.1), South Wigston School (Case Study 7.3) and Pershore High School (Case Study 10.1) demonstrated these leadership qualities. A further dimension of the leadership role is the management of school mentoring coordinators. It is important that they are encouraged to develop their knowledge and skills through training and visits to 'beacon' mentoring programmes. There should also be regular performance reviews as part of the general management of staff, where senior staff can identify issues that need to be addressed with the coordinator.

PLANNING AND MANAGING A MENTORING PROGRAMME FOR YOUNG PEOPLE

Successful mentoring programmes, those that achieve their aims and objectives, are likely to be those that are well planned and efficiently managed. In this chapter we have set out some of the parameters and considerations that need to be borne in mind when establishing mentoring programmes for young people. These are generic observations that apply to most programmes and the specific good practice points associated with each of the separate forms also need to be taken into account.

Planning

- Use a model of the mentoring programme processes (such as that produced by RPS Rainer) to help in scoping the task.

- Identify the pre-planning tasks that need to be conducted.
- Consider whether mentoring is the 'right' solution to the problem that has been identified.
- Undertake background research, use the World Wide Web (see the Web guide at the end of the book) and visit local 'beacon schemes'.
- Join a mentoring network organization for further advice and support.
- Build relationships with appropriate partners who are able to supply resources or mentors.
- Consult widely on the aims and objectives of the mentoring programme and involve young people from the target group in these discussions.
- Try to limit and prioritize the aims and objectives of the programme.
- Reflect which form or forms of mentoring are likely to be most effective in achieving the aims of the programme.

Managing

- Develop a mentoring policy statement setting out the rationale for the programme, and its aims and objectives.
- In educational institutions, develop a vision for the development and role of mentoring in the school.
- In educational institutions, ensure that links are made to related policies, such as those on equal opportunities, community links or inclusion.
- Ensure that the policy or programme handbook spells out the roles and responsibilities of everyone concerned with the programme.
- Develop information for mentors that will help them make considered judgements about whether your scheme is for them.
- Ensure that mentoring and school coordinators are allocated sufficient time to undertake their tasks properly in support of the scheme.
- Develop service level or partnership agreements for cross-institutional programmes and where mentoring organizations are working in partnership with schools.
- Identify all the resources required by the programme and calculate the costs involved.
- Secure funding, ideally from a range of sources, and produce a project budget.
- Ensure that someone is taking the identifiable lead in the development of the mentoring programme.
- In educational institutions, make sure that individual mentoring coordinators are regularly managed and appraised by their line managers, and that they have an opportunity to share regularly problems and solutions.

FUTURE TRENDS

There are several positive predictions that we can offer about the development of mentoring for students and young people over the next few years. The number of people with experience in managing mentoring programmes will increase and a new profession of mentoring manager will develop. There will be increasing amounts of guidance for people setting up and managing mentoring programmes. There will be a growth in partnership approaches to mentoring between voluntary organizations and schools. Schools will have a greater understanding of the resource implications of offering mentoring programmes, and funding for school coordination will become more commonplace. An increasing number of schools will develop multiple mentoring programmes and will view the mentoring culture as part of their appeal to parents.

11

Focus on mentors

INTRODUCTION

In this chapter the focus is on all aspects of mentors, from aims to accreditation. Inevitably this involves a discussion about the generic role of mentor and generalizing about different elements of mentoring programmes. The chapters on the forms of mentoring give further good practice advice on handling mentors. We begin with a review of the characteristics of the 'good' or 'effective' mentor, which involves listing the attributes and skills of mentoring. A related issue is the link between mentoring and emotional intelligence. Then we raise the question of why people might choose to become mentors and what objectives mentors might achieve through their involvement. This is followed by a review of a series of the key processes shared by organizations in setting up and running the majority of mentoring programmes: mentor recruitment, screening, induction, training and ongoing support. The issue of how mentors can be accredited for their work with students is raised. We conclude with a summary of good practice points and speculation about possible future trends.

MENTOR AIMS

Why do people volunteer to become mentors? There are many reasons why people respond to the call to become mentoring volunteers. Many of these will be linked to their personal and family histories. In Chapter 1 we saw how the origins of mentoring in the last century were philanthropic or linked to the youth-justice system. There is often a strong altruistic motivation on the part of many volunteers coupled with a desire to help the less fortunate. However, this is far from the whole picture.

Far from purely 'doing good', today's volunteers are also building up their own skills, improving services, sticking up for consumers, and challenging the way things are done....Volunteering is one of the best expressions of active citizenship. It is a powerful measure of the health of civic society.

(Levy, in foreword to Mensah-Coker, 2000: 2)

Box 11.1 summarizes possible aims for mentors when volunteering to work with students.

Box 11.1 Possible aims for mentors

Personal development

1. *Self-worth*: to improve their own self-esteem and self-worth through the positive feelings that mentoring can engender.
2. *Interpersonal skills*: to develop their interpersonal and mentoring skills.
3. *Inclusion*: to increase their feelings of inclusion through the relationships developed in the programme.
4. *Citizenship*: to make a visible and tangible contribution to their own community.
5. *Emotional intelligence*: to develop emotional intelligence through mentor training and the mentoring relationship.

Work-related

6. *Professional*: to raise students' sights and broaden horizons towards furthering their education or career in a similar area of work as the mentor.
7. *Employability*: to develop knowledge, skills and personal qualities that are valued by employers, such as reliability, honesty and motivation.

Academic

8. *Academic*: to reinforce their subject knowledge and skills through being involved in a mentoring, tutoring or teaching role.

MENTOR CHARACTERISTICS

Mentoring manuals and Web sites frequently devote attention to listing the characteristics of people who are likely to make 'good' mentors. This is in order to enable would-be mentors to make a judgement about whether they possess the necessary qualities when making the decision to volunteer. It also gives mentoring coordinators some criteria by which to judge the people presenting themselves as mentors during the

Table 11.1 *Ten attributes of 'good' mentors*

Ten attributes of 'good' mentors	Rationale
1. Enthusiastic volunteer	Their interest in helping the mentee and setting personal gains aside communicates itself.
2. Accessibility	Mentees should be able to contact mentors easily, but within defined, agreed limits.
3. Sensitivity	Mentors need to be aware of and sensitive to cultural and gender differences.
4. Self-awareness	Mentors need to know their own weaknesses and values, and to be honest about them. They should be able to share values without imposing them.
5. Discretion	Confidentiality is the key to building trust in the relationship.
6. Willingness to learn	Mentoring should be a mutual learning experience, not purely one way.
7. Non-judgemental	Mentors should try to use positive reinforcement and encouraging behaviours.
8. Patience	Patience is especially important in the early stages of relationship building
9. Positive expectations	Mentors should have high or positive aspirations for their mentees.
10. Kind, tolerant and understanding	These are important qualities in sustaining the relationship during inevitable highs and lows.

screening process. Table 11.1 shows desirable attributes of 'good mentors' drawn from the operational literature, together with a rationale about why each attribute is deemed to be important.

A review of the literature suggests a wide range of other characteristics that ideal mentors might possess (see for example, Dondero, 1997; Farmer, 1999; Songsthagen and Lee, 1996; Withers and Batten, 1995; Golden and Sims, 1999), such as the capacity to:

- see the mentee as a special individual and be comfortable with cultural or socio-economic 'distance';
- set high standards and be able to instil confidence to aim high;
- respect the mentee's ability and right to make his or her own decisions;
- empathize with and understand the mentee's struggle;
- see solutions not just problems;
- be flexible and open;
- be able to accept and link to other values, cultures and viewpoints;
- share resources, experience and knowledge;
- show interest, mutual respect and affection;
- show enthusiasm for particular subjects, interest areas and moral issues.

Mentor roles

An alternative way of looking at what makes for effective mentors is to consider the roles that mentors are asked to fulfil. Table 11.2 illustrates various roles for mentors, and would-be mentors can reflect on their effectiveness in each of these roles. The table shows the kinds of behaviours and activities associated with each role. Mentoring programmes do not generally require all these roles to be played. Some are specific to particular types of programme; for example, the role of advocate is often associated with youth-justice mentoring.

Mentor behaviours

One useful way of defining mentor behaviours is to identify behaviours that mentors should always, sometimes or never use (Clutterbuck, 1998). Mentors should:

- *Always*: listen with empathy; share experience; form a mutual learning friendship; develop insight through reflection; be a sounding board; and encourage.
- *Sometimes*: use coaching behaviours; use counselling behaviours; challenge assumptions; be a role model; open doors or sponsor.
- *Never*: discipline; condemn; appraise formally; assess for a third party; supervise.

MENTORS AND EMOTIONAL INTELLIGENCE

Emotional intelligence (EI) is 'the capacity for recognizing our own feelings and those of others, for motivating ourselves, for managing emotions well in ourselves and in our relationships' (Goleman, 1990). EI has been popularized in the United States and United Kingdom through the work of Daniel Goleman (1995), which was based on earlier work by Mayer and Salovey (1997), who put forward a four-part model:

Table 11.2 *Roles of mentors*

Roles of mentors	Associated mentor behaviours
1. Teacher or tutor	Helping with homework, coursework, projects. Supporting basic skills practice. Reinforcing concepts and subject understanding.
2. Coach	Helping to demonstrate skills. Offering feedback on mentee's use of skills. Arranging work experience/internship to develop employability.
3. Befriender	Listening and talking. Helping work through problems. Attending social gatherings and student activities. Meeting family and friends.
4. Counsellor	Listening, asking questions, confronting, supporting and probing.
5. Information source	Providing information and investigating solutions on behalf of mentee.
6. Nurturer	Acting as a sounding board. Giving encouragement and support. Listening to frustrations.
7. Adviser	Drawing on their own experience to identify possible courses of action. Asking catalytic questions.
8. Networker	Linking the mentee to wider networks of associates and acquaintances who can offer further help.
9. Advocate	Representing and accompanying the mentee in appropriate situations.
10. Role model	Sharing and discussing own values. Discussing own experiences and the lessons drawn from them.

- *Perceiving and recognizing emotions*: to recognize how you and others around you are feeling.
- *Assimilating and using emotions*: the ability to generate emotion and to reason using this emotion.
- *Understanding emotions*: the ability to understand complex emotions and emotional 'chains', or how emotions follow transitions from one stage to another.
- *Managing emotions*: the ability to manage emotions in yourself and others.

Hay McBer model

The approach to EI most associated with Daniel Goleman (1995) is the so-called Hay McBer model, which divides EI into personal competence, or how we manage ourselves, and social competence, or how we manage relationships (see Figure 11.1). Personal competence is subdivided into self-awareness and self-management, and social competence is subdivided into social awareness and social skills. EI is of growing interest to employers as the model suggests that self-management and social skills flow out of social awareness and self-awareness. In other words people who demonstrate a lack of social or self-awareness in interviews or assessment centres are likely to have relatively poor social and self-management skills. These are key features of employability, but they are also highly relevant to mentoring. The most effective mentors are likely to be those with strong EI, and poor self-awareness could be used as a criterion for screening out would-be mentors at an early stage.

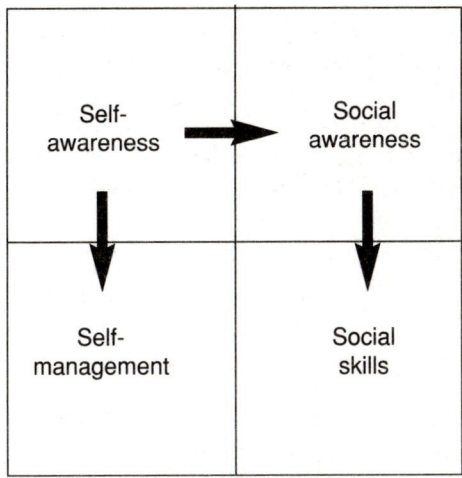

Figure 11.1 *A model of emotional intelligence*

The various elements of the Hay McBer model of EI are as follows:

- Self-awareness includes:
  - emotional self-awareness: recognizing one's emotions and their effects;
  - accurate self-assessment: knowing one's strengths and limitations;
  - self-confidence: a strong sense of one's own worth and capabilities.
- Self-management includes:
  - self-control: keeping disruptive emotions and impulses under control;
  - adaptability: flexibility in adapting to changing situations or barriers;
  - conscientiousness: demonstrating the capacity to manage oneself;
  - trustworthiness: showing integrity, consistent behaviour and maintaining confidentiality;
  - initiative: the readiness to act;
  - achievement orientation: the drive to reach high standards set by oneself.
- Social awareness includes:
  - empathy: understanding others and taking an active interest in their concerns;
  - service orientation: meeting the needs of other people;
  - organizational awareness: empathy at an organizational level.
- Social skills include:
  - leadership: inspiring and guiding individuals and groups;
  - influence: being able to use interpersonal influencing skills;
  - developing others: sensing others' development needs and progressing their abilities;
  - change catalyst: being able to initiate and manage change;
  - communication: sending clear and convincing messages.

Mentoring offers opportunities for mentors to develop their own EI and this can be used as a selling point in recruitment. Mentors can also develop the EI of their mentees through the mentoring process. This can also be seen as a contribution to improving the mentee's employability, as EI is viewed as a desirable set of traits for future employees.

RECRUITMENT

This section addresses the issue of recruitment of external mentors from the local community, whether they are business people, senior citizens, students or other members of the community. In making a decision to volunteer there are usually two steps in the process (Jucovy, 2001a).

People think generally about becoming volunteers and then a 'trigger event' propels them into a particular course of action. This hypothesis suggests that it is important in recruiting mentors to create local awareness of the programme, so that people recognize its name and purpose. Then it is vital to target recruitment at those who are ready to volunteer and have an awareness of and interest in the programme.

Recruitment plans

Mentoring manuals recommend the creation of a recruitment plan. Jucovy (2001a) suggests that programme organizers:

- Record the number of mentors they hope to recruit and the deadlines for recruiting them.
- Plan the timeframe for scheduled activities from the start of the recruitment campaign to the beginning of the mentoring programme.
- Plot staff responsibilities for each activity on a time chart.
- Identify the resource needs in terms of budget and staff time needed to implement the plan.
- Define eligibility criteria for mentors and their preference for the type of mentor the campaign aims to attract.
- Identify what factors would attract mentors to join the programme.
- Develop a mentor job description and person specification.
- Create a clear recruitment message and develop materials that have diverse appeal.
- Create a presentation to use in speaking to community groups.
- Decide on the recruitment strategies they will use.
- Identify and build links with organizations that can give them access to potential mentors.

In general there is a shortage of mentors compared with the number of students who would benefit from a programme. This often means that there is a waiting list or a number of disappointed students. There is also a particular shortage of male mentors. This is a general problem, but it tends to be less acute in business mentoring where there is a partnership between a school and a large company, or in higher education or college programmes linked to schools (MacCallum and Beltman, 1999).

'Word of mouth' recruitment

The main issue for mentor coordinators is whether or not there is a budget for recruitment, as this will constrain the range of techniques used. The fact that many programmes have little or no budget probably explains the popularity of 'word of mouth' as a means of recruiting mentors. In a UK study, mentoring coordinators reported that the best means of recruiting mentors was through a personal, 'word of mouth' approach (Golden and Sims, 1999). The risk of this approach is that it can exclude certain groups of people who are not part of the current networks. Minority ethnic programmes have recognized the importance of employing minority ethnic members of staff to facilitate recruitment. This point has been reinforced by American research (see Chapter 5)

Community mapping

A wide range of techniques has been used to recruit mentors. However, it is important for mentoring coordinators to think about what their needs are in terms of the number and profile of mentors. A key feature of many programmes is community mapping, that is, identifying the resources in the community that might provide a source of mentors. Potential mentors can be sought through:

- local education-business partnerships or chambers of commerce;
- local volunteer bureaux;
- local colleges and universities;
- community organizations, including those for senior citizens and minorities;
- trade unions and teachers' unions (to recruit retired teachers);
- parents, governors, support staff and teachers using their own networks;
- older current students and former students.

Barriers to volunteering

It is helpful to think through any particular barriers facing groups of people targeted by the recruitment campaign (Jucovy, 2001a). For example, college students face a number of concerns that reduce the time available for mentoring; these include the long vacations, the need to undertake part-time work and examination periods (see Chapter 9). Transport costs, and other incidental costs associated with mentoring, and the difficulties of travelling to schools may act as further barriers. This means that college students are more likely to volunteer for programmes that: limit the mentoring period within the academic year; have set times for meetings in one location, usually the school; provide ongoing support and structure; and offer additional incentives, such as course credits for participation. Older adults also may have particular barriers which deter them from volunteering as mentors including: fear about safety; a lack of self-confidence in their abilities as mentors; transport and mobility problems; and financial concerns about incidental costs of mentoring (see Chapter 4). Thus when targeting this group, programme managers need to stress that meetings will take place in a safe location that volunteers can reach easily, that training will help develop their confidence and ongoing support will help them cope with any problems that arise.

Recruitment campaigns

A steering group can be helpful for promoting the mentoring scheme across a number of networks. In some cities there are arrangements for coordinating recruitment across a city through campaigns and advertising toll-free numbers for signposting mentors to particular programmes. For example, the city of Chicago ran a tutor and mentor recruitment campaign over a number of weeks in 1998. This included a celebrity manifesto letter signed by the Mayor, leading actors and sports figures, and a series of 20 volunteer recruitment fairs. Altogether 87 mentoring programmes were involved in the campaign, which generated a lot of media coverage and enquiries from the public. A different approach is the so-called Mentor Point initiative in England, which aims to provide a one-stop-shop approach to recruitment across an area (see Chapter 1 and below).

Marketing literature

Most mentoring programmes develop a flyer or leaflet to attract mentors to the scheme by providing background information, key messages about mentoring and contact information. It is important to think through the features of the programme that might appeal to potential mentors, such as the opportunity for free training and accreditation, the structured nature of the programme, the chance to make a difference or the limited time commitment required. It is important to avoid the use of jargon and to use simple language that can be understood by a wide range of people. Some programmes have developed a catchy 'strapline', which will help communicate the message. Leaflets often include photographs of mentors and mentees. It is important that photographs are chosen with care to include as wide a range of mentors as possible, and that images of students reflect the diversity of the school community.

There is a wide range of places where recruitment leaflets can be left or posted on noticeboards:

- supermarkets;
- libraries;
- doctors' waiting rooms;
- day-care centres;
- colleges and university campuses, including halls of residence;

- community centres;
- places of worship;
- emergency services buildings;
- local authority buildings;
- shop windows;
- gyms and sports centres;
- canteens of large companies.

Diverse recruitment methods

Other methods that are used by mentoring programmes to recruit mentors include:

- *Press releases*: local newspapers are often looking for copy and mentoring is a 'good news' story.
- *A Web site* can be attached to the main school or college Web site and should allow potential mentors to register their interest and complete an application form.
- A mentoring *'open day'* can be held to publicize the programme when the head teacher, and other senior staff from partner organizations, are available to launch and discuss the mentoring scheme.
- *Partners*: programmes can contact people who are involved in other partnerships with the school, such as employers offering work experience or internships.
- *Advertisements* can be placed in the local press, radio or cable TV station.
- *Mentoring breakfasts*: these events can include short presentations about the mentoring programme.
- *Social gatherings*: existing mentors can be invited to bring a friend along to social events involving mentors and mentees.
- *Careers fairs and industry days*: these kinds of events attract employers who can be approached about becoming champions of mentoring in their businesses.
- *Empty shops*: put a display in an empty shop window in the town centre, working through the town centre manager.
- *Videos*: some schools have produced videos about the programme that can be lent out for viewing by individuals and community groups.

It is especially important that there is good 'customer service' for people who make an enquiry. This means that they should be able to telephone or e-mail and receive a swift response from someone who can answer their immediate questions and explain the next stages in the process. Mentoring projects also need to develop information packs that can be given out to prospective mentors; these should include the flyer, a job description and person specification.

MENTOR POINT

The proliferation of mentoring programmes targeted at young people has prompted attempts to coordinate the recruitment and training of mentors. The existence of a large number of voluntary-sector and institutional mentoring programmes in an urban area means potential competition between projects for a finite supply of adult mentors. When many of the projects are publicly funded, this raises the issue of waste of resources and highlights the need for 'joined up' solutions. One such approach in England is the Mentor Point Initiative (NMN, Summer 2000). The idea of Mentor Point is to act as a 'one-stop shop' to recruit, train and support volunteers and to put them in touch with organizations requiring mentors (O'Donnell *et al*, 2001).

The objectives of Mentor Point as defined by the Department for Education and Employment were to:

- bring coherence to mentoring for young people across the locality;
- work in partnership with existing programmes and to support new ones;
- recruit, train and support new and existing volunteers;
- raise the profile and awareness of mentoring;
- employ and promote quality standards in the delivery of mentoring programmes;
- link with learning mentors and the Connexions Service personal advisers.

Problems

In principle, Mentor Point is a sensible idea to reduce costs and to coordinate mentor recruitment and training. However, there are several difficulties that need to be resolved. First, Mentor Point is a partnership of different organizations, and relations can be awkward when partners have differing priorities. Second, there are often different philosophies of mentoring between schemes, and these have to be reflected in the recruitment and training strategies. Third, there is a tension between the offer of a general, generic service and the specific, targeted programmes of certain mentoring providers. Fourth, Mentor Point can bring to the surface competition between mentoring providers. A national evaluation is being undertaken that will shed light on whether Mentor Point is the way forward for mentor recruitment and training in the United Kingdom.

SELECTION

Clearly, not everyone volunteering to become a mentor will be suitable for the type of student targeted by the programme. 'Screening' refers to the processes that projects use to select some mentors and to reject others. It is good practice for projects to draw up a screening policy, as police checks alone do not guarantee that all undesirable characters will be screened out. Guidance is available in the United Kingdom on screening volunteers to ensure the safety of children (Smith, 1993; National Centre for Volunteering, 1997). Police checks were proposed in the United Kingdom in 1984 following the case of a male volunteer with a history of offences against children who murdered a four-year-old child. Projects differ in the length and number of screening processes used. Community-based programmes working with vulnerable young people are likely to have the most rigorous screening, whereas school-based programmes where teachers supervise mentors closely may have less strict procedures (see Case Studies 6.1 and 6.2). Peer mentoring within educational institutions does not need elaborate screening procedures, as mentors are known individuals. However, teachers will generally supervise peer mentor meetings taking place in school.

Stages of screening

There are several stages in screening and the following points are noted in the operational literature:

- *Application forms*: mentor-briefing packs usually contain an application form that provides basic details. It is helpful if projects consider the criteria they might be looking for in selecting or screening out mentors and put these on the application form or supporting literature. Potential mentors should be informed of factors that will preclude their involvement as a mentor. They should be asked to give their reasons for wanting to become a mentor, which should not be entirely self-interested.
- *Initial briefing*: many programmes invite interested mentors to attend a briefing session to hear more about the programme and to ask questions. This offers an opportunity to identify those mentors who are heavily committed and unlikely to be able to invest the necessary time commitment to their mentees. Mentors who miss appointments are a key factor limiting the effectiveness of many programmes.
- *References*: application forms generally ask for a minimum of two references, which should then be checked.
- *Proof of identification*: volunteers can be asked to supply a minimum of two pieces of evidence as a means of identification.

- *Police checks*: these should be carried out and can be made locally or nationally. Local police check processes vary between local authorities and the cost also varies from £10 to £40 per check. When working with children all convictions, cautions and bind-overs must be declared. From 2002 the Criminal Records Bureau will be able to conduct criminal record checks and the fee will be reduced or eliminated depending on the level of check required. In the United States, state checks are carried out and in some cases these are backed up by federal checks.
- *Interviews*: some projects insist on interviews for all mentors, to allow further probing questions to be asked. An interview guide will need to be produced to support staff and to ensure good equal-opportunities practice.
- *Training*: some projects use successful completion of the training programme as a final way of screening mentors.

'Red flags'

Some schemes use the training programme as a means of screening out unsuitable mentors by watching for 'warning signs' (see, for example, Divert 1999) such as:

- dogmatic personalities;
- those showing intolerance, aggression or negative stereotyping;
- people using the mentoring as a vehicle for pursuing another agenda;
- people who are unable to demonstrate mentoring skills, for example displaying an inability to listen, lack of empathy or poor self-awareness.

A final aspect of screening concerns what is sometimes referred to as 'intuition' or 'gut feelings'; in other words, in spite of everything appearing safe and secure something seems 'not quite right' with a would-be mentor (Graff, 1999). These feelings of uneasiness are not in themselves sufficient reason to exclude someone, but they are an indication that further investigations should be undertaken. This might involve obtaining a second opinion, rechecking a reference, asking for an additional interview or requesting a probationary period. It is important to err on the side of caution, but also to be able to defend the position taken, if accused of being discriminatory.

TRAINING

There are wide variations in the amount of training required in different mentoring programmes for students and young people. It is generally the case that business mentors have shorter training sessions than community mentors (Miller, 1998). A balance has to be struck between the level of training that is desirable and that which is realistic, given the time mentors have to give and the resources a programme has to fund the training. Table 11.3 sets out the kinds of content that are covered in mentoring training and some of the training processes that are used. There are generally three main aims of mentor training (Golden and Sims, 1999):

- to explain the objectives and context of the mentoring programme, and to outline the needs of the students involved;
- to establish the ground rules and procedures followed by the mentoring programme;
- to develop the skills of mentoring.

There are clearly a large number of things that could be covered within a mentor training session. Some mentor training is linked to accreditation programmes and the training therefore tends to be more rigorous. The most extensive training tends to be associated with preparation for mentoring with young people at risk of social exclusion (see Case Studies 6.1 and 6.2) or for holistic mentors (see Case Study 1.2). Training sessions are often broken down into an initial induction session that introduces the objectives, the context of the programme and the requirements of mentors, for example having to undergo a police check. Volunteers then have an opportunity to reconsider their involvement before engaging in the full training programme. Rather than an 'overkill' amount of training at the outset, some programme managers prefer to offer ongoing 'top-up' training during the course of the programme as and when particular training needs arise. It is also useful to put a lot of the factual information and guidance in the mentor handbook, which can be used within the training session but also provides a source of further support during the programme (see Chapter 10).

Training styles

The style of training is important; as mentoring is essentially about one-to-one interaction, training should reflect this by being informal and interactive (Miller, 1998). Other commentators make various suggestions about the processes of training mentors (Lauland, 1998):

- Experienced, enthusiastic mentors make excellent trainers.
- A mentor panel can share their experiences.
- A variety of methods can help maintain interest including: role play, case studies, witness sessions, video, teamwork exercises, and 'what if' discussion exercises.

Table 11.3 *Mentor training topics and processes*

Content of mentor training	Possible training processes
Aims of the programme and needs of the students:	
Programme aims and objectives	Input on aims, objectives and outcomes. Witness sessions from current or former mentors and mentees describing outcomes and benefits for them.
Role of mentor: characteristics of effective mentors	Brainstorm: what is a good mentor? Reflection: mentors we have had and their special qualities. What do people expect of mentors? What do mentors expect of mentees? What does the programme expect of mentors?
Accreditation	Input on opportunities for accreditation of mentors.
Characteristics of the target group	Discussion of anonymized case studies of students.
Stages of child development	Input on development needs of children and young people.
Background on the school/college, the school year, examination system	Input from senior member of staff.
Issues facing young people	Input and discussion on social exclusion – drug abuse, child abuse, teen pregnancy, school exclusion, alcohol abuse. Films, plays and photographs.
Programme ground rules and procedures:	
Child protection	Input on child protection procedures. Input on police check requirements.
Contracting	How to make a mentoring agreement with the mentee. Role play on forming a mentoring contract. Discuss examples of written mentoring agreements.

Boundaries	Case studies to examine the limits to the role of mentor; 'what if' examples. Referral agencies and individuals.
Cultural sensitivity and diversity	Input and discussion on ethnic, socio-economic and cultural diversity.
Involving parents	Policy on parental links. Case study examples.
Developing mentor skills:	
Stages of the mentoring relationship	Suggestions on how to build the relationship. Lists of possible activities. Advice on endings and closure.
Values	Reflection on values. Role play on sharing and discussing values.
Emotional intelligence	Self-review exercises. Discussion of strengths and weaknesses.
Listening skills	Exercises in active listening – listening, summarizing and feeding back. Rules for active listening and how to kill a conversation.
Non-verbal communication	Role play, video and feedback. Modelling non-verbal messages.
Questioning skills	Taxonomies of questions. Role plays in using catalytic, open-ended and other question types.
Giving and receiving feedback	Rules for giving and receiving feedback. Fishbowl role play and discussion. Two-person role plays plus observer.
Action planning and goal setting	Action planning/goal setting pro formas. Discussion of examples of appropriate and inappropriate goals. Setting SMART targets: specific, measurable, achievable, realistic, targeted.
Confronting	'What if' examples.

- Mentors should be enabled to practise their current skills and to develop new skills.

There is a need for more research into mentor-training programmes to address questions such as what, when and how much training is essential or desirable (MacCallum and Beltman, 1999).

CODES OF PRACTICE

Some programmes have developed codes of practice to guide the behaviour or mentors in the programme. Box 11.2 provides extracts from a code of practice that formed part of draft Occupational Standards for a National Vocational Qualification in Mentoring in the UK (Wood and Reynard, 2000). This code is addressed to both mentors and their mentees. However, the US example shown in Box 11.3 provides a code of practice aimed at mentors.

Box 11.2: An ethical code of practice for mentoring

- The mentor's role is to respond to the mentee's developmental needs and agenda; it is not to impose a personal agenda.
- Mentors must work within the current agreement with the mentee about confidentiality that is appropriate within the context.
- The mentor will not intrude into any areas the mentee wishes to keep private until invited to do so.
- Mentor and mentee should aim to be truthful with each other and themselves about the relationship.
- The mentoring relationship must not be exploitative in any way, nor must it be open to misinterpretation.
- Mentors need to be aware of the limits of their own competence and operate within these limits.
- Mentors have a responsibility to develop their own competence in the practice of mentoring.
- The mentee must accept increasing responsibility for managing the relationship; the mentor should promote this development and must generally promote the mentee's autonomy.
- Mentor and mentee should respect each other's time and other responsibilities, ensuring that they do not impose beyond what is reasonable.
- Mentor and mentee share responsibility for the smooth winding down of the relationship when it has achieved its purpose; they must both avoid creating dependency.
- Either party may dissolve the relationship. However, both mentor and

---

mentee have a responsibility to discuss the matter together, as part of mutual learning.

- Mentees should be aware of their rights and any complaints procedures.
- Mentors must be aware of any current law and work within it.
- Mentor and mentee must be aware that all records are subject to statutory regulations under the Data Protection Act, 1984.

George W Bush, when Governor of Texas, published Quality Assurance Standards for Mentoring Organizations, which were aimed at ensuring safety for mentees, support and retention of mentors and long-term operational stability for mentoring organizations. The standards represented guidelines based on what the Texas mentoring field considered to be the essential elements of any high-quality mentoring programme. The Texas quality standards also laid down quality standards of behaviour, to which mentors should subscribe (see Box 11.3).

Box 11.3 Governor of Texas Mentoring Initiative: Mentor Guidelines

1. *Preparedness*: Mentors are prepared to be a friend to the young person and demonstrate consistent, dependable, trustworthy, accepting, honest and respectful behaviours.
2. *Integrity*: Mentors consistently act in ways that are ethical, earning the respect and trust of their mentees and supporting community partners.
3. *Commitment*: Mentors are steadfast in their commitment to the policies and procedures of the guiding organization.
4. *Knowledge builder*: Mentors actively seek out shared opportunities that enhance the knowledge, skills and abilities of their mentees.
5. *Inclusive attitude*: Mentors value the diverse racial, ethnic, and cultural and religious traits of their mentees.
6. *Maintain confidentiality*: Mentors act in the best interest of the mentoring organization and ensure confidentiality, taking care to protect against inadvertent disclosure.
7. *Accountability*: Mentors make regular contact with the mentoring organization to ensure effective mentoring practice.
8. *Appropriate*: Mentors refrain from profanity, criticism of school, faculty or staff, inappropriate physical contact, violations of law or school code of conduct.
9. *Eligible screening*: Mentors authorize the completion of required background checks to cover criminal history, driving records, personal interviews and other forms of screening as deemed appropriate.

> 10. *Service to communiy*: Mentors maintain a steady presence in the lives of youth and in community efforts, and strive to encourage others toward participation in volunteer efforts.
>
> (What is the Governor's Mentoring Initiative –
> www.governor.state.tx.us/mentoring/quality)

SUPPORT AND SUPERVISION

Programme managers are failing in their responsibilities if, after matching, mentors and mentees are left to their own devices. US research (Sipe, 1999; Herrera, Sipe and McClanahan, 2000) found that:

- When project workers provide regular support to mentors, then pairs are more likely to meet regularly and be satisfied with the programme.
- When mentors are not contacted regularly by project workers there are the highest percentage of failed matches.
- Mentors benefit a great deal from support from programme staff in the form of ongoing monitoring, training, support-group meetings and related practical support.

Clearly, the extent of support and supervision will vary with the nature of the programme, with programmes for at-risk youth generally requiring the greatest amount of input from project workers.

Check-in schedule

The purposes of monitoring are to ensure that meetings are held regularly, to monitor progress in the relationship towards its goals and to address any problems that have arisen. A schedule of 'check-in' conversations is recommended as follows (Jucovy, 2001b):

- within two weeks of the match to ensure that things have begun well;
- then every two weeks for the first few months to make sure meetings are being held and to identify problems;
- finally monthly check-ins to discuss the quality of the relationship and progress towards goals.

In addition, programmes should have a parallel check-in schedule for the young person and monthly contact with parents or guardians, especially in community-based programmes.

Many programmes find that once the mentoring has begun additional training needs for mentors are identified. These might be addressed through in-service training workshops for mentors on such themes as diversity and cultural sensitivity, target-setting skills, dealing with family-related issues, alcohol or drug problems, and domestic violence. Mentor-support programmes are also a useful vehicle for sharing common frustrations and difficulties provided that they are facilitated by an experienced practitioner (Jucovy, 2001b). Other methods to support mentors include interactive Web sites where problems can be discussed. In school-based programmes it is important that mentors receive feedback from the teaching staff on positive changes that have occurred in their mentee as this can strongly reinforce commitment to the programme and mentor retention. In any mentor support strategy it is important to recognize that not all mentors will have the same support needs or amount of time to devote to the programme.

ACCREDITATION

Most people do not volunteer to become mentors in order to gain accreditation, and most UK programmes do not yet offer accreditation to mentors as part of their scheme (Golden and Sims, 1999). Good practice advice from the operational literature increasingly suggests that schemes should at least inform mentors about the opportunities for accreditation through the programme. Indeed some people see mentoring as a first step into a new career working with young people and hence they are very interested in the issue of accreditation. There is a growing number of mentor qualifications on the market in the United Kingdom, and these have been recently mapped by the National Mentoring Network (Drury, 2001). In the United Kingdom, peer mentors are able to gain recognition in various ways, for example through the Awards Scheme Development and Accreditation Network (ASDAN) Youth Award.

There are a burgeoning number of qualifications available for adult mentors. These tend to vary along several variables including:

- The *level* of the award: there is a national framework of qualifications in England from entry level to level 5 (post-graduate), and mentor qualifications are available at all levels.
- *Time* needed to achieve the award: general parameters are usually set out giving a range of minimum times required. For example, the Oxford School of Coaching and Mentoring qualifications typically take around 72 hours over 6–7 months.
- *Activities* involved in gaining the award. These can include: distance learning, with tutor support; mentoring practice; seminars and tutorials; mentor training; mentor supervision; and building a portfolio.

- *Modes of assessment*. These can include: self-, peer- and tuto. ment; portfolio assessment; use of journals, learning logs an. reflection; observation; reflective practice assignments; wit. statements; and appraisal.
- *Costs*: these can vary depending on the level of the award from £125 for a level 2 or 3 Accredited Mentoring Certificate Programme from the European Mentoring Centre, through £650 for a Certificate of Professional Practice in Mentoring from Goldsmith's University London, to over £3,000 for a Masters Degree in Coaching and Mentoring Practice from the Oxford School of Coaching and Mentoring.

Qualifications available in the United Kingdom tend to come in two main types, distinguished by the mode of assessment. Those forms of accreditation that are based on competency-based modes of assessment tend to favour portfolios of evidence to demonstrate the achievement of specified performance criteria (see Case Study 11.1). In contrast, mentoring qualifications developed by universities tend to prefer mentors to write extended reports on their experience of mentoring (see Case Study 11.2).

Case Study 11.1 Mentoring Draft Occupational Standards (UK)

Over 300 organizations across the United Kingdom were involved in piloting the Mentoring Draft Occupational Standards drafted by the Women's Development Programme of the University of North London (Wood and Reynard, 2000). This competency-based approach divided the mentoring process into five units:

- Unit 1: Facilitating learning and development.
- Unit 2: Preparing to be a mentor.
- Unit 3: Personal interaction between mentor and mentee.
- Unit 4: Monitoring and evaluating the process.
- Unit 5: Self-development of mentor.

Each unit was broken down into various elements. For example, Unit 3 was divided into four elements that define a series of closely related activities:

- Element 3.1: starting the mentoring relationship.
- Element 3.2: developing and maintaining the mentoring relationship.
- Element 3.3: operating within an ethical code of practice.
- Element 3.4: ending the mentoring.

For each element, there were several performance criteria, calling for practical demonstrations of knowledge and skills. These establish the contexts within which the skills must be demonstrated and the knowledge requirements, which underpin the performance criteria. Performance criteria within Element 3.3 (operating within an agreed ethical code of practice) included:

- The mentor's own practice demonstrates a commitment to best practice.
- Any conflicts between agreed ethical code and own values and beliefs are recognized and managed.
- Feedback is sought from appropriate people within agreed timescales.

Underpinning knowledge included: understanding of relevant organizational and national good practice information; awareness of the impact of their own values, beliefs and life experience on working with the mentee; and knowledge of sources of support.

In competency-based approaches to mentor accreditation, the usual approach to assessment is for mentors to assemble a portfolio of evidence to demonstrate that they have achieved the required competencies. Sources of evidence include: a log or journal; mentoring agreements or action plans; witness statements; feedback forms from the mentoring supervisor; mentee's action plans; and reports.

Case Study 11.2 Diploma in Mentoring at Leeds Metropolitan University (UK)

Leeds Metropolitan University offers a suite of three mentoring qualifications, which are generic and can be used in corporate, school-based or other mentoring contexts. They are the Vocational Certificate, the Professional Diploma and the Advanced Diploma in Mentoring. The qualifications are suitable for people who are engaged in mentoring, as the assessment requires work-based learning, that is, systematic reflection on the mentoring process. There are two main units: the Framework for Mentoring and the Dynamics of Mentoring. The qualification is delivered via distance learning with peer and tutor support, and mentoring practice. The assessment method is a 5,000–8,000 word reflective practical assignment, which gains credit currency at undergraduate and Masters' levels. The qualification typically takes about 100 hours to complete over a 30-week period. By 2001, in the six years in which the qualification had been available, around 200 mentors had gained qualifications.

(Adapted from Drury, 2001)

SUMMARY OF GOOD PRACTICE POINTS

The following are a distillation of the main points raised in this chapter.

Planning

- When planning mentor recruitment, consider what motivates people to become mentors in your kind of programme.
- Decide what you think are the most important characteristics of 'good' mentors, as a guide to selection and training.
- Identify the roles that you want mentors to play within the programme, and those roles that you do not want them to take on.
- Divide mentor behaviours into those that mentors should always, sometimes or never use.
- Reflect on the kinds of emotional intelligence necessary to make your programme a success.
- Identify potential 'triggers' that might encourage mentors to join your scheme.
- Develop a clear recruitment message and plan that fits in with your budgetary constraints.
- Consider the equal-opportunities issues that may arise from over-reliance on a word-of-mouth recruitment strategy.
- Draw up a community map to identify potential sources of mentors in the local community.
- Carry out a force-field analysis to identify the barriers and facilitators that will hinder or help people in the targeted group who might come forward as mentors.
- Produce attractive mentoring literature that reflects the diversity of the student and local populations.
- Consider the range of recruitment methods that could make the campaign a success.

Implementing

- Develop a comprehensive screening policy, appropriate to the form of mentoring, and the age and vulnerability of the young people.
- Streamline police check procedures as far as possible to reduce 'waiting' times for mentors to start the programme.
- Plan for several stages of screening and use training as an opportunity to have a closer look at mentors in action.
- Do not ignore 'red flags' or 'gut instincts', but undertake further inquiries.
- Plan mentor training to reflect the aims of the programme, but do not treat mentors as 'empty vessels'. Try to draw on their experience when planning and delivering training programmes.
- Consider breaking up the training programme into 'bite-sized' chunks and scheduling it throughout the programme, rather than all at the beginning.
- Use participatory and informal methods in the training.

- Develop a mentor supervision and support strategy.
- Plan a mentor check-in schedule and processes for identifying ongoing training needs.
- Hold regular mentor support group meetings and arrange for feedback to mentors on the positive changes in their mentees.
- Investigate opportunities for mentor and mentee accreditation and how these might be funded.

FUTURE TRENDS

In the future it is likely that research will provide better evidence on volunteering, which will help mentoring programmes to target potential mentors more effectively. There will be increased government support for marketing the benefits of volunteer mentoring and possibly national campaigns. An increasing proportion of the population will have experienced the benefits of being mentored while at school and will be more willing to become adult mentors. Increased understanding of the use of emotional intelligence in all settings will make the development of emotional intelligence a key element of mentor training and a desirable goal for mentors. There will be greater coordination of mentor recruitment and training across towns and cities where there are many mentoring programmes competing for adult mentors. Police-vetting procedures will be streamlined to reduce costs and waiting times for mentors. Mentor training will increasingly be available online. More universities and awarding bodies will offer a range of mentor qualifications up to Masters level.

12

Mentoring processes

INTRODUCTION

This chapter follows the chronology of the mentee's experience from selection through to the end of the mentoring programme. We begin by examining the issues associated with the selection and preparation of mentees. This is followed by a discussion of the basic parameters of mentoring, such as ground rules, duration and frequency of meetings. A further issue is the extent to which mentor meetings stand alone, complement or are complemented by other activities. The bulk of the chapter is devoted to entering the 'secret garden' of mentorship to investigate different stages and models. Gender issues are raised as part of the description and analysis of the matching of mentors to mentees. The links between mentors, the programme and parents are discussed, along with potential relationship problems. Next, we examine questions arising from the closure of mentoring relationships. We conclude with a summary of the main good practice points described in the chapter and speculation about possible future trends.

MENTEE SELECTION

One of the main problems with school-based mentoring programmes in particular is the selection of mentees. Selection is generally necessary, because there are often more young people who would like a mentor than there are mentors available. It is important to have a clearly identified target group in mind when designing the mentoring programme. The 'target group' consists of students who meet one or more criteria defined by the programme managers. Programmes vary in the number and specificity of referral criteria. On the one hand some programmes for at-risk students may have several criteria and detailed referral forms, whereas others may ask tutors to identify 'underachieving' students, leaving it to the teachers to decide what is meant by that term. The JUMP mentoring programme in the United States has a model of risk and protective factors that is used when referring young people to the programme (see Figure 12.1). Other school information is usually taken into account when considering potential mentees, including:

- disciplinary, attendance and punctuality records;
- test and examination grades;
- classwork, coursework effort and achievements.

However, some guidelines stress the need to take into account the positive aspects of young people that can be developed through mentoring (Skinner and Fleming, 1999). As we have seen (see Case Studies 5.1 and 5.3), there also schemes which are 'aspirational' or for 'gifted and talented' students, which have very different referral criteria. Selection criteria can include a commitment to the mentees' areas of interest, self-motivation, organizational ability and willingness to be open to advice and feedback (Farmer, 1999). In school-based schemes, the programme manager, school coordinator and typically a head of year draw up a short list from the long list of potential mentees.

Most school programmes invite would-be mentees to a meeting where the aims and benefits of mentoring are communicated. It is very important to put a positive 'spin' on the mentoring programme to avoid any sense in which there might be a stigma attached to being chosen. Students and teachers should be made to feel that it is a privilege to have a mentor. It is helpful to involve current or previous mentors and mentees in explaining the benefits of mentoring to the potential mentees. Most mentoring guidelines stress the importance of all mentees being willing volunteers. Some programmes offer a follow-up interview to students following the briefing session.

MENTEE PREPARATION

In order to gain the maximum benefits from mentoring at an early stage of the relationship, mentees need to be prepared (Struchen and Porta, 1997). Such preparation can take various forms (Lauland, 1998). At its simplest, an induction for the whole group is probably most typical involving:

- an outline of the aims, objectives and limitations;
- presentation of potential benefits, perhaps through a talk from former mentees;

- the level of commitment required;
- completion of matching forms;
- standards of behaviour;

Community
Risk factors:
- Easy availability of drugs and guns
- Extreme economic deprivation
- High mobility and transitions

Protective factors:
- High neighbourhood attachment
- Proactive community organization
- Community norms unfavourable toward crime and drug use

Family
Risk factors:
- Parental alcohol or drug abuse
- Lack of adequate supervision
- Family conflict or violence

Protective factors:
- Parental disapproval of delinquency and ATOD (alcohol, tobacco or drug) use
- Feeling of warmth, love and caring parents
- Clear standards and consistent discipline

Positive youth development supports JUMP goals

Reduce juvenile delinquency

Reduce gang participation

Improve academic performance

Reduce drop-out rate

Personal peers
Risk factors:
- Friends who use drugs, engage in delinquent behaviours
- Working more than 20 hours per week
- Low impulse control, or sensation-seeking behaviour

Protective factors:
- Perceived importance of religion or prayer
- Sense of social belonging
- Meaningful, challenging opportunities to contribute to family/ community

Schools
Risk factors:
- Poor grades
- Being behind grade level
- Sense of isolation from/prejudice by peers

Protective factors:
- Realistically high parental expectations for achievement
- Positive engagement with school
- Perceived caring from teachers

Figure 12.1 *Examples of risk and protective factors in the JUMP programme*

- guidelines and rules, for example concerning contact with mentors and regularity of meetings;
- an introduction to key processes and pro formas to be used, such as action plan forms, review forms and mentoring agreements;
- an explanation about how the relationship will end.

In some schemes mentors have advocated pre-mentoring training in interpersonal skills, so that shy, introverted or inarticulate mentees have an opportunity to practise talking and listening in one-to-one situations (Miller, 1998). Some programmes for at-risk students include one-to-one briefings with students to ask them why they believe they were selected and to explain more specifically how mentoring can help them. In a school situation it is important that staff are aware of the students who have mentors, as well as an understanding of the aims of the programme and how it fits into the ethos and curriculum of the school.

MATCHING

Although some programmes, particularly those for at-risk youths, allow students to select their mentors, the majority of student mentoring programmes match according to similarities between mentors and students (Lauland, 1998). Such similarities include:

- gender, ethnicity and language;
- shared background, interests and experiences;
- likelihood of personal compatibility;
- relationship between the mentor's area of expertise or career and the mentee's interests, careers aspirations and needs;
- logistical issues that facilitate regular meetings.

Matching events and activities

Some programmes hold social events to bring all mentors and mentees together for an informal gathering prior to matching (Golden and Sims, 1999). Some programme managers observe the behaviour and personal style of mentors and mentees during training and preparation and test out their intuition about suitable matches during subsequent residential experience (Divert, 1999; see Case Study 6.2). An alternative approach used in the Across Ages project (see Case Study 4.3) was for the project staff to observe the mentors and mentees interacting in the classroom environment before matching.

In the majority of student mentoring programmes, mentors and mentees complete a matching form that asks for the kind of information listed above. The forms are then used by the programme manager in consultation with school staff to make the match, based partly on the rational approach indicated, and partly on the intuitive use of emotional intelligence to match personalities (Golden and Sims, 1999).

GENDER ISSUES

Two major issues discussed in the literature are cross-gender and cross-ethnicity matching. The issue of cross-ethnicity matching was discussed in Chapter 5 with the conclusion that there were merits in same-ethnicity and cross-ethnicity matching, depending on the aims of the scheme. Same-gender matching is a priority for some programmes, as it is an essential aim of some schemes in which:

- women with science, technology, engineering or maths backgrounds act as role models to young women with interests in traditionally male areas of academic work and careers;
- men act as male role models to male students who come from female-led households;
- men 'who are reformed characters' mentor at-risk male students to address the anti-learning, anti-schooling subculture, which results in underachievement.

Mentoring for male students

There is also evidence that schools' perceptions of the benefits of mentoring to male and female students is gendered. Schools tend to think that mentoring can address specific weaknesses that boys typically display in learning, for example, poor organizational, study, revision or basic skills. Many mentoring programmes are based on the assumption that boys, particularly those from one-parent families, require a male adult role model (Philip, 2000). This in turn is based on the assumption that a female environment in the home can arrest male development. This approach to mentoring has been challenged by the work of Gilligan (Philip, 2000). In spite of the increasing number of references to the role of mentoring in developing emotional intelligence, there are still risks for boys in expressing emotions (Mac an Ghaill, 1994). The preponderance of female mentors and the importance of developing emotional intelligence in young people suggest that the need for male role models may have been overemphasized.

The relative imbalance in the ratio of male to female mentors means that in most schemes where the majority of mentees are male, the most common match will often be female mentor to male mentee. Programmes usually have little difficulty in ensuring that girls only have female mentors. However, in some business schemes where mentors are drawn from a company where there is an imbalance of men in management positions, it is sometimes the case that there is a shortage of female role models. This can mean that male mentors are paired with female mentees, which is not always a successful match, as young women may be reluctant to talk honestly with an older male mentor (Miller, 1998).

Mentoring and female students

In the case of female students, mentoring is more likely to focus on coping with pressure, weaknesses in particular subjects and lack of aspirations (Sukhnandan, Lee and Kelleher, 2000). Sullivan argues that the 'classical' or 'male' model of the mentoring relationship may not be suitable for girls (quoted in Warren-Sams, 2001). The so-called 'male model' is when more experienced mentors instruct and guide less experienced mentees in order to develop their character and competence. The mentors demonstrate their personal, social and work skills and operate by challenging and encouraging their mentees. Sullivan argues that the kind of mentoring that concentrates on teaching, socializing and role modelling is not appropriate for women mentors working with adolescent girls. She maintains that a more two-way relationship, with the mentor confirming and enhancing rather than challenging and discounting the knowledge and experience of the younger woman, must be established before mentoring guidance can occur. It has also been argued that small-group mentoring may be more appropriate for young women, as they are likely to value such group affiliation highly (Warren-Sams, 2001).

Sullivan found in the Understanding Adolescence study that girls could benefit from mentoring relationships where mentors:

- give advice, not lectures;
- create a therapeutic relationship that provides a safe haven for speaking one's mind;
- look for a basis of partnership and mutual benefit;
- allow girls to voice their concerns about social issues, prejudice and discrimination;
- are aware of what is helpful and harmful as they teach, challenge and act as role models;
- listen to and validate what young women think and feel;
- share adult experiences.

MEETING PARAMETERS

Duration of meetings

The parameters of mentoring meetings are the basis of all mentoring relationships, including their duration, frequency and location. The case studies give examples of many different models regarding contact time between mentors and mentees. This depends on the form of mentoring, the aims and objectives, decisions made by programme managers and the agreement made by mentor and mentee. For example the UK Mentoring Strategy Group, in a position paper submitted in 2000 to the DfEE on business mentoring, suggested that a minimum level of contact was 12 hours over six months, in other words a one-hour meeting every two weeks.

Frequency of meetings

The frequency of meetings is a second key variable determining the amount of contact time. Greater frequency is generally recommended at the start of programmes while relationships are being established, but frequency may reduce towards the end, when mentees' needs have been largely met or they are increasingly independent. Some schemes do have relatively infrequent meetings, say every three weeks, and problems can occur when a meeting is missed and there is then sometimes a six-week gap between meetings. This tends to undermine the entire mentoring relationship. The problem that some mentors have in keeping to their time commitment is a major cause of the failure of mentoring relationships.

Inevitably, mentoring programmes for at-risk students tend to be much more intensive and generally take place weekly or more frequently. Similarly mentoring which focuses on the development of basic skills needs to happen on a weekly basis. For example, the National Mentoring Pilot Project (see Case Study 9.1) required two-weekly meetings between the higher education student mentors and their secondary-school mentees. However, some programmes, for example those for gifted and talented students, may thrive on non-intensive contact. Some writers have observed that when the focus of the mentoring is the development of skills, then mentoring pairs meet more frequently and over a longer period of time (Songsthagen and Lee, 1996). Where the mentoring is more concerned with befriending and sharing interests, however, meetings tend to be less frequent and there are more terminated relationships.

Location

The issue of the location of meetings is tied to the problem of child protection, and the degree of police checking and screening which has been applied to mentors. Many student-mentoring programmes are site-based in the school, because this allows for greater levels of teacher supervision. Students are also then not involved in travelling to unfamiliar destinations – often at the end of the school day – with the inherent risks that this brings. Schools often have space problems, so that it is difficult to afford mentors and mentees the privacy to engage in confidential conversations. Many business and community mentoring meetings take place in the school hall or library at the end of the school day. However, business mentoring programmes often yield greater benefits to students in terms of their employability and self-confidence when mentees travel to meetings at their mentor's workplace (Miller, 1998). Community-based mentoring requires more rigorous approaches to mentor and mentee support and supervision than site-based programmes, although meetings are often held in community centres where there is some measure of supervision.

THE MENTORING RELATIONSHIP

Another way of describing differences between mentoring programmes is to examine the nature of the relationship between mentor and mentee. According to Garvey (1994), there are five dimensions to the mentoring relationship:

- *Open–closed* dimension: this concerns the issues for discussion. In open mentoring relationships there is total freedom to talk about anything, whereas in closed relationships 'off limit' topics are specified and boundaries are clearly delineated. Boundary setting is a standard feature of mentor training and mentee preparation in which scheme organizers try to impose, with legitimate reasons, limits to the degree of openness.
- *Public–private* dimension: this is the extent to which scheme organizers or teachers have access to information about what is discussed. For example, some telementoring schemes are public, because the online facilitator monitors communications. In some school schemes, mentees and mentors keep diaries and other recording tools that are made accessible to others (see Case Study 6.2).
- *Formal–informal* dimension: most mentoring programmes are formalized and meetings are planned and recorded. However, in more informal mentoring there are few ground rules and meetings can occur at any time. For example, peer mentoring or 'buddy schemes' may exhibit this degree of informality, which is more akin to natural mentoring. Programmes that have been running for a number of years can move along the continuum from formal to informal (see Case Study 3.3).
- *Active–passive* dimension: in active relationships both parties take action as a result of the mentoring meeting; this could involve investigating options, target setting and review of targets. In some programmes the mentee is active and the mentor passive, and in others both might be passive between meetings.

- *Stable–unstable* dimension: in some relationships partners are predictable and commitment and trust is in evidence, but in others there is a lack of trust and commitment.

Programmes vary according to the degree of structure that the project organizers attempt to impose on relationships. The stance taken by the project on the dimensions of the relationship needs to be addressed during mentor training and mentee preparation.

OTHER ACTIVITIES

When setting up a mentoring programme it is important to decide whether one-to-one mentoring through regular meetings is to be a stand-alone activity that will in itself make a difference to the student. Many school-based schemes in the United Kingdom take this approach, which carries less risk and demands lower levels of supervision than the alternative. In contrast, many US and US-influenced programmes encourage mentors and mentees to undertake a potentially wide range of activities together. These can include:

- a peer mentor and mentee undertaking a joint service-learning project in the local community;
- peer mentor and mentee attending the School Council, library and certain classes together (see Case Study 7.1);
- cultural activities, such as theatre or cinema visits or visits to heritage attractions (see Case Study 5.3);
- mentor support for art and craft projects (see Case Study 6.1);
- the mentor attending school plays, school trips and assemblies (see Case Study 4.3);
- visits to a learning centre at a football club to practise IT skills (see Case Study 5.1);
- sporting activities, such as playing a sport together or watching a game;
- business mentors offering work-experience placements at their workplace;
- academic summer camps (see Case Study 3.3) and activities weekends or residentials (see Case Study 4.3).

These kinds of activities are designed to help build the relationship through shared experiences, positive memories and fun. They all have a focus on learning by doing. Some programmes also arrange social events when mentors and mentees can meet and share a common experience.

Mentoring-plus activities

Some programmes recognize that on their own mentoring meetings may not achieve all the goals of the programme. A range of other interventions, designed to develop the knowledge, skills or attitudes of the student accompany mentoring in many schemes. This applies particularly to programmes for at-risk young people and those sustained over a long period of time. For example, the GEAR UP Program led by Rutgers University (see Case Study 9.3) involved:

- tutoring and academic counselling;
- essay workshops;
- company tours, job shadowing and internships;
- community service and cultural outings;
- home visits and workshops for parents.

The Dalston Youth Project (see Case Study 6.2) for at-risk youth offered:

- key skills, counselling and conflict-handling sessions with project staff;
- after-school clubs on curriculum-linked work;
- learning new skills, such as photography;
- English as an additional language for parents, and workshops on how to support their children's learning;
- parenting-skills workshops to help parents build better relationships with their children.

When there are a range of other interventions in addition to mentoring, then it becomes virtually impossible to disentangle the relative contribution of different activities to any positive changes in the student. However, many programme managers have found that building in additional activities in the ways described helps to improve the success rate of the programme. Many programmes are limited by budget constraints on the supporting activities they can offer. Schools are also cautious about encouraging mentor and mentee meetings in the community, where supervision becomes more difficult and greater levels of monitoring are required.

STAGES OF THE MENTORING RELATIONSHIP

There are several ways of conceptualizing the stages of the mentoring relationship. In this section we introduce four models that have been advanced to describe the stages of the mentoring relationship:

- the mentor-protégé relationship model;
- the chronological model;
- the life cycle model;
- the career development model.

The models only describe ideal-typical mentoring relationships; actual mentoring relationships will vary from these types. However, such models do provide programme managers with a language for discussing what is likely to happen during the course of the mentoring relationship in training sessions and during mentor support group meetings.

Mentor–protégé relationship model

One of the earliest approaches was based on adult mentoring in a corporate context, the so-called 'Mentor–Protégé' relationship model (Gray, 1986). This model was the foundation for Gay's discussion of the continuum of mentoring behaviours (see Chapter 2). The relationship can pass through four levels, suggesting that as the competence and experience of the mentee grows, then so does the equality between them and their mentor:

- Level 1: the mentee has limited experience and displays little competence. In this situation the mentor may act more in a teacher role and assume greater direction for what happens in and between mentoring meetings.
- Level 2: the mentor acts as a guide to the mentee, based on greater experience and expertise.
- Level 3: the mentor acknowledges the mentee's growing competence and experience and facilitates a more equal contribution during meetings.
- Level 4: the mentor and mentee are both engaged in learning from each other and there is a relationship of equals.

Chronological model

A more common approach to discussing the stages of the mentoring relationship is to take a chronological view. Here the stages can range from three to eight. At its simplest there are three obvious stages to a successful relationship, which mirror the familiar stages of group formation:

- Stage 1: 'forming and storming' includes the first meeting, developing trust and rapport, making an agreement and some 'testing out' of each other. Students who lack trust in adults owing to their previous experience may test out the commitment of their mentor through missing appointments, not returning calls, making unreasonable requests or being sullen in meetings.

- Stage 2: 'norming and performing' includes the bulk of meetings where goals are set, reached and reviewed and a good relationship is formed. Some relationships may become 'stuck' at Stage 1, because of a poor match, prior 'damage' to the students' capacity to trust adults, students being stuck at the testing out stage or dropping out of school for a variety of reasons.
- Stage 3: 'closing' the relationship when targets have been achieved, the mentee has developed and become more independent as a learner.

The 'life cycle' model

At its most complex, some writers elaborate on the stages of mentoring and compare it to life or relationships. For example, the so-called 'Mentoring Life Cycle Model' has eight stages (Swansea College, not dated):

- Stage 1: gaining commitment to the mentoring process ('conception').
- Stage 2: getting involved through selection and matching (giving birth').
- Stage 3: getting together at the initial meeting ('babyhood').
- Stage 4: getting to know each other at the start of the relationship ('childhood').
- Stage 5: working together to action-plan and address issues ('adolescence').
- Stage 6: learning together that involves mutual learning and development ('adult maturity').
- Stage 7: looking back together on what has been achieved through the relationship ('old age').
- Stage 8: saying goodbye when goals have been achieved and it is time to move on ('death').

A ninth stage of 'rebirth' or redefinition could be added for all those mentoring pairs that decide to continue meeting as friends after the end of the formal mentoring scheme (Kram, 1985). Other writers would argue that it is not possible to define a stage model to which complex mentoring relationships will conform. For example, after initial enthusiasm there may be 'lulls' or stages of irrelevance when initial objectives appear to have been achieved.

The 'career development' model

One of the main aims of mentoring is for career development. The Mentoring Action Project (MAP) coordinated by the Institute of Careers

Guidance between 1995 and 1997 explored the potential of one-to-one mentoring in career guidance for disengaged young people (Ford, 1998). The MAP project produced a six-stage model for career development through mentoring.

- Stage 1: mentoring for survival included helping to meet the basic needs of the mentee (health, family relationships) and supporting the mentee in negotiations with other agencies.
- Stage 2: mentoring to improve social and life skills included time-keeping, appearance, coping strategies, and strategies to overcome barriers to progress, mini-action plans and phased steps.
- Stage 3: mentoring to improve self-awareness included reflecting on and learning from past behaviour, determining more positive behaviour and relating past and future behaviour to the expectations of others, including employers and learning providers.
- Stage 4: mentoring to improve self-image included helping the client to recognize achievements, providing opportunities for the young person to succeed, and celebrating, recording and accrediting success in non-formal situations.
- Stage 5: mentoring for career exploration included initial and continuing assessment, computer-aided and psychometric testing, learning 'tasters' and short internships.
- Stage 6: mentoring for career management included support in decision-making, action planning and implementing action plans, ongoing support and follow up, while passing the initiative gradually to the young person.

LEARNING MENTORS IN ACTION

We observed in Chapter 1 that learning mentors in the United Kingdom were a possible example of holistic mentoring in action. In spite of the existence of national guidance and training for learning mentors, there has been considerable autonomy in how they have been used in schools. In the absence of a national evaluation report, evidence of the variety of the role is inevitably anecdotal. The examples here give a flavour of the varied roles and processes being undertaken by learning mentors.

Case studies

The learning mentors at South Camden Community School in London have helped a student with a terrible attendance record by ringing his home each morning and meeting him each day to try to motivate him. They have also visited students' homes when they have been absent. In one case they found a student and his mother sharing a one-bedroom flat where they were taking it in turns to sleep in the bed. The learning mentors have also offered careers guidance to students on progression into higher education (Coughlan, 2001).

The three learning mentors at All Saints Catholic High School on Merseyside managed a mentoring programme that included 49 volunteers from teaching and non-teaching staff, business people, police, governors and the Education Business Partnership. Personal support plans, session notes, evaluation data and 'emotional literacy' information were provided to each mentor. The mentors also organized peer mentoring for Year 8 and 11 students to mentor others, as part of the anti-bullying strategy (Jones, 2000).

More detailed case studies of learning mentors at work are beginning to appear (Birmingham Local Education Authority, 2001). A learning mentor at Hodge Hill School in Birmingham described her work with a 15-year-old female student who was disruptive in lessons, had a poor relationship with her peers, was breaking school rules and was low-achieving. The intervention involved:

- an initial interview for relationship building and target setting;
- classroom observation to look at strengths, weaknesses and attitudes to staff and peers;
- baseline teacher assessment and analysing specific lesson assessment forms, which showed patterns of motivation in some subjects and disruption in others;
- regular feedback to teaching staff in written form;
- meetings with the student's family to gather information on the family context, and regular telephone conversations to discuss targets and attitude;
- a visit to the student at an off-site centre and negotiating disapplication from the National Curriculum;
- brokering meetings between the student and individual teachers;
- arranging a visit to a nursery (linked to her career interest).

This clearly goes beyond the role of most external mentors that we have described in the book. It remains to be seen whether at the end of the learning mentor initiative the mentors are subsumed within the role of personal advisers under the new Connexions Service, or continue to be funded, because of their success in supporting individual students.

EXPERIENTIAL LEARNING

Some authors have compared the processes used by the mentors in meetings to debriefing processes employed within experiential learning or experience-based learning. Following Kolb, the experiential learning cycle illustrated in Figure 12.2 suggests that in order to learn from experience the learner needs to reflect on that experience in order to draw out lessons or generalizations. These constitute guides to future behaviour and can then be applied in new situations, giving rise to new experiences. The experiential learning cycle provides a model for mentoring meetings and a learning model that can be used in mentor training. This can be described as a mentoring learning cycle (Carr, 2000). In essence, mentors are helping to process the mentees' learning through the use of open-ended questions designed to draw out the mentees, to help them understand the experiences they have had and to give them some future options based on a real understanding of their situation (see Table 12.1). This has been describing as the mentor 'chasing' the learner around the cycle by asking questions that encourage description, reflection, conceptualization and ways of testing out ideas.

The mentoring learning cycle

The process of a typical mentoring learning cycle involves the following mentor behaviours. In mentor meetings, the first step is to encourage

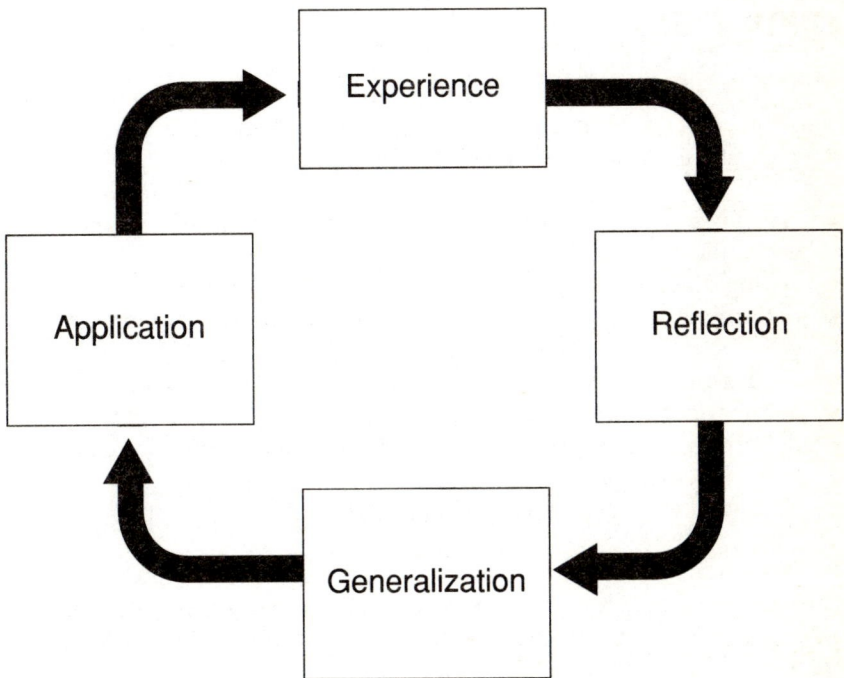

Figure 12.2 *The experiential learning cycle (adapted from Kolb)*

mentees to describe their experiences since the last meeting. This can be focused around, for example, the targets that were set last time, aspects of personal development or class work. It may involve describing a situation that occurred in class where they lost their temper, feelings of inadequacy in making a presentation to the class or problems with completing classwork targets. Mentors can ask catalytic questions to encourage a full description of the situation and an exploration of the context. Second, in order to encourage reflection, mentors can ask questions which invite the mentee to examine the experience from different perspectives. The third stage of processing experience-based learning is to generalize from the concrete experience to other similar situations. Primarily every experience and situation can be used for the purposes of learning provided that there is an opportunity for reflection and analysis with a sympathetic mentor. Finally, the mentees will show they have learned from their experience and from the mentoring relationship when they are able to apply this learning in new situations. This stage can involve considering various courses of action, discussing their advantages and disadvantages, and the mentees taking ownership of particular courses of action.

CONTRACTING

At or soon after the initial mentoring meeting, some programmes advocate both parties signing a mentoring contract. A mentoring contract or agreement has a number of benefits, which can include:

- clarifying what both parties expect from the relationship and from each other;
- setting down what roles and tasks each will undertake;
- defining the frequency, timing, duration and location of meetings;
- establishing rules of confidentiality;
- setting out the specific goals that the mentee hopes to achieve;
- listing proposed activities;
- defining the circumstances in which the relationship can be terminated by either party;
- stating when the contract can be renegotiated.

If either party has failed to keep to what they have agreed, then the contract may be brought into play. Either party or the programme manager can refer to the contract in order to put the relationship back on track.

Table 12.1 *The mentoring learning cycle: key questions*

Stage	Mentor questions
Experience	Tell me about what has happened since our last meeting. Describe the best and worst experiences you have had. Describe the situation. What did you feel at the time? What led up to this situation?
Reflection	What were other people saying/thinking/feeling? When have you felt like that before? Is this the first time this has happened? In what ways was this similar or different to other experiences? What made them good and bad experiences?
Generalization	Why did it happen? What are the factors that led to these situations? What are the consequences of particular actions? How can these bad situations/mistakes be avoided? What kinds of behaviour lead to a good result? What kinds of things do you need to work on? What are the most important/least important things about this situation/experience? What have you learned from the experience?
Application	What are the different choices that are available? What are the pros and cons of each choice? How can I support you in this course of action? What do you need to do first? What is the action plan? How will you know if the plan is successful? What are you going to do and by when?

THE ROLE OF PARENTS

The programme manager's stance on relations between mentors and parents is important. Some forms of mentoring tend to exclude parental contact, as in the case of peer, business, higher education students and telementoring. Other forms such as socially excluded, community and minority ethnic mentoring tend to encourage contact between mentors and their mentees' families. Contact is also more likely in longer-term, community-based programmes than in shorter-term, site-based programmes where all meetings occur in the school. Even if the mentor and family do not physically meet, the mentees may talk about family problems and the mentors need to consider how to respond.

Parental orientation

Mentoring programmes are unlikely to be effective if parents do not support them (Struchen and Porta, 1997). Schools generally ask for signed parental permission, but in many cases this is as far as involvement is taken. However, some schemes recognize that parents may be concerned about a relationship between their child and an adult stranger. Others may be worried that the mentor will try to usurp their role or authority (Lauland, 1998). For these reasons some programmes run orientation sessions for parents, which provide opportunities to:

- explain the nature, goals and benefits of the programme;
- gain parental support for prompt attendance at mentoring meetings and for sticking with the programme to the end;
- inform parents how they can support the aims of the programme, for example through support for homework;
- meet the mentors to be reassured about what is being proposed, namely that the mentors do not intend to impose their own values;
- provide contact details if any problem or further questions should arise.

Parental involvement

Programmes for at-risk young people, who may have been excluded from school or be on the verge of exclusion, may have a more holistic approach that includes work with parents (Divert, 1999). Such strategies are based on the assumption that students with problems at school also tend to have problems at home and that the two are inter-related. The Divert Trust in the United Kingdom supports socially excluded mentoring programmes and has developed a three-pronged approach to parental support:

- Support and advocacy: parents are given training to enable them to act as advocates for their children with schools and other agencies. They are also offered support, for example through 'village forums' or self-help groups.
- Knowledge acquisition: parents are offered training and information to enable them to understand and overcome obstacles they face that may prevent them exercising their rights.
- Skills development: parents are provided with courses on parenting skills to assist them in handling their children in more positive ways (see also Case Study 6.2).

Other ways of involving parents include: setting up a parental advisory council; arranging parental workshops on common problems facing young people; encouraging parents to meet mentors regularly; sending out programme newsletters to parents; and telephoning parents to share children's successes (Lauland, 1998).

Maintaining distance

The operational literature offers advice to mentors on maintaining distance and boundaries between themselves and the family, largely on the grounds that the relationship is with the mentee not the family (Jucovy, 2001a).

- Distance: maintain cordial but distant contact with the family.
- Focus: keep the main focus on the mentee, as forming other relationships will take time away from the key relationship.
- Friendship: resist the family's efforts to extract help beyond providing friendship for the student, particularly in the area of discipline. If there is an obvious problem in the family that is affecting the student's behaviour, then this should be referred to the programme staff.
- Non-judgmental attitude: be non-judgmental about the family, even if the student criticizes them. Listen and be supportive and explore ways of overcoming problems, but do not agree with the youth's criticism.
- Confidentiality: do not disclose to the family any conversations with your mentee, and do not feed back anything the family may have said about their child.

Some long-term programmes (see Case Study 3.3) actively involve siblings in project activities, so that they do not feel excluded from and antagonistic to the main purposes of the programme.

RELATIONSHIP PROBLEMS

As with all forms of human relationships, things can and do go wrong in mentorships. Programme managers should be familiar with the most common problems so that these can be addressed in preparation, training, support, supervision and review. Table 12.3 draws on the operational literature (Lauland, 1998; Jucovy, 2000a; Divert, 1999) to identify some of the main problems, the control measures that projects can put in place to prevent them and measures that can be taken once they have happened. These are only a sample of general, potential problems and each form will tend to generate specific difficulties that need to be planned for.

Sometimes unsuitable mentors do start programmes, and some commentators refer to 'drive-by' mentors, who may start a relationship and then abandon their mentees, creating more problems for those young people. Another problem is 'cloning', where mentors attempt to mould mentees in their own image through shaping their attitudes in a prescriptive way. Problems can also originate from mentees, who may make allegations or complaints against teachers to their mentors and encourage their mentors to intervene on their behalf. It is important that mentors are able to keep their distance and to avoid collusion. Training should stress that they will only be gaining one perspective of their mentee's school career. The lesson for programme managers is that it is better to anticipate problems, to put control measures in place and to write down clear procedures so that all parties know what they should do when particular circumstances arise.

ENDINGS

There are differences between programmes in terms of whether they have pre-defined end points. Most student mentoring programmes have a clear end date, but some are open-ended and leave it up to individual pairs whether to end mentoring when goals have been achieved or continue the relationship on the same or different footing (see Case Study 3.3). Mentors and mentees need to know from the time when they enter the programme how long their commitment is expected to last.

Even when students understand that the programme will come to an end, some may still feel rejected. It is important, therefore, that mentors receive some training in how to handle this final stage of the mentoring relationship, and that programme staff and teachers are prepared to offer some support to the student. At or near the final meeting, mentors should take the opportunity to recall the progress made by the student, highlighting their strengths, what they have learned, experienced and developed (Jucovy, 2000a). Mentors are urged to reiterate their confidence in the student and to identify future positive actions and directions. It is also using emotional intelligence for the student and the mentor to describe their feelings at the end of the relationship, which might include sadness, guilt, relief or satisfaction.

Celebratory events

Most schemes have a formal end-of-mentoring celebratory event where sometimes awards or certificates are given to mentors and mentees. They generally include speeches and some form of entertainment. This is sometimes referred to as graduation, marking a public ending of the mentorship. They are also a means of involving stakeholders in the programme and of securing ongoing commitment from sponsors.

Table 12.2 *Common relationship problems and programme responses*

Problem	Control measure	Possible response
'Bad' match.	Matching to include residentials, pre-matching meetings, or mentee guided choice.	Encourage mentor to be patient and to try a few more meetings. Mentor or mentee to approach supervisor about re-match on a no-fault divorce basis.
Mentee seems to lack enthusiasm for mentoring.	Brief mentors to be patient and to take time to build up trust.	Encourage mentors to make regular contact through notes or calls and to be proactive and creative. Suggest a link up with another mentor and mentee for joint activities.
Mentee presents with serious problems, eg drug or alcohol abuse.	Careful briefing of mentors and clear procedures.	Mentors should refer the problem to the programme manager.
Unrealistic expectations by mentee or mentor.	Briefings for both parties should counsel against over-optimistic expectations.	Support groups for mentors and mentees. Ongoing counselling of mentees by programme manager.
Problems in taking the initiative.	Clear briefing for mentors to take the early initiative in fixing appointments.	Programme managers to make one party clearly responsible for setting meetings.
Missed or irregular meetings by mentor.	Monitoring of meetings and follow up when meetings are missed.	Identify why meetings are being missed: logistical problem or lack of commitment. Find new meeting time or close match and find more reliable mentor.
Mentor is frustrated at perceived lack of impact on mentee.	Emphasize in mentor training that change takes times.	Provide regular feedback to mentors at support meetings or via telephone contact.

It is also desirable for the programme manager to write to mentees, parents and mentors to thank them for their contribution and to mark the end of the programme. Some student mentoring programmes support the continuation of relationships as friendships, provided that both parties agree and the parents have given their consent. In some forms, particularly peer mentoring and socially excluded mentoring (in a community context), programme managers may recruit 'graduate mentees' to become mentors. Dalston Youth Project, for example, invited ex-mentees to become advocates for the programme by giving talks about it to students in the target group in local schools.

SUMMARY OF GOOD PRACTICE POINTS

The following summary offers a checklist of the main points raised in this chapter.

Pre-matching

- Develop clear referral criteria and referral forms to help other people identify members of the target group.
- Make sure that mentees are willing volunteers and thoroughly briefed about the aims, objectives and processes of mentoring.
- Build positive messages into mentee briefings so that mentoring is not viewed as an activity for students and young people who are failing to achieve.
- Plan an induction programme for mentees and, if appropriate, build in pre-mentoring training in interpersonal skills.
- Draw up a mentoring agreement or contract for both parties to sign.
- Consider carefully the role of parents in the programme and how the relationship between mentee, mentor, parents and project staff will be managed.
- Decide whether the programme will offer training, support or activities to parents and siblings.

Matching

- Identify matching criteria and devise matching forms.
- Decide on the degree of mentor and mentee influence over who they are matched with, and consider pre-matching events or activities.
- Be clear about your policy on cross-gender and cross-ethnic matching. Think through the implications of an imbalance in the gender and ethnicity of mentors compared to mentees (eg preponderance of female mentors and male mentees).

- Consider the implications for mentor training of the research on females and mentoring.

Post-matching

- Ensure that the duration, frequency and location of meetings set out in the mentoring handbook or programme ground rules are consistent with the aims of the scheme.
- Decide on the degree of structure that the programme manager wishes to try to impose on mentoring relationships. This will determine how the relationship is defined to participants in terms of the dimensions of the relationship (ie is the relationship open, private, active, stable or relatively closed, public and passive?).
- Decide whether the mentoring process is a stand-alone activity or whether there are other elements that aim to achieve overall goals (eg basic skills work, residential experience, group counselling).
- Decide whether to confine mentor-mentee interactions to the mentoring meetings, or to encourage a range of social and education-related activities.
- Consider how the mentoring process appears to you and whether it is possible to define stages. What model of the stages of the mentoring process provides a best fit with your own experience?
- Use the model to inform briefing, training, monitoring and support sessions.
- Produce case studies of successful mentoring relationships to use in recruitment and training.
- Use the experiential learning model to provide a framework for mentors to use during mentoring meetings. Introduce the mentoring learning cycle in mentor training.
- Identify the main relationship problems that are likely to occur given the nature of the target group. Plan to reduce the risks of these problems appearing and have strategies in place to deal with them when they happen.
- Be prepared to support mentors and mentees when the programme reaches an end.
- Plan a memorable, end-of-programme celebratory event.

FUTURE TRENDS

As the forms of mentoring proliferate it will be easier to sell the positive benefits of mentoring to young people and their parents. Mentoring will be regarded as something that can benefit all young people. There will be a move towards combining mentoring with other activities in a mentoring plus approach. Social activities for mentors and mentees in the community will be constrained by continuing worries over child protection. It will be seen as increasingly important to include parents within mentoring programmes. Mentoring processes will be explored through research and evaluation studies and more will be known about the ingredients of successful matching and mutually beneficial relationships.

Evaluation and quality

INTRODUCTION

In this chapter we explore the related questions of 'How do we know what works in mentoring?' 'How can we measure the outcomes of mentoring programmes?' and 'How do we improve the quality of mentoring schemes?'

In our discussion of the different forms of student mentoring there has been a section on research and evaluation evidence at the end of each chapter. We begin by defining some key terms used in the evaluation of public programmes and the evolution of measures of performance in the voluntary sector, drawing on US experience. This is followed by an account of various approaches to the evaluation of mentoring programmes. An important aim of most mentoring evaluations is to improve the quality of the scheme through changing practices in order to achieve better outcomes. In the final part of this chapter we examine the issue of measuring and assuring quality in mentoring programmes. We conclude with a summary of good practice points and an outline of possible future trends in evaluation and quality assurance.

THE LANGUAGE OF PROGRAMME MEASUREMENT

In order to evaluate the success of mentoring programmes and to make comparisons between programmes, it is important to use a common language for describing elements of the mentoring programme (Hatry *et al*, 1996). Some of the terms we will use are as follows:

- *Inputs* are the resources – human, financial and physical or material – that are used to deliver the main processes of the mentoring programme.

- *Processes or activities* are the main elements of the mentoring programme, such as mentor recruitment, training and mentor meetings.
- *Outputs* are essentially quantitative products, which derive directly from the various elements of the mentoring programme. These would include, for example, the number of trained mentors, the number of mentoring pairs and the number of pairs successfully completing the programme.
- *Outcomes* are the changes that occur in the beneficiaries of the programme during or after the mentoring. Outcomes can include changes in knowledge, skills, attitudes, values, behaviour, or status. Outcomes can be those intended by those planning the mentoring scheme or unintended outcomes, which were unforeseen. Outcomes can also be assessed at various points, for example, during a mentoring programme, at the end of the programme and at some date in the future to see if the gains are long term.
- *Outcome indicators or key performance indicators* are the measures of the success of a mentoring scheme. Indicators are numerical measures, which show the proportion of beneficiaries who show evidence of having changed in the way the programme planners intended.
- *Outcome targets* are numerical objectives applied to the success of the mentoring programme. For example, a mentoring programme may set a target based on their prior experience that '90 per cent of mentees will show improvements in their school attendance'.
- *Benchmarking* is when the mentoring programme uses outcome targets for the purpose of making comparisons. Mentoring programmes that operate on an annual cycle can seek to improve on outcome indicators on a year-on-year basis. For example, a scheme where 60 per cent of students showed improvements in basic skills may want to set a target of a 70 per cent improvement for the following year. Funders may set benchmarks for different mentoring programmes to attain.

MEASURING PERFORMANCE IN THE VOLUNTARY SECTOR

Over the past twenty years there have been a number of different approaches to measuring the performance of non-profit or voluntary sector activities (Plantz and Greenway, 1997). In chronological order by their use in the United States, these approaches were:

- *Financial accountability*: programmes were asked to account for how they spent their funds.
- *Output measurement*: programmes were then asked to identify their

key outputs, for example, the number of 'beneficiaries' or in this case the number of mentees or mentoring pairs.

- *Quality standards for service delivery*: following expressions of concern about the quality of services being delivered, many programmes developed quality standards and quality assurance bodies were created to assess and accredit organizations for complying with the standard.
- *Participant-related measures*: data on clients was sought to ensure that programmes were effectively targeting the people that the scheme was aimed at. For example, for mentoring 'at-risk' students what proportion had been temporarily excluded from school, were drug and alcohol abusers or were persistent truants (see Case Study 6.3 for examples of risk factors and Figure 12.1).
- *Key performance indicators*: public accounting companies working for the voluntary sector created many of these indicators. They are often expressed in terms of ratios, for example, between inputs, processes and outputs. For example, the percentage of mentors initially recruited who complete the mentoring programme.
- *Client satisfaction surveys*: surveys of participant satisfaction were required to judge the extent to which they were satisfied with the service provided. Again these provide benchmarking data and the opportunity to create outcome targets to improve the client satisfaction ratings.
- *Outcome measurement*: in mentoring terms, this requires measuring the actual changes in the mentees produced by the programme during or after the mentoring programme.

'GREY' EVALUATION

Much of the evidence discussed earlier in the book is drawn from so-called 'grey literature', that is, research and evaluation that has limitations as an objective study. First, some of the evaluations have been internal, that is carried out by the staff of the programme, who tend to have an interest in highlighting positive outcomes. Second, the methodology used in internal and external evaluations is often based around questionnaires or interviews with mentors and mentees. Outcomes are, therefore, largely self-reported and subject to problems of response bias. Third, many of the external evaluation reports have been commissioned and paid for by mentoring projects. There is always a risk that programme managers can influence data gathering instruments and final reports for their own purposes, which may be to exaggerate positive claims, particularly when continued funding is dependent on evidence of impact. For these reasons 'grey literature' on mentoring does not convince either academics or governments that there is evidence that 'mentoring works'. It is often treated in the same way as the abundant, anecdotal evidence provided by the testimonies of mentors and mentees.

Nevertheless, it is still good practice for mentoring programmes to have an internal monitoring and evaluation strategy. Self-evaluation may have its limitations, but it does engage the people running the programme in questions of how to improve effectiveness and it involves asking those involved what they think. So although internal evaluations may not produce generalizable findings, they do identify 'promising approaches', which are in need of further investigation. Empowerment evaluation also provides a democratic process for including staff in the evaluation of their own projects (see below).

EVALUATION AND RELATED CONCEPTS

Monitoring can be external or internal. External monitoring is generally conducted on behalf of funders or sponsors and its main purpose is accountability. Auditors often carry out external monitoring by following the financial 'paper trail' to ensure that work that has been claimed for has been undertaken and that the numbers of 'beneficiaries' of the programme claimed actually exist. Auditors' visits are likely to be arranged at short notice and their findings usually appear in reports, which highlight any problems. Clearly it is important for mentoring projects to ensure that they satisfy the requirements of funders for financial probity and accountability. So satisfactory external monitoring reports based on sound internal financial systems and quality procedures are important 'hygiene factors' for any mentoring programme.

Distance travelled

The aims of mentoring are to bring about desirable changes in mentees. These can be changes in knowledge, skills, attitudes and behaviour. A key task of the mentoring coordinator is to monitor these changes during the course of the programme. Generally this requires the collection of baseline information from mentees at the start of the programme, and further information during and at the end of the programme, in order to assess so-called 'distance travelled'. Such internal monitoring does not, however, tell the whole story, because there are always a number of variables that could have influenced the changes that are being measured. This non-experimental approach to evaluation fails to address the central question of what would otherwise have been, as it is impossible to observe the young person both with and without a mentor (Grubb and Ryan, 1999). The improvements in attendance or behaviour may have happened anyway without the intervention of a mentor, and so cause and effect cannot be established.

Key performance indicators

One means of gauging the effectiveness of mentoring is to monitor the impact on key performance indicators (KPIs). Programme managers should ask themselves the question, 'If the success of the scheme were to be judged on one or two indicators, then what would they be?' In order to be able to identify KPIs it is important to be precise in defining and prioritizing objectives. For example, a common developmental objective of mentoring programmes is 'to improve self-esteem'. This could be measured in various ways, for example, there are psychometric tests of self-esteem that could be used. However, it is more likely that most mentoring programmes will use ratings by mentees, mentors, parents or significant others, such as teachers, to assess how self-esteem has improved. KPIs could, therefore, include the number or percentage of mentees reporting that their self-confidence has improved. Mentors can also rate the extent to which mentees have demonstrated improved self-confidence during meetings as a way of triangulating or verifying claims made by mentees. These are all essentially soft indicators or non-experimental approaches to evaluation that focus on outcomes, but which fail to address the question of what would otherwise have been.

Table 13.1 *Examples of key performance indicators for student mentoring*

Objectives	Approaches to measurement	Examples of key performance indicators
To improve school behaviour	School disciplinary records	Percentage reduction in temporary exclusions, detentions, referrals etc.
To improve motivation to learn	Student self-rating Subject teacher rating	Percentage of students reporting more time spent on coursework. Percentage of students showing improvements in effort grades in different lessons.
To improve basic skills	Reading tests	Percentage of students showing improvements in reading scores.
To raise aspirations	Students' career action plans	Percentage of students with firm career action plan or plans for progressing into further or higher education, where there were none before mentoring.

Evaluation

There is an extensive literature on evaluation, but in this section we will focus on how to undertake practical evaluation of mentoring programmes. A broad definition of mentoring provides a useful starting point for our discussion.

> The practice of evaluation involves the systematic collection of information about the activities, characteristics and outcomes of programmes, personnel and products for use by specific people to reduce uncertainties, improve effectiveness, and make decisions with regard to what those programmes, personnel, or products are doing and affecting.
>
> (Patton, 1982:15)

This definition highlights the importance of the systematic gathering of data on mentoring programmes, which must be planned and intentional. It illustrates the diversity of evaluation, which can focus on objectives, inputs, processes, or outcomes. Evaluation, unlike some research, always has an end user to make use of the findings and recommendations to change the programme in a variety of ways.

Purpose

A critical question to ask before embarking on evaluation of a mentoring programme is 'what is the purpose of the evaluation'? There are at least three types of purpose (Chelimsky, 1997).

- *Accountability*: to satisfy funders and stakeholders; to meet contractual agreements; to gauge if programme objectives are being met; and to identify successes and failures;
- *Development*: to improve processes and outcomes; and to improve the quality of the programme;
- *Knowledge*: to understand how mentoring processes impact upon outcomes; and to understand better what forms of mentoring achieve which outcomes.

On a macro-level, evaluation is used to inform government policy decisions about what programmes should be expanded and which terminated. It is also used to generate information which is used to stimulate public debate as results are acted upon, reinterpreted, ignored or supplemented by further research (Grubb and Ryan, 1999: 28). On a micro-level evidence of impact is an important way of providing positive reinforcement for mentors that they are in fact making a difference (Lauland, 1998). It can also serve in the recruitment of mentors and external organizations, which provide mentors to schools (Miller, 1998). In this way the results of evaluations can inform individuals about their options.

Formative evaluation

There are various ways of categorizing evaluation, but perhaps the most common is the distinction between formative and summative approaches. Formative evaluations are largely concerned with the development of the mentoring scheme. They involve learning from the scheme in action and are often undertaken informally by programme staff when reflecting on their own practice in order to make improvements. Rather than focusing solely on whether the programme works, formative evaluation poses the question, why does it work? Simple formative questions, which reflective practitioners might ask include:

- Are things going according to plan?
- What do mentors and mentees think about the scheme?
- How can we change things to make the programme run more smoothly?

Mentoring coordinators can engage in informal, formative evaluation by asking these kinds of questions. The main aim is to improve the processes being used during the course of the mentoring programme. For example, during a periodic review and support meeting with mentors they might report that meetings are too infrequent. This may result in a decision to increase the frequency of the programme. People involved in running the programme most often undertake formative evaluation, however, external evaluators from within or outside the project can also be involved. The outcomes of formative evaluations are likely to be informal taking the form of verbal or short written briefings to steering groups or the senior management team of the project.

Summative evaluation

Summative evaluation is usually associated with accountability and is more likely to involve external evaluators. This is because funders and stakeholders value the greater objectivity of data gathering and reports from external organizations with a reputation for objectivity. Public/Private Ventures in the United States have established a reputation for undertaking objective, large-scale summative evaluations of Big Brothers/Big Sisters and other mass mentoring programmes (see Case Study 13.1). The main focus of summative evaluation is on identifying the strengths and weaknesses of the programme and making recommendations for improvement. Summative evaluations involve data gathering at the end or after the end of a programme, so that evidence of impact can be assessed. Formal reports are the main outcome. A pragmatic definition of the purpose of summative evaluation is 'to answer practical questions of decision-makers and programme implementers who want to know whether to continue a programme, extend it to other sites, modify it, or close it down' (National Crime Prevention Council, 1986).

However, summative, external evaluations generally have to be paid for from the programme budget. The quality of the evaluation is partly related to how much money is available to fund it and the 'political context' for the evaluation. It has been suggested that when limited funds are available for a mentoring programme, organizers tend to be reluctant to divert scarce resources into assessing the effectiveness of the programme (Struchen and Porta, 1997). Mentoring coordinators, who manage and support programmes in different institutions will sometimes have to brief external evaluators. It is important for them both to understand evaluation practice, but also to reflect upon their own motivations and relations with the evaluator.

Outcome evaluation and measurement

Mentoring programmes exist to provide beneficial outcomes for students, therefore, the prime aim of any mentoring evaluation should be upon whether and to what extent desired outcomes are achieved. This is an issue that has not been well dealt with in the UK, but it is a problem that affects programmes across the world (MacCallum and Beltman, 1999). Some programmes use standardized instruments and questionnaires to measure pre- and post-mentoring scores on various measures. However, such instruments tend to be expensive, often do not tap the most important outcomes, can be culturally biased and are set at too high a reading age for many mentees.

Classical experimental design

Comparatively few mentoring evaluations use the classical experimental design. However, we have seen that some large-scale US programmes have used this model (see Case Studies 4.3 and 13.1). The main problem of evaluating the impact of mentoring upon students is the range of other influences that can account for the improvements in the identified outcome. How do we know that it is the mentor that has led to the improvement and not some other factor such as better teaching or more attention from staff in the school? The classical experimental design applied to mentoring would involve taking a large population of students and randomly allocating them to a mentored and a non-mentored group. Care is taken to make sure that the mentored group and the control group have similar characteristics. All students would be given a pre-mentoring instrument to gather data or data would be collected on key variables such as attendance and punctuality. Half the students would then go through the mentoring programme while the 'control group' would not. At the end of the programme the baseline instrument and other indicators would be compared with any significant differences being attributed to the mentoring.

Difficulties

There are several reasons why it is difficult to use the experimental design in mentoring evaluations. First, when the evaluation is focused in one school or college there is likely to be a relatively small number of mentored students involved. In other words the size of the sample is too small to yield generalizable results. Second, it is often not desirable to take the whole cohort of students as the target group for mentoring (although GEAR UP Programs provide an exception here, see Chapter 9). Mentoring programmes are usually targeted at the students in most need. An experimental design would mean denying some of the students a mentor, even though they have been deemed to be in need of a mentor. Third, there are often multiple activities going on in a school designed to produce similar outcomes to the mentoring programme. Mentoring schemes are also often accompanied by other activities, such as group residential experiences or basic skills support, in what we have termed a 'mentoring-plus' approach. It is difficult to disentangle the relative contributions of the different activities to any improvements seen in the mentee. Fourth, collecting evidence from the control group adds significantly to the costs of the evaluation. Finally, larger samples can be identified, but often across a range of different institutions in which case there are likely to be significant differences in the ways in which the mentoring schemes operate.

Pre- and post-testing

For these reasons there is a lack of examples of classical experimental design in evaluations of mentoring programmes. It is much more common for mentoring evaluations to use pre-and post-tests and questionnaires to compare the mentees before and after the mentoring. This is an example of what has been described as a weakly experimental approach to evaluation (Grubb and Ryan, 1999). It has the advantage of being able to demonstrate that positive changes have occurred, but it cannot be inferred that mentoring has been the cause or sole cause of the change. There are also quasi-experimental designs, for example, the evaluation described in Chapter 3 where schools had groups of mentees and were asked to select students who matched them to form a control group (Miller, 1998).

In experimental designs, pre- and post-testing designs and quasi-experimental designs, various things can threaten the validity of the results. In particular the normal processes of maturation in young people may account for some of the positive changes. Tests and instruments may not precisely measure what they are supposed to measure and actually taking a test can affect the behaviour of the students. Any events in or outside of school may have an impact on the students and the measurement of outcomes. Distortion can be introduced by important, but unnoticed differences between the mentored group and the control group. The loss of mentees from the study or 'attrition rate' as it is called, can also adversely affect the results.

Case Study 13.1 Experimental Evaluation Design – Big Brothers/Big Sisters of America

Big Brothers/Big Sisters of America is probably the best-known mentoring programme in the United States with 75,000 mentoring pairs in 1996 (see Chapter 1). It is estimated that there will be 300,000 pairs involved in school-based programmes by 2004 (Curtis and Hansen-Schwoebel, 1999). There is a national office that sets standards and procedures to guide local projects. The standards cover:

- screening and acceptance of mentors and young people (mostly from single parent families);
- training of mentors;
- matching;
- frequency of meetings (3–4 hours three times per month for a year);
- supervision of matches including contact with mentor, young person and parent.

Public/Private Ventures conducted a comparative study of 959 10 to 16-year-olds who applied to join the programme in1992/93 (Tierney, Grossman and Resch, 1995). The sample was 60 per cent male and over half were from minority groups. Eight local agencies were chosen on the basis of their size of operation and geographical spread. Baseline interviews were conducted with young people at the start of the evaluation. Half the group was assigned mentors and half was placed on waiting lists. After eighteen months the two groups were re-interviewed. The evaluators had generated six hypotheses that one-to-one mentoring would make a difference in the following outcome areas:

- anti-social activities;
- academic performance;
- attitudes and behaviours;
- relationships within the family;
- relationships with friends;
- self-concept;
- cultural enrichment.

All findings were based on self-reported data obtained from the baseline and follow-up interviews or from forms completed by project staff.

Comparisons were made between the mentored group and the control group controlling for baseline characteristics. The main findings were that the mentored group:

- was 46 per cent less likely to start using drugs and 27 per cent less likely to start using alcohol;
- was about 33 per cent less likely to use violence;
- had improved school attendance and performance (truanted about half as much as control group);
- had modest gains in grade points as a measure of academic achievement;
- had improved peer and family relationships with greater trust in the parent.

The evaluators argued that the strong impacts were largely due to the rigour of the standards used and the support provided by the local agencies to the mentoring pairs. They also observed that this cost an average of $1,000 a match and that these costs could not be met from private sources.

DEVELOPING AN EVALUATION STRATEGY

Everyone involved in running a mentoring scheme should develop a strategy for evaluation. In order to encourage this process the National Mentoring Network has published a guide to effective evaluation based on current evaluation practice in diverse projects across the UK (Miller, 1999b). The simplest approach to developing an evaluation strategy is using the so-called 5WH method. This involves responding to the following six questions.

- Why do we need to evaluate the mentoring programme?
- What evidence needs to be collected on what aspects of the programme?
- How will this evidence be gathered?
- Where will the data be gathered?
- When will the evidence be gathered?
- Who will collect the evidence?

Probably the most important question to resolve is the first, as this will determine whether external or internal, outcome or process, summative or formative evaluations are required. It also focuses attention on what will be done with the results of the evaluation and helps in selecting which aspects of the programme to concentrate on. The second question is important in developing a sharp focus, because mentoring programmes are complex interventions with many elements. It is easy to collect masses of data and then to find it impossible or difficult to make sense of that data. Evaluation novices tend to become preoccupied with the third question of methodology. Common mistakes are to borrow evaluation instruments from other projects and to use them with minimum adaptation or to ask too many questions. An important issue for the evaluation is whether most of the data is collected at the end or whether the evaluation is ongoing during the course of the programme. Finally, the decision over external or internal evaluation is most likely to be constrained by funding. Internal evaluation is likely to be seen as less reliable and objective than external evaluation.

Good practice in programme evaluation

During 1998 members of the National Mentoring Network were surveyed to see the extent to which their mentoring programmes met ten good practice criteria (see Box 13.1).

Box 13.1 Good practice in developing an evaluation strategy

1. There is a strategy in place to evaluate whether the objectives of the mentoring programme were met.
2. Funding for evaluation has been factored into the programme budget.
3. There is a strategy in place to assess outcomes for mentees and benefits for mentors.
4. Baseline data is collected on mentees before the start of the mentoring.
5. End of programme data on mentees is compared to the baseline.
6. There are review meetings with mentors to discuss progress.
7. There is an end-of-programme review with mentors and mentees.
8. Mentors and mentees complete end-of-programme questionnaires.
9. An evaluation report is written with recommendations for improvement.
10. Evaluation evidence is used to change practice in following programmes.

(Adapted from Miller, 1999b)

A MODEL FOR EXTERNAL EVALUATION

A long-established framework for evaluation is the so-called 'countenance model' (Stake, 1967). Mentoring projects that operate over a

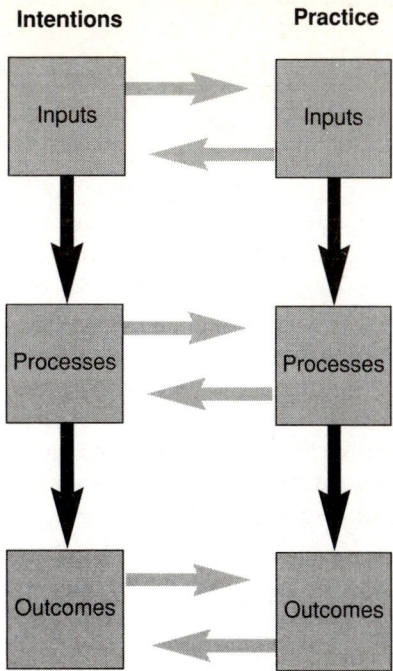

Figure 13.1 *The countenance model of evaluation*

number of educational institutions generally have project guidelines, which explain to practitioners how the programme is supposed to run. Such project guidelines set out aims, inputs, processes and outcomes. However, when practitioners use these guidelines they will tend to make compromises and changes when translating them for local circumstances. In this way the practice begins to diverge from the project's ideal model. One way of viewing a programme is to divide it into three elements: inputs, processes and outcomes (see Figure 13.1).

The first task for the evaluator is to examine the logical relationships between these three elements. For example, the evaluator should consider whether the proposed inputs of people and resources are likely to have the desired impact on the target group in order to produce hoped-for outcomes. The second stage is to examine the programme in practice. Where there are several aims for a programme, practitioners often prioritize these in different ways. Processes are often changed to suit particular circumstances. There are also unintended outcomes as well as planned outcomes from mentoring programmes. The role of the evaluator is to compare and contrast the planned model with the actual practice observing and commenting on differences.

EMPOWERMENT EVALUATION

Empowerment evaluation represents a kind of 'third way' approach to the evaluation of mentoring programmes. In empowerment evaluation the evaluator acts as a coach or facilitator to encourage self-evaluation by programme managers and participants (Fetterman, 2000). There are three steps in empowerment evaluation. The first step is to set out the mission or vision for the mentoring programme or, as an alternative, to state the results, which the programme hopes to bring about in the mentees (in 'managing change' language – 'Where do we want to get to?').

The second step is to identify and prioritize the most important processes in achieving the mission or results. The external evaluator brings the programme managers and participants together to rate how well the programme is performing on each of the key activities. This offers a way of describing where the programme is now and a summation of its strengths and weaknesses ('Where are we now?'). Table 13.2 shows one method of rating aspects of the mentoring programme to identify

Table 13.2 *Empowerment evaluation: self-evaluation*

Mentoring programme: key processes	How well are we doing? Ratings 1 = low 10 = high
1. Pre-planning of the mentoring programme	
2. Programme management	
3. Promotion and recruitment of mentors	
4. Selection of mentors and mentees	
5. Preparation of mentors and mentees	
6. Matching	
7. Mentoring meetings	
8. Mentor and mentee support	
9. Monitoring, quality and evaluation	
10. Ending the mentoring programme and progression	
11. Accreditation	

elements that need attention and, perhaps, those where mentors, mentees and programme staff have different views over effectiveness.

The third step involves the group stating their own goals and the strategies to address these issues. The role of the external evaluator is to help the programme managers and participants to identify the type of evidence required to demonstrate progress towards their goals ('How are we going to get there?'). Thus, evaluation is built into the planning and management of the mentoring programme.

There are several advantages of empowerment evaluation over more traditional approaches to external evaluation. First, it is essentially a more democratic process, as the evaluator acts as a critical friend to the group of programme managers and participants. Second, it empowers programme managers, because they can see how self-evaluation is linked to external requirements. Third, external evaluators are also empowered, because there is an internal evaluation process, which means that they can operate at a more sophisticated level than is generally the case. Finally, it acknowledges that people can create knowledge about their own programmes and generate their own solutions to problems.

Empowerment evaluation offers one way forward for mentoring evaluation. Many student-mentoring programmes are organized by voluntary sector organizations and schools where there is often no budget for external evaluation. Mentoring projects operating in a number of locations could offer empowerment evaluation as a lower cost, democratic approach to fostering a culture of self-evaluation and honesty about the mentoring programmes. It provides a means of embedding self-evaluation in the on-going practices of programme operations.

PROGRAMME VERSUS SYSTEMS EVALUATION

There is a tendency to want to evaluate a programme before it has properly been implemented. In this case the evaluation may produce inaccurate conclusions. It is, therefore, conventional to recommend a process or formative evaluation before an outcome or summative evaluation (Grubb and Ryan, 1999). There is a second tendency to see a mentoring programme as discrete and independent of other programmes or mainstream activities. The focus is largely on the benefits to mentees, and to a lesser extent to mentors. Indeed most of our discussion about the evaluation of mentoring has focused on the 'programme' in isolation from the context in which it is situated.

In contrast to this narrow perspective, a wider systems view would examine the mentoring programme in a wider context (Grubb and Ryan, 1999). This might include asking questions such as the following. How easily could the programme be expanded to include many more mentees and mentors? What would be the constraints on replicating the programme across the country? To what extent does the programme stand alone, or is it part of a larger scheme, which includes a range of strategies for bringing about the desired change in the mentees? What is the relative impact of these different strategies including mentoring? To what extent do school-based mentoring programmes align with other school strategies and policies for raising achievement, inclusion and equal opportunities? What impact does the programme have on the ethos of the school? How does the programme affect social capital? These wider questions are seldom examined in current evaluations of mentoring programmes. However, they are extremely relevant to programmes that have evolved in the way described in Chapter 14.

QUALITY STANDARDS

The proliferation of mentoring programmes since the early 1990s has stimulated the demand for quality standards. Once a new field has developed more and more is known about what constitutes good practice. This encourages the production of guidance by regional and national bodies setting out the characteristics of high quality programmes. This has been the case in the evolution of mentoring programmes (see Chapter 2). Mentoring projects also tend to set down their own recommended structures and procedures for achieving the desired results. Quality standards are generally a collection of statements in the form of prescriptions about a mentoring programme. The production of quality standards is one dimension of the increasing professionalization of the field (Miller, 2000b). Being able to demonstrate compliance with an external and nationally agreed quality standard is also a good way for mentoring programme managers to demonstrate their personal competence in managing the scheme.

Benefits of quality standards

The demands for quality standards are partly generated by government and other external funders of mentoring programmes (see Chapter 1). They want to know that the programmes that they are funding are meeting certain minimum standards, on the assumption that programmes that meet quality criteria are likely to be more effective at achieving results than those that do not. Poorly run mentoring programmes may not only waste public money, but also put young people at risk. For people running mentoring programmes being able to demonstrate compliance with a recognized quality standard is also a good way of maintaining funding or winning extra resources. They can also provide a tool for self-evaluation as projects are encouraged to match their own practice against the recommended, good practice criteria.

Mentoring programmes also raise a number of equality issues, and it is important that managers can show that the programme addresses equality, for example in the recruitment and selection of mentees and mentors. Developing a quality standard can be an effective way of disseminating good practice to others wishing to establish new mentoring programmes. Quality standards can also be directed at mentors to enable would be mentors to distinguish between well- and poorly managed programmes.

Quality standards in the United Kingdom

In the United Kingdom, the NMN has taken the lead in developing and disseminating quality standards. These are often described as quality frameworks, because good practice criteria are categorized under the main stages or processes of a mentoring programme. The first such framework published by the NMN was for mentoring with socially excluded young people (Skinner and Fleming, 1999; see Chapter 6). The quality framework sets out 30 statements, which are further broken down into recommended core practices. These criteria were developed following visits to 20 mentoring programmes working with socially excluded young people. Following the success of this framework, the Minister for School Standards announced that a generic quality framework should be produced offering a minimum quality standard for all forms of mentoring (Morris, 2000; and see Box 13.2).

Box 13.2 UK Generic Quality Standards for Mentoring

1. When new or expanded mentoring projects are proposed, other local programmes targeting the same client group are investigated.
2. When developing a proposal for a new, modified or expanded mentoring programme, individuals or representatives from the client group are consulted.
3. The mentoring programme has a clear statement of aims and a restricted set of specific, measurable, achievable, realistic and targeted objectives.
4. All personnel involved in managing and operating the mentoring programme are committed, appropriately trained and have clearly defined roles and responsibilities.
5. The mentoring programme is adequately resourced in terms of funding, staffing, premises and equipment.
6. There is a support structure in place across the mentoring programme – for the programme manager, project workers, institutional coordinators, mentors and mentees.

---

7. The promotional materials communicate the aims and benefits of the programme, are appropriate, clear and accessible for the target groups of mentors and mentees, and include important information, such as the role of mentor, personal commitment, police checks, vetting procedures and training requirements.

8. The mentoring project uses a range of recruitment strategies to attract mentors and, when appropriate, encourage diversity in mentors recruited.

9. There is a formal application procedure that meets good equal opportunities practice, with clear criteria for acceptance or rejection.

10. There are clear referral/eligibility criteria for potential mentees directly related to the objectives of the programme and the target/client group; and all mentees demonstrate a willingness to participate in the programme.

11. Mentor training is interactive and, at a minimum, includes: the context for the mentoring; how to form a successful mentoring relationship; policies, procedures and guidelines of the programme; and the support structures available.

12. Mentees are prepared for the mentoring relationship so that they are able to gain maximum benefits.

13. Matching is undertaken by the programme manager, taking into account recent information supplied by mentors and mentees including: statements of preference; family/cultural criteria; common interests; mentor life/work experiences.

14. Mentors and mentees reach agreement on the basic mentoring contract covering: when, where and for how long they meet; the structure of meetings; action planning and respective commitments between meetings; confidentiality and boundaries.

15. The mentoring project offers individual and group support for mentors and mentees.

16. There are strategies in place for monitoring mentee development, improving the quality of the programme, and both formative and summative evaluation.

17. There is an exit strategy for both mentor and mentee and a defined ending to the scheme, which is celebrated.

18. The project has explored opportunities for accreditation for mentors and mentees, and, where appropriate, these are encouraged and supported.

(Draft prepared for the National Mentoring Network by Andrew Miller, 2001)

QUALITY ASSURANCE

Quality assurance is the process of assessment and accreditation of programmes against a quality standard. It is usually a combination of self-evaluation and external assessment. Quality assurance is one step away from quality standards, because it involves the use of external assessors to visit and to quality assure the programme. The judgement of the assessors, and usually an awarding panel, determines whether the programme has reached the required level or standard and, therefore, merits the award of the quality kitemark or 'standard'. This is often in the form of a plaque, certificate and/or logo that serves as a quality mark to say that this mentoring programme has reached a particular standard of quality. Such quality assurance programmes generally last for a period of about three years before some form of reassessment and renewed accreditation must be sought. In 2001, the NMN introduced so-called Approved Provider status for mentoring programmes as a response to government requests for a minimum quality standard (NMN, September 2001).

Business Excellence Model

In 1998, a national bursary was awarded for the development of a quality assurance system for mentoring in schools (Miller, 1999a; and see Chapter 1). The quality assurance framework developed was based around the Business Excellence Model (BEM) (British Quality Foundation, 2001). The BEM is being widely used by businesses across Europe to benchmark the quality of their organizations. It is a standard representing an idealized business. Its generic categories have been shown to be applicable to any organization or part of an organization. Using these categories in conjunction with an assessment process an organization can evaluate, develop and mature to become the best in its class. The BEM was developed by the European Quality Foundation for Management and subsequently was adopted by the British Quality Foundation. It forms the basis for awards schemes associated with each of these organizations: the European Quality Award and the British Quality Award.

BEM is beginning to be used by schools in this country alongside Investors in People to improve school performance and effectiveness. The BEM is based upon the premise that:

Customer Satisfaction, *People Satisfaction* and *Impact on Society*
are achieved through
Leadership
Driving
Policy and Strategy, *People Management*, *Resources* and *Processes*

255

Leading ultimately to Excellence in
Business Results.

The nine elements of BEM are divided into Enablers and Results. Enablers are concerned with how the organization runs. Results are concerned with what it is and has been achieving. Each BEM 'element' is given a weighting representing the importance attached to it in respect of its contribution to the model overall. Totalling 100, the weightings are equally assigned (50 per cent-50 per cent) to the Enabler and Results categories.

Excellence in Mentoring

The Excellence in Mentoring quality framework applies the BEM model to the school-based mentoring programmes. The five Enablers, applied to school mentoring programmes, are:

- *Leadership and Management*: this includes the commitment by senior management to the mentoring programme, the effective allocation of roles and responsibilities, level of staff awareness, partnership building, celebration of achievements.
- *Policy and Strategy*: includes the development of a set of aims, staff awareness of aims, SMART targets, policy statements, mentoring culture and stakeholder involvement.
- *People Management*: includes the role and responsibility of mentoring coordinator, training of coordinator, mentor training, appraisal and recognition.
- *Resources*: includes human resources supporting the scheme, physical space, finance, use of good practice guidance, access of students to means of communication and company financial support.
- *Processes*: includes briefing for students, training for mentors, structuring of mentoring meetings, mid-programme reviews and evaluation.

Results include:

- *Mentor and Mentee Satisfaction*: includes customer satisfaction ratings, evaluation feedback from mentors, mentees and equal opportunities.
- *Staff Satisfaction*: includes satisfaction of teachers and other staff, motivational effect on staff and the wider impact of the mentoring culture.
- *Impact on Society*: includes the views of parents, spin off benefits to the school, impact on social exclusion.
- *Outcomes*: includes the impact of mentoring on students, minimum targets for successful outcomes, completion rates, self-reported and mentor reported outcomes, impact on behaviour and attainment.

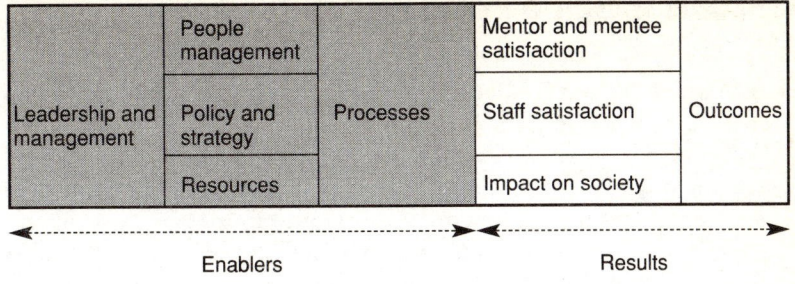

	People management		Mentor and mentee satisfaction	
Leadership and management	Policy and strategy	Processes	Staff satisfaction	Outcomes
	Resources		Impact on society	

◄--►◄--►

Enablers   Results

Figure 13.2 *The Business Excellence Model applied to school mentoring*

Using the BEM, in conjunction with a self-assessment approach, schools operating mentoring schemes can derive one of the model's key benefits. By carrying out a series of assessments, awareness is raised as to the strengths and opportunities for improvement. This growing self-knowledge throughout the school can lead to greater effectiveness. It is from a cyclic application of the assessment (usually annually), over a period of time that the full benefits of using the BEM model accrue.

Benefits of quality assurance

There are a number of benefits to schools from undertaking a quality assurance process such as the one described. First, there are often a variety of mentoring programmes within one school and the process enables an overview to be gained of the relationship between mentoring and the whole curriculum. Second, the compilation of the portfolio provides a comprehensive body of evidence about the work being undertaken and the wider impact of the mentoring programmes. It can then be used with a wide range of audiences to raise the profile of the programme and even to gain extra resources. Third, it can highlight resource needs such as the need for extra non-contact time for the coordinator. Fourth, it can raise the status and visibility of mentoring and the mentoring coordinator within the school. Finally, it can involve external mentoring support staff and advisers in offering an objective sounding board, which will aid the future development of the programme.

SUMMARY OF GOOD PRACTICE POINTS

- Become familiar with the language of programme measurement and evaluation. Make a list of the main measures or terms that are or could be used in describing the mentoring programme.
- Consider the ways in which programme performance has been measured in evaluating the voluntary sector. Which of these measures are or might be used in the mentoring programme?
- Refer back to the evaluation evidence in Chapters 3 to 7 and make a note of those findings that are most relevant to the mentoring programme.
- Read carefully any contractual requirements and ensure that arrangements are in place for the 'paper trail' required by external auditors.
- Develop an evaluation strategy for the mentoring programme.
- Collect baseline information on mentees.
- Develop a database to record information on the main beneficiaries, the mentees.
- Identify some key performance indicators on which the mentoring programme can be judged by people inside and outside the project.
- Consider the main purposes of evaluating the mentoring programme and the uses to which any findings will be put.
- Decide whether external or internal evaluation is appropriate depending upon levels of funding and views of stakeholders.
- Consider using an empowerment model of evaluation to embed evaluation practices within the organization.
- Agree the type of evaluation methodology that will be used depending on the extent to which findings are required to be generalizable and to stand up to critical scrutiny.
- Consider the moral and social implications of the use of control groups that will not benefit from the mentoring programme.
- Postpone a full outcome evaluation until the programme is fully implemented.
- Think through the implications of evaluation findings for future funding decisions. Consider the implications of evaluation processes upon programme managers and participants.
- Undertake formative or process evaluation before summative or outcome evaluation.
- Investigate the external quality standards that can be applied to the mentoring programme.
- Consider the costs and benefits of compliance with an external quality assured mentoring standard.
- Use the quality assurance process to encourage a self-review and a culture of continuous improvement.

FUTURE TRENDS

As increasing amounts of public money are used to support mentoring programmes for students and young people, there will be pressure for national quality standards. Mentoring kitemarking schemes will be introduced as marks of quality that sponsors, mentors, mentees, parents, teachers and members of the community will recognize. The tendency for local kitemarking schemes to proliferate will eventually be resolved with the introduction of national systems to assure the quality of the range of mentoring programmes. Government will fund longitudinal studies of mentoring programmes for young people to examine the effects of mentoring on future learning, development and employability. More programmes will build evaluation into their practices and some programmes will experiment with empowerment evaluation. There will be more evaluation that takes a systems approach examining the impact of mentoring programmes, for example, on social capital, school ethos and peer relationships.

Part IV

Conclusion

14

The future of mentoring for students and young people

We have examined many different forms of student mentoring and seen how it has developed in the United States and UK. Case studies of programmes have illustrated aspects of good practice in mentoring. The research and evaluation evidence supports the view that student mentoring can bring many benefits to students, schools, mentors and communities. In this chapter we set out a vision of mentoring for young people in the future and explore how a mentoring culture might serve to transform schools and improve life for individuals. What if schools began to build on their mentoring programmes, to introduce other forms of mentoring and to develop stronger mentoring partnerships with their local community? What would a school with a mentoring culture be like? The case study of Telemachus High School in the year 2015 describes a whole-community approach to mentoring. What would the benefits be to all parties involved? What policies need to be introduced by government and what actions need to be taken by schools to move towards this vision?

Case Study 14.1 Telemachus High School 2015

The school is part of a sustained partnership that includes local business, the local council, voluntary and community groups, churches, neighbouring schools and the local college and university. The partnership aims to use the resources of its people and constituent members to benefit the entire community, and to include all young people in that community. Mentoring is viewed by all as a key strategy for school improvement, for social inclusion, for bringing the community together and for improving people's lives. The improvement of social capital is widely seen as a major goal of mentoring programmes for students and young people. The school has an open door policy to working with the community, and there is a mentoring ethos and culture in evidence. The school's mentoring policy is closely linked to other policies for raising standards, for community links and for student support. Mentoring procedures ensure that students have a mentor who can best meet their particular needs. The overall management of mentoring brings coherence and ensures that staff, students and mentors are not overburdened.

Mentoring for all

Student volunteering is seen as an important part of the curriculum and students of all ages are involved in active citizenship projects in school and the local community. Peer helping, peer mentoring and peer tutoring are embedded into the life of the school. Every student in need of extra support has an older buddy who befriends and supports the student's academic work in libraries and after-school clubs. Being in the role of mentee is a key part of the training to take on the role of mentor. Students from the high school are paired with children from local primary schools and during their weekly visit they encourage the pupils and support their learning. In between visits the pairs communicate by e-mail about mutual interests. All students receive recognition and accreditation for their peer mentoring work. Older students need to have undertaken mentoring assignments in order to graduate. Tiered mentoring involves older students mentoring younger students throughout the year groups or grades.

School–community mentoring partnerships

The school has an adult and community learning centre that is used by a wide range of people and community organizations. Adults visiting the centre are mentors for students experiencing difficulties in school. The school offers its resources to local mentoring organizations that provide community-based mentoring for young people. There is a synergy between school-based and community-based programmes, including joint mentor recruitment and training. Cross-cultural mentoring by adults and among peers promotes racial harmony within the school and in the local community. Students who would benefit from role models of the same cultural background are able to access them through the minorities mentoring programme. The school specializes in the arts, media and sports, and the faculties have databases of local achievers in these fields who are prepared to volunteer to support the school. Staff from the local radio station mentor small groups of students taking media studies courses. Local artists are paired with talented students following arts courses. People from local sports teams support teachers in coaching and mentoring students and teams. Two large local employers provide business mentors to work with students taking business courses and those interested in entering the work-force at age 19.

School–university partnership

Lecturers from the local university act as telementors to students who are undertaking projects as part of academic and vocational courses. In particular, the science and technology faculties provide assignments and ongoing support for teachers and students. Students in the early grades are targeted for stretching work and university mentors, as the research shows that this has the most impact in raising achievement and aspirations. Students undertaking higher degrees in the education faculty carry out evaluations of mentoring programmes as part of their academic training and as a subject of research. Service learning is well established at the university and many students volunteer to mentor high school students, to run workshops for them on higher education and to host visits to the university. The local college has a similar programme aimed at supporting students taking vocational courses. A gifted-and-talented programme pairs high-flying undergraduates with able students from low-income families who may be wavering about going to university.

Management and teacher involvement

A group of senior volunteers, including former teachers, provides coordination of the external mentoring programmes. They work closely with the personal advisers, who provide diagnostic assessment and ongoing support for at-risk students, and all students who are new to the school. A steering group includes representatives of students, teachers and organizations providing mentors to review programmes, resourcing, monitoring and evaluation outcomes. Senior teachers mentor all new members of the teaching and support staff. All teachers are expected to take on an academic mentoring or tutoring role, working with four or five individual students throughout the year. Staff view mentoring as a key skill for all people to have and an important means to achieve the aims of the school. The head teacher acts as a champion of the mentoring culture by acting as a mentor to a new local head teacher, and by ensuring that mentoring is resourced and celebrated. Regular awards recognize outstanding achievements by mentors and mentees, but all mentors are acknowledged.

BENEFITS

Individuals

Individuals taking on the role of mentor develop their emotional intelligence. They develop empathy and the ability to listen, but also the skills to challenge and motivate others. These benefits have repercussions in improving their own personal relationships at work and in the family. Students serving as peer mentors see helping the learning of other people as a key responsibility of everyone. Mentoring experiences promote a culture of lifelong learning among students, mentors and teachers. The lives of adult mentors without children, or whose children have grown up, are enriched by contact with young people. Students benefit from the pool of experience, knowledge and skills that specialist mentors bring to subjects and courses. The caring ethos of the school and mentor support for all undermine bullying, reduce behavioural problems and end school exclusions.

Businesses

Businesses find that their employees are motivated to work for companies that allow them time for volunteering to support their local schools. Company appraisals highlight the gains employees have made in their interpersonal skills, mentoring skills and emotional intelligence. Students from the school have good interpersonal skills and are strong on employability skills and qualities, in part as a result of their experience as mentees and mentors. The school has developed effective systems for welcoming business people and other adult visitors, and keeping them informed about the progress of their mentees.

Teachers

Teachers find that they have given up some of their autonomy. There are lots of other people with an interest in young people's learning in the school all the time. Teachers find that they are no longer alone in discussions about teaching and learning. Peer tutors and mentors reinforce learning and support homework. Specialist mentors from business, particular employment sectors and the university enrich the curriculum. Higher education students raise the aspirations of students to attend university. These people reflect the ethnic diversity of the local population and bring many more role models into the school. Adult volunteers take after-school clubs, which reduces the demands on teachers' time.

Community members

Senior citizens and people from minority ethnic communities feel welcome and valued by the school staff and students. They have a role in providing their experience to help students in need of adult support. Bonds are strengthened between older people working in the school and between minorities. Intergenerational bonds are created and informal groups of mentor friends develop. Mentoring serves as a unifying mechanism to include all sorts of people in the school community. In these ways the social capital of the local community is enhanced. Volunteers work in teams to manage external mentoring and make the teachers' job easier.

University

The university is able to increase the number of students from the school who wish to apply to go there. Undergraduates are able to undertake service learning through mentoring at the school and related activities. Mentoring and the school curriculum provide vehicles for academic staff and students' research and evaluation work. The evaluation strategy adopts a wider 'systems' rather than a narrow 'programme' approach. This effectively captures the richness of the impact of mentoring programmes in the school and the community. Staff from departments with declining popularity play a direct role in increasing demand for their subjects through involvement in telementoring and curriculum development.

Senior management team

Senior staff and the head teacher benefit from a school that is working closely with the local community. The partnerships and the large number of adults involved with the school bring in extra resources, both human and financial. Students and teachers are happier. Aspirations are high and achievements are steadily raised. The quality of learning for all students has improved as a result of the mentoring programmes. The school's emphasis on people helping each other through mentoring relationships means that the school is popular with parents. It serves as a beacon to other schools, showing what can be achieved through adopting a mentoring culture from top to bottom of the organization. The strong partnerships developed with other educational institutions, businesses and the community place the school at the centre of local life.

TOWARDS A MENTORING CULTURE

The case studies in this book show what can be achieved through mentoring. No schools currently have a mentoring culture of the kind described in the case study of Telemachus High School. However, we have encountered all these ingredients of mentoring, curriculum and community in the case studies drawn from schools in the United States, United Kingdom and Australia today. In this final section, We highlight some of the actions of government and schools that will support the move towards a mentoring culture.

Government

Government is important in setting the context in which mentoring for young people can thrive. High profile government support for mentoring can draw the attention of local government and school governors to the importance of mentoring in transforming schools. Government can support volunteering through funding for voluntary sector organizations wishing to establish school- and community-based mentoring programmes. They can also support education for citizenship through opportunities for accreditation of mentoring work and links to gradua- tion. The cost of mentoring programmes can be reduced by ending charging for police checks on mentors and by speeding up the process.

Mass-mentoring programmes require large-scale government funding. These provide mentoring programmes with which schools can form a link. Funding can support mentoring programmes targeting particular groups, such as senior citizens and minority ethnic communities. Govern- ment can also encourage corporate community investment and volun- teering through adjustments to the tax system. It can set national quality standards and support quality assurance systems to ensure that mentor- ing programmes are well managed and benchmarked. Government can set out a vision for mentoring that is based upon local partnerships of schools, businesses, universities and colleges to bring about economies of scale and a mentoring culture in an area. This will serve to generate social capital both within and between schools and communities.

Schools

School decision makers can support the development of the mentoring culture in a number of ways. It is important that senior staff act as mentors and as champions of mentoring. They need to make sure that there is a strategic plan in place to move towards the mentoring culture over, say, a five-year period. This will require financial and human resources. Strong partnerships have to be formed with local business, the voluntary sector and community organizations, as part of a wider com- munity links strategy. Bonds need to be strengthened between the school and local colleges and the university. Partnership agreements can be put in place to document the roles and responsibilities of all the partners.

The mentoring policy needs to complement other school policies, for example on raising standards and inclusion. Staff roles and responsibili- ties need to be reviewed to ensure that the mentoring coordination team is enthusiastic, well trained and resourced to do an effective job. Volunteer resources need to be welcomed and seen as key to running effective external mentoring programmes. A steering group with broad representation needs to be established to move the mentoring programmes forward. Young people need to be represented on the steering group and centrally involved in decision making about develop- ments in mentoring. University support can help set up effective moni- toring and evaluation strategies. Peer mentoring programmes can begin with pilot schemes and then broaden to include whole grades of students. Above all senior staff should celebrate mentoring successes and the achievements of both mentors and mentees. These are the kinds of measures that can place one-to-one mentoring relationships at the heart of school transformation and community regeneration.

Challenges

It is also true that the actions of government and schools can undermine the move towards a mentoring culture. Government funding cuts borne out of recession or a change of administration can remove the infrastructure needed to support the 'fervour' we have described above. Support for volunteering and the voluntary sector organizations that manage mentoring programmes needs to be sustained. The tendency of government to fund pilots or provide annual funding makes it difficult to build the kinds of sustained partnerships and programmes that are required. A move to politicize mentoring or to link it too closely to the school dropout or social exclusion agendas may result in many schools, parents and teachers viewing mentoring as only suitable for a minority of young people or for schools in poor neighbourhoods. A failure to sustain support for active citizenship or to link it to the curriculum and graduation could undermine the supply of young mentors.

Schools too can undermine the development of a mentoring culture. School decision makers are sometimes reluctant to open the school up to the local community. Teachers can be suspicious of what might be perceived as unqualified people and do-gooders interfering with the professional business of education. Teacher shortages and the overburdened curriculum make it more likely that teachers will view mentoring as one more initiative that they can do without. School mentoring coordinators may be given inadequate time or support to do the job properly, and mentors can feel let down as a result. In such circumstances, companies may start to withdraw support as school-based programmes gain a bad name.

In spite of all these potential blockages, mentoring has gained a lot of support from among the army of mentors and mentees, who are both current and future voters, as well as users of the education system. There are also promising signs that governments have seen the benefits of mentoring and the potential advantages of a move towards the mentoring culture. More research needs to be done on what forms of mentoring are most appropriate for supporting the learning of students with particular sets of needs. Government could create beacon schools from those wanting to extend their mentoring programmes in the ways we have described. Research efforts could focus on the beacon schools to provide evidence of the impact and benefits of the mentoring culture on students, mentors, schools and the local community. *Mentoring Students and Young People: A handbook of effective practice* aims to encourage governments, schools and communities to take the steps necessary to create this mentoring culture for the benefit of young people, schools and society.

Glossary of mentoring terms

Academic mentoring is used in three ways: first, mentoring where the prime goal is to improve the academic achievement of the mentee; second, as an alternative phrase for academic tutoring, where teachers support students, often in the run up to examinations; third, mentoring in a higher education context, where staff mentor students.

Business mentoring is used in two ways: first, mentoring of students by people from the private sector; second, mentoring of young people starting a business by experienced business people or professional business advisers. **Enterprise mentoring** can be used to describe the latter form.

Career mentoring is where the main focus is on the career development of the mentee and in addition, sometimes, where the mentor is a careers specialist.

Classical mentoring refers to the one-to-one relationship between an older, wiser person and a younger, less experienced person (as in the myth of Mentor and Telemachus).

Community mentoring is where mentors are drawn from the local community, such as residents, church representatives, community groups, police. **Community-based mentoring** is when mentoring meetings take place outside of the school setting (eg in youth clubs, workplaces, cafés).

Contract mentoring refers to the situation where mentors and mentees reach an individual agreement or contract about what each will hope to achieve through the mentoring process.

Corporate mentoring occurs within corporations, generally with a work-related or career-related focus.

Cross-age mentoring is when mentors are drawn from a different age group to mentees. **Cross-cultural mentoring** is where mentors and mentees are from different cultural backgrounds. **Cross-gender mentoring** is when males and females are paired.

Developmental mentoring occurs when the prime aim is the personal development of the mentee.

Drive-by mentoring is a pejorative phrase used to describe situations where mentors only engage with their mentees either superficially or for a very short period of time, which can result in reduced self-esteem and further damage.

External mentoring refers to circumstances where mentors are drawn from outside the education institution, eg from business or the community. In contrast, **internal mentoring** involves peers, teachers, support staff or paraprofessionals, such as learning mentors, who are members of the school or college community.

Friend-to-friend mentoring is a form of **natural mentoring** occurring within one-to-one friendships.

Gifted-and-talented mentoring refers to schemes targeted at students with special abilities or potential.

Group mentoring or **small-group mentoring** is when the mentor is matched with two or more students (usually up to a maximum of between four and six). **Telementoring** can include **whole-class mentoring** when the mentor communicates by e-mail with up to 30 students. Some people would regard these forms as **pseudo mentoring**, because mentoring is defined as only including one-to-one support.

Higher education student mentoring refers to programmes where university or college students mentor younger students, generally in schools.

Holistic mentoring is when the mentor is a highly skilled, possibly professional, person deploying the full range of helping behaviours to develop their mentee.

Individual–team mentoring is a form of **natural mentoring** in which a group of young people looks to an individual or small number of individuals for advice and support.

Intergenerational mentoring generally involves a 'skipped' generation between mentors and mentees. Hence, it is usually applied to the over-50 generation mentoring students.

Long-term relationship mentoring is a form of **natural mentoring** similar to **classical mentoring**, however, in this case the adult concerned has a history of rebellion and risk-taking.

Mass mentoring refers to large-scale, statewide or national programmes, and/or programmes that have been replicated or franchised over a wide area, eg Big Brothers/Big Sisters of America.

Minority ethnic mentoring or **Black and minority ethnic mentoring** is where the programme is targeted at mentees and mentors from specified **minority ethnic** communities.

Natural mentoring is a term applied to mentoring relationships that occur from time to time in people's lives, outside of a structured mentoring programme.

Near-age mentoring is a form of **peer mentoring** when mentors are one to three years older than mentees. **Same-age mentoring** is peer mentoring by students in the same year group.

Paid mentoring is contrasted with **volunteer mentoring** to reflect possible differing motivations on the part of mentors. Some argue that only unpaid volunteers can be mentors and that programmes where mentors are paid are **pseudo mentoring**.

Peer group mentoring is a form of **natural mentoring** when groups of friends explore an issue together, often involving risk behaviour.

Peer mentoring literally means mentoring by equals, but usually refers to people with the same status, ie teacher-teacher or student-student pairings.

Primary mentoring is sometimes used for programmes involving primary aged pupils as mentees. It can also be used to describe mentoring of teachers by teachers in primary education.

Professional mentoring is when mentors are specially trained, experienced and paid. External corporate mentors and learning mentors would fall into this category.

Pseudo mentoring can be applied to programmes which fall outside definitions of mentoring. However, different people draw the boundary between mentoring and other activities, such as coaching, teaching and tutoring, in different places. Others would argue that mentors must be unpaid volunteers.

Reciprocal mentoring is the situation in **natural or structured mentoring** when mentee and mentor alternate their roles.

Site-based mentoring is when the location of meetings is within the educational institution, rather than community-based.

Socially excluded mentoring is when the target group of young people are, or are at risk of, being excluded from society. Sometimes this is called **at-risk mentoring**.

Sports mentoring is a term used in programmes where experienced sports people mentor individual students or teams. Some would say that this is better described as coaching.

Structured mentoring or **planned mentoring** or **intentional mentoring** is when a third party organizes the mentoring relationship in contrast with **natural mentoring**.

Student-led mentoring refers to a student-centred mentoring philosophy where mentees set the agenda for mentoring meetings. This is contrasted with **school-led mentoring** where the school sets goals, targets and processes that pairs are expected to follow. In **mentor-led mentoring**, it is the mentor who is encouraged to set the agenda.

Student mentoring is used as a generic phrase to cover all the forms of mentoring where young people in educational institutions are mentees.

Teacher mentoring is used in two ways: first, where experienced teachers mentor other less experienced or newly qualified teachers, often as a formal part of their training or induction; second, where teachers act as mentors to students, although some people would describe this as academic tutoring or a form of **pseudo mentoring**.

Team mentoring refers to the situation when two or more people mentor a young person, for example, a learning mentor and a business mentor. The two mentors are required to work together rather than independently.

Telementoring is when the mentoring programme uses telecommunications – telephone, e-mail or teleconferencing – as the main means of contact between mentors and mentees. **E-mentoring** is a particular form of **telementoring** that focuses on the use of e-mail.

Tiered mentoring refers to programmes where the mentees act as mentors to other students.

Transition mentoring describes mentoring programmes that target young people during times of transition, eg transfer from primary to secondary school, from secondary school to college, or from school or university to employment.

Workplace mentoring or **work-experience mentoring** refers to the practice of allocating a mentor to students undertaking internships or work placements.

Youth justice mentoring usually involves young people being given a mentor as part of a court order. Some people argue that the compulsory nature of **youth justice mentoring** means that this is another form of **pseudo mentoring**.

Web guide

Big Brothers, Big Sisters of America
Find out about the world's oldest, and probably largest, mentoring organization.
www.bbbsa.org

Crime Concern Mentoring Knowledgebase
Useful UK site for beginners and experienced practitioners on running mentoring programmes.
www.mentoringknowledgebase.com

Department of Education, Training and Youth Affairs
Location of the excellent 1999 mentoring report by Judith MacCallum and Susan Beltman.
www.detya.gov.au

Home Office
The UK government department that has responsibility for mentoring and volunteering through its Active Community Unit. Site is useful to track policy and funding opportunities.
www.homeoffice.gov.uk

Informal Education
Useful UK site for articles on mentoring research and learning mentors.
www.infed.org

International Telementor Center
Interesting site addressing telementoring and business mentoring with case studies of school projects.
www.telementor.org

Gaining Early Awareness & Readiness for Undergraduate Programs
Main site for exciting and ambitious US initiative with links to local GEAR UP projects.
www.ed.gov/gearup

Juvenile Mentoring Program
Find out more about mentoring in a youth justice context.
www.ojjdp.ncjrs.org

Learning Mentors – Birmingham Education Service
A good site for finding out more about the work of the UK's learning mentors in schools.
www.mentor.bham.org.uk

Mentoring Leadership & Resource Network
Useful site created by the prolific Barry Sweeny with articles and links.
www.mentors.net

Mentors' Forum
Interesting network site with good European mentoring links and information on adult mentoring.
www.mentorsforum.co.uk

National Mentoring Association of Australia
Site of the national Australian network contains benchmark quality standards and links.
www.mentoring-australia.com

National Mentoring Network
The national UK network for mentoring with information on events, policy developments and publications.
www.nmn.org.uk

National Mentoring Pilot Project
Home site of the UK's major project for higher education students mentoring in schools.
www.ncl.ac.uk/sis/nmpp

National School Network
Links to useful articles and 'how to' guides on telementoring.
www.nsn.bbn/com/telementor

North West Region Educational Laboratory – National Mentoring Center
An invaluable site with many free downloadable documents, mentoring

guides and technical packets by Linda Jucovy and others.
www.nwrel.org

Peer Resources
Excellent Canadian-based site has many good, free materials, and access
to more through joining the network.
www.peer.ca

Public/Private Ventures
The organization that has conducted the most evaluation and research
into mentoring programmes.
www.ppv.org

References

Alexander, S and Day, G (1995) *Roots & Wings Mentoring Scheme: Information pack for prospective mentors*, SBC Warburg, London

Amis, K and Marsh, N (2001) Small group mentoring in secondary schools: focus on higher education, in *Mentoring for Social Inclusion: Report on the Second Annual Conference of the London Region of the National Mentoring Network*, ed A D Miller, pp 43–45, NMN and Learning and Skills Council, London

Anderson, E M and Shannon, A L (1995) Toward a conceptualisation of mentoring, in *Issues in Mentoring*, ed T Kerry and A S Mayes, pp 25–34, Routledge, London and New York

Anderson, J (1994) Launch of the National Mentoring Network, in *Report on the Third National Mentoring Conference*, Salford Business Education Partnership (SBEP), Manchester

Appiah, L (2001) *Mentoring: School–business links*, Runnymede Trust, London

Audit Commission (1998) *Misspent Youth*, Audit Commission, London

Barber, M (2001) Welcome to *The Mentor*, in *The Mentor*, **1**, National Mentoring Pilot Project, Cardiff, p 2

Beattie, R M and Sanborn, C (1999) Mentoring is not a black and white venture, in *The Mentoring Connection*, International Mentoring Association (www.wmich.edu/conferences/mentoring/black_white.html)

Beiswinger, G (1985) *One to One: The story of the Big Brothers/Big Sisters Movement in America*, Winchell Company and Big Brothers/Big Sisters of America, Philadelphia

Ben-Avie, M, Steinfeld, T R and Vergnetti, M L (2000) *Documenting the Impact of the ScholarshipBuilder Program on the Lifepaths of Students*, Yale Child Study Center, New Haven

Benioff, S (1997) *A Second Chance: Developing mentoring and education projects for young people*, Crime Concern and the Commission for Racial Equality, London

Binik, Y M, Cantor, J, Ochs, E and Meana, M (1997) From the couch to the keyboard: Psychotherapy in cyberspace, in *Culture of the Internet*, ed S Kiesler, pp 71–102, Lawrence Erlbaum, Mahwah

Birmingham Local Education Authority (2001) *Learning Mentors Good Practice Examples*, on Birmingham Learning Mentors' Information Site (www.mentor.bham.org.uk)

Boateng, P (2000) *Keynote Address to London Mentoring Matters! Conference*, National Mentoring Network, Manchester (mimeo)

Borredon, L (1995) A pilot year of mentoring students at a French business school, in *Mentoring in Action*, eds D Megginson and D Clutterbuck, pp 63–84, Kogan Page, London

Branden, N (1994) *Six Pillars of Self-Esteem*, Bantam, New York

British Quality Foundation (1998) *Guide to the Business Excellence Model for TECs/CCTEs*, DfEE/British Quality Foundation, London

British Quality Foundation (2001) *Manage Your Organisation Using the Excellence Model*, British Quality Foundation, London

Brown, J S, Collins, A and Duguid, P (1989) Situated cognition and the culture of learning, *American Educator*, **18** (1), pp 32–42

Business and the Community (BITC) (1997a) *Roots & Wings Mentoring Guide*, BITC, London

BITC (1997b) *Roots & Wings Mentoring Guide and Case Studies*, BITC, London.

BITC (1998) *Aim High: 1998 Examples of Excellence*, BITC, London

BITC (not dated) *Roots & Wings Mentoring in the Community*, BITC, London

Cahalan, M and Farris, E (1990) *College Sponsored Tutoring and Mentoring Programs for Disadvantaged Elementary and Secondary Students: Higher education survey reports*, Westat, Rockville

Cardenas, J A *et al* (1991) *Valued Youth Program, Dropout Prevention Strategies for At Risk Students*, Paper presented at the Annual Meeting of the American Educational Research Association, Chicago

Cardow, A (1998) Mentoring at light speed, *Mentoring and Tutoring*, **5** (3), pp 32–45

Carmeli, A (1999) *Perach: Involving students in the community*, Keynote Address at the Second Regional Conference on Tutoring and Mentoring, Perth, Western Australia (mimeo)

Carr, R A (2000) *The Mentoring Cycle*, Peer Resources Papers (www.peer.ca)

Carr, R (2001) *The Changing Nature of Mentorship in Canada*, Peer Resources (www.peer.ca)

Carrad, L (2002) Policy developments in mentoring and volunteering, in *Mentoring, Citizenship and the Community: Report of the third annual conference of the London Mentoring Network*, ed A D Miller, Learning and Skills Council, London (forthcoming).

Center for Children and Technology (1996) Telementoring: using tele-communications to develop mentoring relationships, *Center for Children and Technology Notes*, **4** (1) (www.edc.org/CCT/)

Chelimsky, E (1997) Thoughts for a new evaluation society, *Evaluation*, 3 (1), pp 97–118

Clark, H H and Brennan, S E (1991) Grounding in communication, in *Perspectives on Socially Shared Cognition*, ed L B Resnick, J M Levine and S D Teasley, pp 127–49, American Psychological Association, Washington

Clarke, A and Tarling, R (1998) *Dalston Youth Project Part B (11–14): An evaluation*, Surrey Social and Market Research, Guildford

Clutterbuck, D (1998) *Learning Alliances: Tapping into talent*, Institute of Personnel and Development, London

Cobb, B (1997) *HP Telementor Program Evaluation 1996–97*, International Telementor Centre (www.telementor.org/hp/hp-evaluation/summary.html)

Cohen, P A, Kulik, J A and Kulik, C C (1982) Educational outcomes of tutoring: a meta-analysis of findings, *American Education Research Journal*, **19** (2), pp 237–48

Coleman, J (1990) *Foundations of Social Theory*, Harvard University Press, Cambridge

Collins, P (1994) Mentoring moving on: a network development, *Education and Training*, **36** (5), pp 16–19

Community Service Volunteers (2000) *Student Volunteering Statistics 1999–2000*, Community Service Volunteers, London (mimeo)

Conway, C (1997) Mentoring in organizations, in *Mentoring: The new panacea?*, ed J Stephenson, Peter Francis, Norfolk

Costigan, M (2000) National Mentoring Network: past, present and future, in *Perspectives on Mentoring: The Report on the Ninth National Mentoring Conference 2000*, ed A D Miller, pp 10–15, Salford Business Education Partnership, Manchester

Coughlan, S (2001) *How Mentors Make a Difference*, BBC News Online, 24 January 2001 (www.news.bbc.co.uk/hi/english/education)

Crime Concern/Youth Justice Board (2001) *Mentoring Work with Minority Ethnic Young People: Briefing paper*, Crime Concern/Youth Justice Board, London

Curtis, T and Hansen-Schwoebel, K (1999) *Big Brothers/Big Sisters School-Based Mentoring: Evaluation of five pilot programs*, Big Brothers/Big Sisters of America, Philadelphia

Day, G and Kannike, Y (1999) *Roots & Wings Mentoring Project: Monitoring report 1998–99*, Lewisham Roots & Wings Mentoring Project, London (mimeo)

Department for Education and Employment (DfEE) (1997) *Excellence in Schools: White Paper*, DfEE Publications, Suffolk.

DfEE (1999a) *Baseline Survey of Mentoring in Schools*, DfEE, Sheffield (unpublished)

DfEE (1999b) *Excellence in Cities: Planning guidance for LEAs on learning mentors*, DfEE, London (mimeo)

DfEE (2000a) *Blunkett Launches Schools Anti-Bullying Strategy*, Press Notice 2000/0582, DfEE, London (www.dfee.gov.uk)

DfEE (2000b) *Community Mentoring as a Means of Support for Underachieving Ethnic Minority Pupils*, (internal paper AGREMPA 99(3)), DfEE, London (mimeo)

DfEE (2000c) *Removing the Barriers: Raising achievement levels for minority ethnic pupils*, DfEE, London

DfEE (2000d) *Schools Plus: building learning communities, a report from the Schools Plus policy action team*, DfEE, London

Dimock, K V (1998) Building relationships, engaging students: a naturalistic study of classrooms participating in the Electronic Emissary Project, in *Electronic Emissary Research Manuscripts* (www.emissary.ots.utexas/edu/emissary/publications)

Divert (1999) *Divert Mentoring Handbook*, Divert Trust, London

Dondero, G M (1997) Mentors: beacons of hope, *Adolescence*, **32** (128), pp 881–86

Drury, C (2001) *Accredited Mentor Training Courses*, NMN, Manchester

Ellis, S W and Granville, G (1999) Intergenerational solidarity: bridging the gap through mentoring programmes, *Mentoring and Tutoring*, **7** (3), pp 181–94

Evans, A (2001) *Mentoring in Action: National Mentoring Pilot Project report Portsmouth conference March 2001*, University of Wales, Cardiff

Evans, A and Dowler, A (1999) *The National Mentoring Pilot Project*, University of Wales, Cardiff

Evans, K and Hoffmann, B (2000) Engaging to learn: situated learning and re-integration initiatives for young people, in *Combating Social Exclusion through Education: Laissez-faire, authoritarianism or third way*, ed G Walraven, C Parsons and D v Veen, Garant, Belguim

Farmer, D (1999) *Mentoring: Meeting the needs of gifted students in regular classrooms* (video/booklet), (www.austega.com/gifted/provisions/mentoring)

Fetterman, D M (2000) *Foundations of Empowerment Evaluation: Step by step*, Sage, Thousand Oaks, California

Field, J (2000) E-mentoring, *Mentoring News, The Newsletter of the National Mentoring Network*, autumn/winter, Manchester

Fletcher, S (2000) *Mentoring in Schools*, Kogan Page, London

Ford, G (1998) *Career Guidance Mentoring for Disengaged Young People*, Institute of Careers Guidance, Stourbridge

Freedman, M (1988) *Partners in Growth: Elder mentors and at-risk youth*, Public/Private Ventures, Philadelphia

Freedman, M (1992) *The Kindness of Strangers: Reflections on the mentoring movement*, Public/Private Ventures, Philadelphia

Fresko, B and Carmeli, M (1990) Perach: a nationwide student tutorial project, in *Explorations in Peer Tutoring*, ed S Goodlad and B Hirst, Blackwell, Oxford

Fresko, B and Kowalsky, R (1998) Helping high school pupils in the Perach project: a comparison of mentoring and tutoring approaches, in *Mentoring and Tutoring by Students*, ed S Goodlad, Kogan Page, London

Furano, K, Roaf, P, Styles, M and Branch, A (1993) *Big Brothers, Big Sisters: A study of program practices*, Public/Private Ventures, Philadelphia

Galbraith, M W and Cohen, N H (1995) Mentoring: new strategies and challenges, in *New Directions for Adult and Continuing Education*, **66**, Josey-Bass, San Francisco

Garvey, R (1994) A dose of mentoring, *Education and Training*, **36** (4) pp 18–26

Gaustad, J (1992) *Tutoring for At Risk Students*, Oregon School Study Council, Eugene, Oregon

Gay, B (1994) What is Mentoring?, *Education and Training*, **36** (5) pp 4–7

Gay, B (1997) The practice of mentoring, in *Mentoring: The new panacea?*, ed J Stephenson, pp 19–28, Peter Francis, Norfolk

Gay, B (2000) *Keynote Address to Mentoring Matters Conference*, National Mentoring Network for the Home Office

Gibb, S (1994) Evaluating mentoring, *Education and Training*, **36** (5) pp 32–39

Gillborn, D and Mirza, H (2000) *Educational Inequality: Mapping race, class and gender*, OfSTED, London

Gilligan, C (1982) *In A Different Voice: Psychological theory and women's development*, Harvard University Press, Cambridge, Massachusetts

Golden, S and Sims, D (1997) *Review of Industrial Mentoring in Schools*, National Foundation for Educational Research (NFER), Slough

Golden, S and Sims, D (1999) *Evaluation of the National Mentoring Network Bursary Programme 1998–99*, NFER, Slough

Goleman, D (1990) Compassion and comfort in middle age: new research finds a flowering of lives marked by generosity and deeper relationships, *New York Times*, 6 February

Goleman, D (1995) *Emotional Intelligence*, Bantam Books, New York

Goodlad, S (1995) *Students as Tutors and Mentors*, Kogan Page, London

Goodlad, S and Hirst, B (1989) *Peer Tutoring: A guide to learning by teaching*, Kogan Page, London

Goodman, R (1997) The Strengths and Difficulties Questionnaire: a research note, *Journal of Child Psychology and Psychiatry*, **38**, pp 581–86

Goodman, R, Meltzer, H and Bailey, V (1998) The Strengths and Difficulties Questionnaire: a pilot study on the validity of the self-report version, *European Child and Adolescent Psychiatry*, **7**, pp 125–30

Graff, L (1999) *Beyond Police Checks: The definitive volunteers and screening guidebook*, Graff and Associates, Dundas, Ontario, Canada

Granville, G (2000) Understanding the experience of older volunteers in integenerational school-based projects, in *Perspectives on Mentoring*:

Report of the Ninth National Mentoring Conference 2000, ed A D Miller, pp 26–33, Salford Business Education Partnership, Manchester

Gray, W (1986) Components for developing a successful formalised mentoring program in business, the professions, education, and other settings, in *Proceedings of the First International Conference on Mentoring*, ed W A Gray and M M Gray, **2**, Vancouver, British Columbia, Canada, pp15–22

Gray, W (1989) Situational mentoring: custom designed planned mentoring program, *Mentoring International*, **3** (1), pp 19–28

Greaves, S (2001) Life support, *Red*, emap Elan Network, London, pp 59–60

Green, J and Rogers, B (1997) *Roots & Wings Mentoring Pilot and Moston Brook High School*, North West Consortium for the Study of Effectiveness in Urban Schools, Manchester

Greeno, J G (1997) Response: on claims that answer the wrong question, *Educational Researcher*, **26** (1), pp 5–17

Gresham, F M and Elliott, S N (1990) *Social Skills Ratings Systems*, American Guidance Service, Circle Pines

Grubb, W N and Ryan, P (1999) *The Roles of Evaluation for Vocational Education and Training: Plain talk on the field of dreams*, Kogan Page, London

Guetzlow, E (1997) The power of positive relationships: mentoring programs in the school and community, *Preventing School Failure*, Spring, pp 100–04

Gulam, W and Zulfiquar, M (1998) Mentoring: Dr Plum's elixir and the alchemists' stone, *Mentoring and Tutoring*, **5** (3), pp 39–45

Hansard (2001) *House of Commons Hansard Written Answers for 26 February 2001*, Ms Estelle Morris in reply to a written question from Mr Coaker (www.parliament.the-stationery-office.co.uk)

Harrington, A (1999) *E-mentoring: The advantages and disadvantages of email to support distant mentoring*, Coaching and Mentoring Network Articles (www.coachingnetwork.org.uk)

Harris, J and Jones, G (1999) A descriptive study of telementoring among students, subject matter experts, and teachers: message flow and function patterns, *Journal of Research on Computing in Education*, **32**, pp 36–53

Harris, J, O'Bryan, E and Rotenberg, L (1996) It's a simple idea, but it's not easy to do: practical lessons in telementoring, *Learning and Leading with Technology*, International Society for Technology in Education, Oregon

Harter, S (1990) *The Self-Perception Profile for Children*, University of Denver, Denver, Colorado

Hatry, H, van Houten, T, Plantz, M C and Greenway, M T (1996) *Measuring Program Outcomes: A practical approach*, United Way of America, Alexandria

Herrara, C, Sipe, C L and McClanahan, W S (2000) *Mentoring School-age*

Children: Relationship development in community-based and school-based programmes, Public/Private Ventures, Philadelphia

Hillage, J, Hyndley, K and Pike, G (1995) *Employers' Views of Education Business Links, Report 283*, Institute for Employment Studies, Brighton

Hofstede, G (1991) *Cultures and Organisations: Software of the mind*, McGraw-Hill, New York

Home Office (2000a) *Report of Policy Action Team 12: Young people*, Home Office, London

Home Office (2000b) *Volunteering and Community Activity Today: Material assembled for the Active Community Cross-Cutting Review 1999–2000*, Home Office, London (www.homeoffice.gov.uk)

Hope, R and Davies, W (2000) Generations in action, in *Perspectives on Mentoring: Report of the Ninth National Mentoring Conference 2000*, ed A D Miller, pp 125–27, SBEP, Manchester

Howells, A (1998) *A Study of Interracial Mentoring*, University of Greenwich, London (unpublished dissertation)

Huddleston, P (2001) Evaluation: the story so far, in *Building in Success: The Second Annual Conference for NMPP School Coordinators*, ed A Evans, University of Wales, Cardiff

Hughes, C and Guth, C (2001) Enlarging one's circle of friends: At McGavrock High School, it's all done on the buddy system, *Breaking Ground: The newsletter of the Tennessee Developmental Disabilities Council*, **5** (4)

Hughill, K (2000) Is e-mentoring e-ffective? Progress report on the e-mentoring pilot, in *Perspectives on Mentoring: Report on the Ninth National Mentoring Conference 2000*, ed A D Miller, pp 86–96, SBEP, Manchester

Iremonger, J (1999) University students act as mentors in schools, *Mentoring News*, **10**, NMN, Manchester

Iremonger, J (2000) Voluntary community service learning programme at Middlesex University, in *Mentoring in Schools: Report on the First Annual Conference of the London Region of the National Mentoring Network*, ed A D Miller, pp 35–37, NMN and Focus Central London, London

Jamieson, I M (1985) Corporate hegemony or pedagogic liberation?: The schools-industry movement in England and Wales, in *Education, Training and Employment: Towards the new vocationalism?*, ed R Dale, Open University/Pergamon, Oxford

Jones, S (2000) Learning mentor programme: The practicalities and the practice, *Mentoring News*, **13**, NMN, Manchester

Jucovy, L (2000a) *The ABCs of School-Based Mentoring: Technical assistance packet 1*, National Mentoring Center at Northwestern Regional Educational Laboratory, Portland

Jucovy, L (2000b) *Jumpstarting Your Program: Strengthening mentoring programs*, National Mentoring Center Northwestern Regional Educational Laboratory, Portland

Jucovy, L (2001a) *Recruiting Mentors: A guide to finding volunteers to work with youth, technical assistance packet 3*, National Mentoring Center at Northwestern Regional Educational Laboratory, Portland

Jucovy, L (2001b) *Supporting Mentor: Technical assistance packet 6*, National Mentoring Center at Northwestern Regional Educational Laboratory, Portland

Kerka, S (1998) New Perspectives on Mentoring, *ERIC Digest*, 194

Klein, R (1999) *Defying Disaffection: How schools are winning the hearts and minds of reluctant students*, Trentham, Stoke on Trent

Kolb, D A (1984) *Experiential Learning: Experience as the source of learning and development*, Prentice Hall, New Jersey

Kram, K E (1985) *Mentoring at Work: Developmental relationships in organizational life*, Scott Foresman, Glenview

Langridge, K (1998) *Harvest Mentoring Scheme*, London Guildhall University, London (unpublished MA dissertation)

Lauland, A (1998) *Yes, You Can: A guide for establishing mentoring programs to prepare youth for college*, United States Department for Education, Washington

Lave, J and Wenger, E (1991) *Situated Learning: Legitimate peripheral participation*, Cambridge University Press, New York

Law, B (1983) The colour-coded curriculum, in *NICEC Training and Development Bulletin*, **23**, National Institute of Careers Education and Counselling, Cambridge

Lee, P and Murie, A (1999) *Literature Review of Social Exclusion*, Scottish Office Central Research Unit, Glasgow

Levinson, D, Darrow, C, Klein, E, Levinson, M and McKee, B (1978) *The Seasons of a Man's Life*, Knopf, New York

Lubove, R (1965) *The Professional Altruist: The emergence of social work as a career, 1880–1930*, Harvard University Press, Cambridge, Massachusetts

Lunt, N, Bennett, P, McKenzie, P and Powell, L (1992) Understanding mentoring, *The Vocational Aspect of Education*, **44** (1), pp 135–41

Mac an Ghaill, M (1994) *The Making of Men*, Open University Press, Buckingham

MacCallum, J and Beltman, S (1999) *International Year of Older Persons Mentoring Research Project*, Department of Education, Training and Youth Affairs, Canberra

McClure, L (1997) The Hewlett-Packard e-mail mentor program, *Reality Check Newsletter*, April, Northwest Regional Educational Laboratory, Portland (www.nwrel.org/edwork/reality/april97/article4.html)

McIntyre, D and Hagger, H (1996) *Mentors in Schools: Developing the profession of teaching*, David Fulton Publishers, London

McNamara, O and Rogers, B (1997) *Roots & Wings Mentoring Programme: Evaluation report*, North West Consortium for the Study of Effectiveness in Urban Schools, Manchester

MacPherson, W (1999) *The Stephen Lawrence Inquiry: Report of an inquiry by Sir William MacPherson of Cluny*, Cm 4262–1, The Stationery Office, London

Maras, P and Bingham, S (2000) *Tutoring and Mentoring in Schools in the London Borough of Greenwich: A preliminary evaluation of two schemes*, University of Greenwich, London

Maras, P, Edgecombe, D, Dobson, S and Tagoe, P (2001) The bad kids are getting rewarded: peer mentoring for school pupils, in *Mentoring for Social Inclusion: Report of the Second Annual Conference of the London Region of the National Mentoring Network*, ed A D Miller, pp 40–42, NMN and Learning and Skills Council, London

Mayer, J D, and Salovey, P (1997) What is emotional intelligence?, in *Emotional Development and Emotional Intelligence: Implications for educators*, ed P Salovey and D Sluyter, pp 3–31, Basic Books, New York

Mensah-Coker (2000) *Giving Time: Volunteering in the twenty-first century*, Community Service Volunteers, London

Mercken, C (1999) Generations together, *Report of the First International Conference on Intergenerational Programmes: 13–14 October 1999 at Maastricht*, OITECC, the Netherlands

Miller, A D (1998) *Business and Community Mentoring in Schools*, Research Report no 43, DFEE, Sheffield

Miller, A D (1999a) *Excellence in Mentoring: School self-review framework*, NMN and Focus Central London, London

Miller, A D (1999b) *Mentoring: A guide to effective evaluation*, NMN, Manchester

Miller, A D (2000a) *Excellence in Mentoring Award: Deptford Green School assessment report*, NMN and Focus Central London, London (mimeo)

Miller, A D (2000b) Mentoring in schools: a quality assurance framework, in *Perspectives on Mentoring: The report on the Ninth National Mentoring Conference*, ed A D Miller, pp 50–61, SBEP, Manchester

Miller, A D (2000c) Employability skills for the twenty-first century: implications for work experience, *Careers Education and Guidance: Journal of the National Association of Careers and Guidance Teachers*, June

Miller, A D (2001) *Excellence in Mentoring Award: Pershore High School assessment report*, NMN and Focus Central London, London (mimeo)

Miller, A D, Fiehn, J and Huddleston, P (1998) *Business and Community Mentoring in Schools: Final report*, University of Warwick, Coventry

Miller, A D, *et al* (1995) *Making Education Our Business: Improving the quality of business-education links*, DfEE, Sheffield

Mitchell, H J (1999) Group mentoring: does it work? *Mentoring and Tutoring*, **7** (2), pp 113–20

Monaghan, J (1992) Mentoring: Person, process, practice and problems, *British Journal of Educational Studies*, **40** (3), pp 248–57

Morris, E (1998) Speech by Estelle Morris MP, Parliamentary Under Secretary of State for School Standards, in *Report of the 1998 National Mentoring Conference*, SBEP, Manchester

Morris, E (2000) The government perspective, in *Perspectives on Mentoring: Report on the Ninth National Mentoring Conference 2000*, ed A D Miller, pp 16–19, SBEP, Manchester

National Centre for Volunteering (1997) *Safe and Alert*, National Centre for Volunteering, London

National Crime Prevention Council (1986) *What, Me Evaluate?* National Crime Prevention Council, Washington DC

National Mentoring Network (NMN) (1999) *Mentoring News*, Summer, NMN, Manchester

NMN (Summer 2000) One-stop mentor pilots announced, *Mentoring News*, **12**, NMN, Manchester

NMN (June 2001) *Mentoring News*, **14**, NMN, Manchester

NMN (September 2001) *Mentoring News*, **15**, NMN, Manchester

National Mentoring Pilot Project (NMPP) (2000) *Mentors' Handbook 2000*, University of Wales, Cardiff

Nellen, T (nd) Education and community: the collective wisdom of teachers, parents and community members, *First Monday: Peer reviewed journal on the internet*, **4** (http://firstmonday.org/issues/issue42/nellen/

Newburn, T (2001) Mentoring and evaluation, in *Mentoring for Social Inclusion: Report of the Second Annual Conference of the London Region of the National Mentoring Network*, ed A D Miller, pp 21–26, NMN and Learning and Skills Council, London

Noe, R A (1988) An investigation of the determinants of successful assigned mentoring relationships, *Personnel Psychology*, **41**, pp 457–79

Novotney, L C, Mertinko, E, Lange, J and Baker, T K (2000) Juvenile mentoring program: A progress review, *Juvenile Justice Bulletin*, Office of Juvenile Justice and Delinquency Prevention, Washington

Odell, S J (1990) *Mentor Teacher Programs: What research says to the teacher*, ERIC Reproduction Service no ED 346 042, National Education Association, Washington DC

O'Donnell, H, Wilcox, J, Ritchie, N and Saint, N (2001) Issues in co-ordinating mentoring recruitment and training across a geographical area, in *Mentoring for Social Inclusion: Report of the Second Annual Conference of the London Region of the National Mentoring Network*, ed A D Miller, pp 52–53, NMN and Learning and Skills Council, London

Odyssee Institute for Training, Education, Coaching and Consultancy (OITECC) (1999) *Report of the First International Conference on Intergenerational Programmes: 13–14 October 1999 at Maastricht*, OITECC, the Netherlands

Office for Standards in Education (OFSTED) (1999) *Raising the Attainment of Minority Ethnic Pupils: School and LEA responses*, OFSTED, London

OFSTED (2000a) *Improving City Schools: Strategies to promote educational inclusion*, OFSTED, London

OFSTED (2000b) *Evaluating Educational Inclusion: Guidance for inspectors and schools*, OFSTED, London

O'Neill, D K, Wagner, R, and Gomez, L M (1996) Online mentors: experimenting in science class, *Education Leadership*, **55** (3), pp 39–42

Parsloe, E and Wray, M (2000) *Coaching and Mentoring: Practical methods to improve learning*, Kogan Page, London

Parsonage, L (2000) TS2K, *Mentoring News, the Newsletter of the National Mentoring Network*, autumn/winter, Manchester

Patton, M Q (1982) *Creative Evaluation*, Sage, Newbury Park, California

Philip, K (2000) Mentoring: pitfalls and potential for young people, *Youth and Policy*, **67**, pp1–15

Philip, K and Hendry, L B (2000) Making sense of mentoring or mentoring making sense? Reflections on the mentoring process by adult mentors with young people, *Journal of Community and Applied Social Psychology*, **10**, pp 211–23

Piper, H and Piper, J (1999) 'Disaffected' young people: problems for mentoring, *Mentoring and Tutoring*, **7** (2), Taylor and Francis, Hampshire, pp 121–29

Piper, H and Piper, J (2000) Disaffected young people as the problem. Mentoring as the solution. Education and work as the goal, *Journal of Education and Work*, **13** (1), pp 77–94

Plantz, M C and Greenway, M T (1997) Using performance measurement to improve public and nonprofit programs, in *New Directions for Evaluation*, **75**, ed K E Newcomer, Josey-Bass Publishers, San Francisco

Pollard, F (2000) Mentoring for young offenders: the challenges of working with young people in the criminal justice system, in *Perspectives on Mentoring: Report of the Ninth National Mentoring Conference 2000*, ed A D Miller, pp 62–71, SBEP, Manchester

Porteous, D (1998) *Evaluation of the CSV On-Line Mentoring Scheme*, Community Service Volunteers, London

Powell, M A (1999) *Academic Tutoring and Mentoring: A literature review*, California Research Bureau, Sacramento

Pringle, B *et al* (1993) *Peer Tutoring and Mentoring Services for Disadvantaged Secondary School Students: An evaluation of the Secondary Schools Basic Skills Demonstration Assistance Program*, Policy Studies Associates Inc for the US Department of Education Office of Policy and Planning, Washington, DC

Putnam, R (1995) Bowling alone: America's declining social capital, *Journal of Democracy*, **6** (1), pp 65–78

Rak, C F and Patterson, L E (1996) Promoting resilience in at-risk children, *Journal of Counseling and Development*, **74**, pp 368–73

Reisner, E, Petry C A and Armitage, M (1989) *A Review of Programs Involving College Students as Tutors or Mentors in Grades K-12*, Policy Studies Associates, Washington, DC

Rhodes, J (1994) Older and wiser: mentoring relationships in childhood and adolescence, *Journal of Primary Prevention*, **14** (3), pp 187–96

Rhodes, J, Ebert, L and Fischer, K (1992) Natural mentors: an overlooked resource in the social networks of adolescent mothers, *American Journal of Community Psychology*, **20** (4), pp 445–61

Rhodes, J E, Gingiss, P L and Smith, P B (1994) Risk and protective factors for alcohol use among pregnant African-American, Hispanic and White adolescents: the influence of peers, sexual partners, family members, and mentors, *Addictive Behaviors*, **8**, pp 555–64

Riel, M (1999) *Telementoring over the Net* (www.igc.org/iearn/circles/mentors.html)

Roberts, A (1999) An historical account to consider the origins of the term mentor, *History of Education Society Bulletin*, **64**, pp 81–90

Roberts, A (2000) Mentoring revisited: a phenomenological reading of the literature, *Mentoring and Tutoring*, **8** (2)

Robson, C (1993) *Real World Research*, Blackwell, Oxford

Rosenroll, D A (1994) *Toward an Operational Definition of Peer Helping*, Peer Resources Papers (www.islandnet.com/-rcarr/peer.html)

RPS Rainer (1999) *Breaking the Cycle*, RPS Rainer, Kent

Salmon, G (2000) *E-moderating: The key to teaching and learning online*, Kogan Page, London

St James Roberts, I and Singh, C S (1999) *Using Mentors to Change Problem Behaviour in Primary School Children: Research findings no 95*, Home Office Research, Development and Statistics Directorate, London

Salford Business Education Partnership (SBEP) (2000) *Generations In Action: Final report*, SOC 98 101673, SBEP, Manchester

Salovey, P and Mayer, J D (1990) Emotional intelligence, *Imagination, Cognition and Personality*, **9**, pp 185–211

Saunders, D and Gibson, M (1998) Peer tutoring and peer-assisted student support: five models within a new university, *Mentoring and Tutoring*, **5** (3), pp 3–13

Sewell, T (1997) *Black Masculinities and Schooling*, Trentham Books, Stoke on Trent

Sherman, L (1999) Reaching out for diversity, *National Mentoring Center Bulletin*, **2**, Northwest Regional Educational Laboratory (www.nwrel.org)

Silburn, J and Box, G (1999) Tell me a story: a new angle on student mentoring, in *Papers of the Second Regional Conference on Student Tutoring and Mentoring*, 30 September to 2 October 1999, Perth, Western Australia

Sims, D, Jamison, J, Golden, S and Lines, A (2000) *Running a Mentoring Programme: Key considerations*, NMN, Manchester

Singh, B (2001) Solution focused mentoring, in *Mentoring for Social Inclusion: Report of the Second Annual Conference of the London Region of the National Mentoring Network*, ed A D Miller, pp 27–31, NMN and Learning and Skills Council, London

Single, P B and Muller, C B (1999) Electronic mentoring: issues to advance research and practice, *Proceedings of the Annual Meeting of the International Mentoring Association*, Atlanta, Georgia, pp 234–50

Sipe, C L (1999) Mentoring adolescents: what have we learned?, in *Contemporary Issues in Mentoring*, ed J B Grossman, Public/Private Ventures, Philadelphia

Skinner, A and Fleming, J (1999) *Quality Framework for Mentoring with Socially Excluded Young People*, NMN, Manchester

Slaven, A (2001) From exclusion to inclusion, in *Mentoring for Social Inclusion: Report of the Second Annual Conference of the London Region of the National Mentoring Network*, ed A D Miller, pp 16–20, National Mentoring Network and Learning and Skills Council, London

Smith, D R (1993) *Safe from Harm: A code of practice for safeguarding the welfare of children in voluntary organizations in England and Wales*, Home Office, London

Social Exclusion Unit (1998) *Truancy and School Exclusion: Report by the Social Exclusion Unit*, Cm 3957, The Stationery Office, London

Songsthagen, L L and Lee, S (1996) America's most needed: real life heroes and heroines, *Schools in the Middle*, February/March, pp 37–42

Southwark Black Mentor Scheme (1998) *Southwark Black Mentor Scheme 1996-1998*, **3**, Peckham Partnership/Southwark Education, London

Sproull, L and Kiesler, S (1992) *Connections: New ways of working in the networked organization*, MIT, Cambridge, Massachusetts

Stake, R (1967) The countenance of educational evaluation, *Teachers College Record*, **68** (7)

Steele, M with Marigna, M (2000) *Strengthening Families, Strengthening Communities: An inclusive parent programme*, Race Equality Unit, London

Stone, R (2000) The business benefits of mentoring, *Mentoring News*, **12**, NMN, Manchester

Struchen, W and Porta, M (1997) From role modeling to mentoring for African-American youth: ingredients for successful relationships, *Preventing School Failure*, **41** (3), pp119–27

Sukhnandan, L, Lee, S and Kelleher, S (2000) *An Investigation into Gender Differences in Achievement: Phase 2 – School and classroom strategies*, NFER, Slough

Swansea College (not dated) *Mentoring: The definitive workbook*, Development Processes Limited, Manchester

Taylor, A S and Dryfoos, J G (2001) Creating a safe passage: elder mentors and vulnerable youth, *Generations Journal*, American Society on Aging (www.generationsjournal.org)

Tierney, J P and Branch, A Y (1996) College students as mentors for at-risk youth: a study of six campus partners in learning programs, in

Mentoring: A synthesis of P/PV's research: 1988–1995, ed C L Sipe, Public/Private Ventures, Philadelphia

Tierney, J P, Grossman, J B and Resch, N L (1995) *Making a Difference: An impact study of Big Brothers/Big Sisters*, Public/Private Ventures, Philadelphia

Tilley, K (2000) Supporting parents, in *Perspectives, in Mentoring: The report on the ninth National Mentoring Conference*, ed A D Miller, SBEP, Manchester, pp 115–18

Tobin, L (2000) *What Makes a Great Mentoring Program? Highlights of USA study tour* (www.mentoring-australia.com)

Topping, K (1994) A typology of peer tutoring, *Mentoring and Tutoring*, **2** (1), pp 23–24

Topping, K and Hill, S (1995) University and college students as tutors for school children: a typology and review of evaluation research, in *Students as Tutors and Mentors*, ed S Goodlad, pp 13–31, Kogan Page, London

Toward, G (2000) Mentoring: a whole school approach, in *Report of the Ninth Annual National Mentoring Conference 2000*, ed A D Miller, pp 78–87, SBEP, Manchester

Vygotsky, L S (1994) The development of academic concepts in school aged children, in *The Vygotsky Reader*, ed R v d Veer and J Valsiner, Blackwell, Oxford

Walker, A (1997) The strategy of inequality, in *Britain Divided: The growth of social exclusion in the 1980s and 1990s*, ed A Walker and C Walker, pp 69–92, CPAG, London

Walther, J B (1992) Interpersonal effects in computer-mediated interaction: a relational perspective, *Communication Research*, **19**, pp 52–90

Walther, J B and Burgoon, J K (1992) Relational communication in computer-mediated communication, *Human Communication Research*, 19, pp 50–88

Walton, J (2001) *Mentoring in Mainland Europe and the Republic of Ireland*, Coaching and Mentoring Network (www.coachingnetwork.org.uk)

Warren-Sams, B (2001) *Bulletin 4: Gender issues in mentoring*, Northwest Regional Educational Laboratory, Portland, Oregon (www.nwrel.org)

Watts, A G (1999) *The Role of the Personal Adviser: Concepts and issues*, Centre for Guidance Studies, University of Derby, (www.derby.ac.uk/cegs/)

Webb, J (1997) *Dalston Youth Project: Programmes 1, 2 and 3 for Young People Aged 15–18 Years: Summary of the evaluations*, Janice Webb Research, Grantham

Webb, J (2000) *Dalston Youth Project: Programme 7 final evaluation*, Janice Webb Research, Grantham

Weiner, S J and Mincy, R (1993) *Guiding Boys Through the Transition to Adulthood: The role and potential of mentoring*, Urban Institute, Washington

Werner, E E and Smith, R S (1992) *Overcoming the Odds: High risk children from birth to adulthood*, Cornell University Press, Ithaca

Wighton, D J (1993) *Telementoring: An examination of the potential for an educational network*, Education Technology Center, British Columbia (http://mentor.creighton.edu/htm/telement.htm)

Wilkin, M (1992) *Mentoring in Schools*, Kogan Page, London

Withers, G and Batten, M (1995) *Programs for At-risk Youth: A review of the American, Canadian and British literature since 1984*, Australian Council for Educational Research, Melbourne, Victoria

Wood, D and Reynard, A (2000) *Mentoring: Draft occupational standards*, University of North London, London

Wood, J (2000) *Research into Performance Indicators for Effective Student Tutoring: Minimising risk and maximising benefit through matching students to schools*, Tyneside and Northumberland Students into Schools Project, University of Newcastle, Newcastle

Yeomans, R and Sampson, J (eds) (1994) *Mentorship in the Primary School*, Falmer, London

Index

academic objective   37, 60, 74,
106, 156, 173–74, 189
accreditation   203, 208–10
Active Community Unit   15, 17,
26
activities for mentors and mentees
78–79, 90, 105, 108, 110, 124,
221
African American
mentors   78–79
natural mentoring   25–26
Age Concern   84
aims of mentoring   33–37, 173–74
career-related   33–34
developmental   33–36, 106
instrumental   33, 136
psychosocial   33
subject   33–34, 37, 41, 65
work-related   33–34, 36–37
A Nation at Risk   5
aspirational objective   36–37, 91,
94, 174
Athena   24
at-risk mentoring   40, 103–19
at-risk young people
definitions   104
attendance   64, 129, 158

attitudinal change objective   36,
106, 109, 174
Australia   10–11, 69, 77–78, 80–81,
160

bandwagon effect   169
basic skills   74, 80, 83, 106, 116,
122, 43–44, 149
befriending   29, 31, 35, 61, 67
behavioural change objective   36,
105–06, 129, 174
Beth Johnson Foundation   79
bi-cultural competence   96
Big Brothers/Big Sisters
evaluation   246–47
of America   4–6, 42–43, 100
of Canada   8–9
origins   4
black mentoring programmes
86–102
Boateng, Paul   14–16
Brown, Gordon   17–18
buddying   31, 62, 121, 124
Bursary Scheme (see NMN)
13–14, 87
business benefits   39, 56–59,
266

Business Excellence Model
255–57
Business in the Community (BITC)
55, 140
business mentoring 12–13, 41, 45,
53–72, 183, 219–20, 264

Campus Compact 6
Campus Partners in Learning
157
Canada 8–9
career development 20, 36–37,
66, 68, 94, 151, 224–25
case studies *see* list on viii
celebratory events 71, 76, 90, 93,
95, 108, 232–34
Chance UK 15
Chicago 197
child protection 119, 147, 200–01,
203, 219, 236
citizenship 132, 148, 152, 189,
264, 269
classical model of mentoring
24–25, 218
classification of programmes
39–43
by aims 40
by mentee characteristics 40
by mentor characteristics 41
by programme characteristics
42–43
Clutterbuck, David 30, 191
coaching 32, 58
codes of practice 205–07
cognitive scaffolding 48
communication problems 61,
70–71, 94, 137, 144, 157
communities of practice 49, 69
community-based programmes
43, 115, 179, 207, 220
community mapping 76, 196

community mentoring 41, 73,
266
Community Service Volunteers
150
company coordinator, role of
55–56, 71
Connexions Service 16, 100, 226
contract mentoring 26–27
contracting 228–29
control group 64–66, 81, 114, 127,
129, 246–47
control measures 232–33
corporate mentoring 5, 32, 39, 62
corporations
BP 94
Citibank 60
Deloitte & Touche 58, 62, 66–67
Hewlett-Packard 72, 138–39
IPC Magazines 60
J C Penney 139
Marks & Spencer 59
Merrill Lynch 63, 67
Warburg Dillon Read 56
costs 70, 109, 115, 130, 177,
179–81, 209
counselling 31–32
Crime and Disorder Act (1998)
15, 105
Crime Concern 106, 109, 115
cross-cultural/ethnicity matching
95, 98–99, 114–15, 264
cross-institutional mentoring
122, 126–27, 130
customer service 198

Dalston Youth Project 15, 95,
109–11, 113–14, 222, 234
Department for Education and
Employment (DfEE) 13, 16,
19, 64, 199
diaries 43, 111, 126

'disaffected' youth   116
disengaged youth   116
distance traveled   64–66, 240
drop-out   9–10, 21, 88, 97, 104, 124
duration   42, 61, 95, 107, 154, 219

Education Action Zones (EAZs)
      18, 151–52
Education Business Partnerships
      (EBPs)   13, 21, 55, 68, 75–76
e-mail   61, 134, 142
e-mentoring   *see* telementoring
Emotional Intelligence (EI)
      38–39, 128, 189, 191–94, 204,
      217
   Hay McBer model   193–94
employability skills   21, 37, 54, 60,
      67, 69, 173–74, 189, 193–94,
      266
empowerment evaluation   250–51
endings   93, 108, 111, 205–06, 235
enterprise mentoring   40
equal opportunities issues   68, 97,
      160
Europe   11–12
evaluation   242–52
   empowerment   250–51
   external   240, 248
   formative   93, 157–58, 243
   outcome   244
   purpose   242
   strategy   247–46
   summative   62, 64, 67, 159
   teacher   62, 64, 90, 96
Excellence in Cities   16–17, 44
Excellence in Mentoring Award
      62
Excellence in Schools   15
experiential learning   48, 226–28

family learning   67, 79

Fenelon   24
Freedman, Marc   3–7, 22, 81
Friendly Visitors   4
funding   91

Gay, Brian   28, 223
GCSE   14, 62, 64–66, 129, 157, 182
GEAR UP   5–7, 150, 155–56,
      159
gender issues   66, 76, 78–79,
      91–92, 112, 114, 149, 153,
      217–18
generations   74–75
gifted and talented mentoring
      40, 265
Goleman, Daniel   192
government policy *see also UK*
      government policy   268–69
ground rules   27, 138, 153, 158,
      175–76, 205–07,   228
group mentoring   41, 44–46, 54,
      218

helping behaviours   31–32, 38
higher education student
      mentoring
holistic mentoring   20, 30–31,
      37–38, 46, 87

identity   88–89, 99
industrial mentoring *see also*
      business mentoring   12–13, 54,
      183
infrastructure   8, 17–18, 22
intensiveness   42
intergenerational mentoring   39,
      73–85
intergenerational programs   18,
      39, 73–74
International Mentor Center   134,
      143

internships *see also work experience*
37, 60, 94
Israel (see Perach)   9–10, 20, 44
issues in mentoring
  ambition and targeting   159
  community-based versus school
    based   115
  coordination   160
  cross-institutional programmes
    130
  cultural matching   98
  developing employability   69
  exclusivity   97
  focus   129, 142–43
  institutionalized racism   97
  mentoring plus   116–17
  mentor selection and training
    130
  one-to-one versus group   45–46
  paid versus volunteer mentors
    44–45
  philosophies   43–44
  project workers   100
  resourcing   143
  selection of mentees   68
  separate or integrated   82
  social capital   82
  supply of mentors   68, 99
  sustainability   69–70
  unreliability and turnover of
    mentors   70

Jeffrey, Howard   93

key performance indicators (KPIs)
  239, 241
key skills   69, 151

labelling   35, 116
leadership   89, 184–85
Learning Mentors   16–20, 42, 44,

225–26
learning skills objective   37,
  173–74
learning theory   47–49
literacy   74, 81, 109–11, 122, 142

MacPherson Report   97
management   108, 167–87
marketing literature   197–98
mass mentoring   6–7, 9, 21–22,
  103, 268
matching   78, 81, 92, 161, 216–18
  ethnicity   92, 98–99
  gender   92, 217–18
  religion   92
materials   61, 175
maturational objective   35–36,
  122, 174
mentee preparation   89, 159,
  214–16
Mentor (Greek myth)   24
mentoring culture   182, 263–69
mentoring, definition of terms *see*
  Glossary 270–74
mentoring for women   5, 11, 26,
  36, 46, 135
Mentoring Fund   18
mentoring learning cycle   227–29
mentoring meetings   218–20
mentoring plus approaches
  105–06, 116–17, 222
mentoring relationships
  (mentorships)   26–27, 220–21,
  231–33
Mentor Point   16, 199
mentors
  aims   38–39, 69, 75–76, 123,
    128–29, 149, 188–89
  behaviours   191
  benefits   58, 151
  effective   191–92, 203

ethics   205–06
information for   175, 203–04
older   74–82
roles   191–92
minority ethnic mentoring   40, 44,
    86–102
motivational objective   10, 35, 54,
    66, 89, 173–74
multi-focused programmes
    37–38

National Mentoring Conference
    14, 16
National Mentoring Network
    (NMN)   13–14, 17, 45, 253,
    255
National Mentoring Pilot Project
    (NMPP)   10, 18, 44, 152–153,
    157
National Urban League   63, 67
natural mentoring   23, 25–26, 97,
    172
New Deal   14–15

occupational standards   209–10
Odyssey   24
online facilitator   139–40, 144
outcomes   238
outputs   238

paid mentoring versus volunteer
    mentoring   10, 27, 44–45, 164
paired reading   74–75, 122
parenting skills   100, 107, 110
parents   61, 63, 67, 78, 92, 97, 110,
    113, 127, 156, 204, 229–31
parrainage   12
partnerships   156, 172, 264–65
peer helping   120
peer mentoring   18, 42, 120–32,
    183, 208

peer tutoring   120, 127
Perach (see Israel)
personal and social skills objective
    35–36, 54, 174
philosophy of mentoring   15–16,
    43–44, 184
planned mentoring   23
    definition   23, 26, 46–47
    continuum approach   28
    key characteristics approach
        28
    phenomenological approach
        29
    popular consensus approach
        27
police checks   89, 153, 200–01, 212
policy borrowing   10, 20
policy statement   173–75, 183, 268
politics of mentoring   21–22
power distance hypothesis
    11–12
power in mentorships   25, 30, 47
pre-planning   139–40, 169–72
President Bush   5
President Clinton   6, 21, 150
President George W Bush   6, 21,
    206–07
Presidents' Summit for America's
    Future   5, 21
primary pupils   12, 39, 88–89,
    107–09, 124–25
primary relationships   80
Project GRAD   159
project workers   60, 89–91, 100
protective factors   78, 215
pseudo mentoring   20, 37, 42, 47,
    105, 116

quality assurance   22, 255–57
quality frameworks   117, 252–54
quality standards   11, 22, 253–54

racism 87–89
  institutionalized 97
recruitment of mentors 60–61, 76–77, 94, 99, 110, 153–55, 194–96
'red flags' 201
referrals 107–09, 213–14
research, need for 12, 115, 172, 251–52, 269
residentials 69, 106, 109, 126
resilience research 79, 81, 115
resourcing 143, 179–80
risk factors 78, 97, 105, 112, 161, 215
role continuity 122
role models 10, 28–29, 32, 35–36, 57, 87–88, 91, 94, 105, 115, 149, 151, 217
Roots & Wings 8, 54, 59–62, 64
RPS Rainer 168

school-based mentoring 59–62, 115
school coordinator 60, 71, 77, 125, 130 138, 157, 160–61,177–78, 214
school exclusion 104–05, 110
schools
  All Saints Catholic High 226
  City of Leeds 140
  Deptford Green 59–62
  Hamilton Senior High 160
  Hodge Hill 226
  McGavrock High 124
  Murry Bergtraum 141
  Pershore High 180–84
  South Camden Community 225–26
  South Wigston 125–27
  Summit Elementary 138
  Telemachus High 263–67

University High Charter 156
screening 68, 77, 200–201
selection of mentees 61, 68, 83, 92–93, 126, 213–14
self-esteem objective 33–35, 54, 80, 89, 109, 123, 125, 149, 161, 173–74
service level agreement 178–79
sexism 24
site-based programmes 43
situated learning 48–49, 69
social capital 82
social events 61, 95, 149, 216
socially excluded mentoring
social exclusion 21, 103–04
Social Exclusion Unit 87, 104–05
social inclusion 14, 21, 39, 74–75, 104, 189
special needs 19, 105, 107–09, 124, 128
staff development 57–59, 69
stages of mentoring
  career development model 224–25
  chronological model 223–34
  engagement phase 108
  life cycle model 224
  mentor protégé relationship model 223
Stay in School Initiative 9
steering group 60, 100, 110, 185
stereotyping 80, 83, 116
structure of programmes 43
subject matter expert (SME) 37, 43, 136, 139–41
supervision 109, 207–08
supply of mentors 22, 60, 68, 99
support for mentors 76, 78, 93, 110, 207–08
sustainability 69–70

target setting   82, 93, 182–84
teacher mentoring   12–13, 41–42,
   179
Telemachus (Greek myth)   24
telementoring   68, 72, 133–47
   problems   143–44
   versus traditional   133,
   136–38
teletutoring   135
tiered mentoring   125–27, 264
training of mentors   78, 92, 153,
   201–05
   manual   153, 175
   styles   202–05
   topics   19, 89, 94, 107, 155,
   202–04, 208
tutoring   32, 127–28, 149
transition mentoring   35–36, 62

UK government policy   13–20
uncertainty avoidance hypothesis
   11–12
underachievement   87–88
university
   Colorado State   141–42
   Leeds   140
   Leeds Metropolitan   210
   Malmo   10
   Middlesex   154–55
   Murdoch   160
   Newcastle   161
   New York-Potsdam   139
   North London   209–10

Rutgers   156
South Bank   152–54
Temple   78
Texas   139
Wales, Cardiff   152
Warwick   xiv
Westminster   162
Yale   67
USA, development of mentoring
   3–8

vocational objective   37, 54
voluntarism   3
volunteering   83, 189
   barriers to   196–97
   company   9, 11, 62, 68, 72
Vygotsky, Lev   47–48

whole-school approach   125–27,
   180–84
widening participation   163
work experience (see also
   internship)   37, 55, 60, 69, 72,
   94
work-related objective   36–37
World Wide Web   20, 26–27, 138,
   275–77

YELLIS   65–66
young offenders   36, 44, 104–06,
   113–14
Youth Justice Board   15
Youth Offending Team   105